In Someone Else's Country

Anti-Haitian Racism and Citizenship in the Dominican Republic

Trenita Brookshire Childers

ROWMAN & LITTLEFIELD
Lanham • Boulder • New York • London

Executive Editor: Nancy Roberts
Editorial Assistant: Courtney Packard
Marketing Manager: Jonathan Raeder
Interior Designer: Ilze Lemesis

Credits and acknowledgments for material borrowed from other sources, and reproduced with permission, appear on the appropriate pages within the text.

Published by Rowman & Littlefield
An imprint of The Rowman & Littlefield Publishing Group, Inc.
4501 Forbes Boulevard, Suite 200, Lanham, Maryland 20706
www.rowman.com

6 Tinworth Street, London SE11 5AL, United Kingdom

British Library Cataloguing in Publication Information Available

Library of Congress Cataloging-in-Publication Data

Names: Childers, Trenita Brookshire, 1983– author.
Title: In someone else's country : anti-Haitian racism and citizenship in the Dominican Republic / Trenita Brookshire Childers.
Description: Lanham, Maryland : Rowman & Littlefield, 2021. | Includes bibliographical references and index. | Summary: "'In Someone Else's Country' details the current situation of racial profiling in Caribbean countries where certain citizens are denied any documentation to become a citizen of the country they were born and raised in"— Provided by publisher.
Identifiers: LCCN 2020006346 (print) | LCCN 2020006347 (ebook) | ISBN 9781538131008 (cloth) | ISBN 9781538131015 (paperback) | ISBN 9781538131022 (epub)
Subjects: LCSH: Haitians—Dominican Republic—Social conditions. | Haitians—Dominican Republic—Legal status, laws, etc. | Citizenship—Dominican Republic—Social aspects. | Racism—Political aspects—Dominican Republic. | Dominican Republic—Emigration and immigration—Social aspects.
Classification: LCC F1941.H3 C55 2021 (print) | LCC F1941.H3 (ebook) | DDC 305.80097293—dc23
LC record available at https://lccn.loc.gov/2020006346
LC ebook record available at https://lccn.loc.gov/2020006347

♾™ The paper used in this publication meets the minimum requirements of American National Standard for Information Sciences—Permanence of Paper for Printed Library Materials, ANSI/NISO Z39.48-1992.

To Miles, Micah, and Maxwell,
my sweet, beautiful boys
I hope that you always seek justice, love mercy,
and walk humbly with your God (Micah 6:8)

Contents

Illustrations

Preface

When I describe this research to people, they often ask, "Are you Dominican?" I am not. Then comes "Are you Haitian?" I am not. My scholarly attention to anti-Haitian policies in the Dominican Republic is born of a deep connection to understanding how people experience blackness across the globe.[1] The fates of Black people in all countries are linked, and our individual freedom is rooted in our collective freedom. Like other African American scholars studying the global experiences of Black people,[2] I believe that our work is to speak truth to the power that maintains racial divisions in all countries.

My analytic lens for this work is born of my varied experiences living in the Dominican Republic. The first time I lived there, in 2008, I was a Peace Corps volunteer. I felt instantly connected to a country where bachata, *la bandera*,[3] and open hospitality warmed my soul. The community I lived in was supportive and welcoming. But I noticed the divisions between neighborhoods within the community: the Dominican and Haitian families interacted very little, if at all. I also noticed birth-registration campaigns. Some people in the Dominican Republic do not have birth certificates for a variety of reasons: they were not born in a hospital; or they were born in a hospital, but overburdened administrators neglected their paperwork; or administrators withheld documents because their mother "looked Haitian."

Perhaps because of my identity as a Black American, I was more attuned to issues of racial inequality.[4] So when I thought about research topics for my dissertation, and my wonderful husband asked, "What would you research if you didn't have children?" my immediate response was "I would go back to the Dominican Republic to learn about race and documentation." And that was the catalyst for the research questions that led to this book.

My second time living in the Dominican Republic was much different from the first. During our time as Peace Corps volunteers, my husband and I lived in the community where we worked, forming deep relationships with friends and host-family members in the country. The second time, during ethnographic research and data collection for this book, we lived about thirty minutes from the field site called La Tierra, and I went there several times each week for about three to five hours at a time. Also, our two small children, then ages four and one, were in the country with us. I learned so much by discussing this work when dropping my children off at daycare or preschool. People were either politely silent or eager to share their own perspectives.

My family was often a point of conversation that led to discussions about race in the Dominican Republic. The four of us—me, my husband, and our two boys—are four different shades of brown. People would often comment on our skin tones, and I took their comments as opportunities to learn about race within Dominican families. Sometimes these conversations remained squarely about skin color. Other times they diverged and became about ancestry. For example, someone might say, "I am *india*, but my sister is darker than me. We have a grandfather who is Haitian."

The way that these conversations looped seamlessly between skin color and Haitian ancestry created a complex picture of race and racism in the Dominican Republic that merits much more nuanced research than this book will offer. But my hope is that the findings from this book will contribute to ongoing conversations about how race and legality are intertwined for immigrant families from marginalized racial or ethnic backgrounds as racism is woven into immigration policies to exclude unwanted groups.

Notes

[1] For a broader discussion about Haiti and global blackness, see Celucien L. Joseph, Jean Eddy Saint Paul, and Glodel Mezilas, eds., *Between Two Worlds: Jean Price-Mars, Haiti, and Africa* (Lanham, MD: Lexington Books, 2018).

[2] See works by Jean Beaman, Kia Caldwell, Christina Davidson, Elizabeth Hordge-Freeman, Tianna Paschel, Vilna Bashi, France Winddance Twine, and many others.

[3] *La bandera* refers to a typical Dominican meal of rice, beans, and meat.

[4] Elizabeth Hordge-Freeman, "'Bringing Your Whole Self to Research': The Power of the Researcher's Body, Emotions, and Identities in Ethnography," *International Journal of Qualitative Methods* 17, no. 1 (2018): 1609406918808862.

Acknowledgments

It would be impossible to name everyone in my village who had a role in ushering this book into existence. I deeply apologize to anyone I have omitted.

This project was born out of the foundational and life-changing experiences I encountered as a Peace Corps volunteer, serving with my husband. Over the course of my time volunteering in the Dominican Republic, I formed meaningful relationships with Peace Corps staff, my fellow volunteers, and community members who loved me, supported me, and formed a second family while I was miles away from my own. Tragically, our family experienced a devastating loss when my brother-in-law, Ricky Childers, drowned while visiting the country during our Peace Corps service. Ricky was a shining light to all he met, and he was gone much too soon. To grieve with family, my husband and I terminated our Peace Corps service early.

In the following year, I enrolled in the graduate program in sociology at Duke University. When it was time to decide on a dissertation topic during my third year in the program, my husband and I decided to go back to the Dominican Republic with our two young children, ages four and one. We wanted to have a chance to close our Dominican Republic story on our own terms. And we also wanted to create new and beautiful memories of the Dominican Republic so that fear and tragedy would not hang so heavily over our love of the Caribbean.

I am exceedingly grateful for the funders that believed in this project and supported this important scholarship at nearly every stage of this research. At critical early stages, I received funding from Duke University in the form of the James B. Duke International Research Travel Fellowship to visit potential field sites. The Center for Latin American and Caribbean Studies also funded a year-long Foreign Language and Area Studies Fellowship that allowed me to learn Haitian Creole and supplement my sociological training with courses on Caribbean history and US policy in Latin America. Data collection for this research was supported by the generosity of the Fulbright Program sponsored by the US Department of State. Although my primary purpose for living in the Dominican Republic was research and data collection, I am so grateful to the Fulbright Program for emphasizing the importance of cross-cultural exchange. This emphasis reminded me to be engaged with our friends and neighbors while we worked, studied, and took our children to school, day care, and soccer practices. I am also grateful to the Ford Foundation and for the National Science Foundation Dissertation Research Improvement Grant that provided funding to transcribe interviews and hire an excellent research assistant, Malena Jean Lamas.

I am incredibly grateful for the support of organizations in the Dominican Republic that embraced a politically charged research topic and offered their guidance and support. This book would not have been possible without the Caribbean Migrants Observatory (OBMICA), La Clinica de Familia, and the Peace Corps Dominican Republic office. At OBMICA, Bridget Wooding and

Allison Petrozzielo offered their invaluable insight and passionate perspective, always centering social justice as the "why" for this research. At La Clinica de Familia, Derrick "Luis" Lewis, Mina Halpern, Honey Mejia, Riqui Rey Rosario, and Omar Hernandez were immensely supportive as I navigated this research space. Special thanks to Adele Williams and Doña Rosina Anglada at the Peace Corps Dominican Republic office for plugging me into a network of researchers and volunteers working tirelessly to improve access to documentation among people of Haitian descent.

I would not be the scholar I am today without the influence of my primary advisors. Always raising the bar and requiring nothing less than excellence of his students, Eduardo Bonilla-Silva pushed me to go above and beyond the data sources I anticipated incorporating at the start of this project. Linda K. George patiently offered feedback on my writing and encouraged me to think critically about the role of social institutions and the intergenerational impact of inequality. An invaluable synthesis of methodological rigor and encouragement, Linda Burton provided a foundational understanding of how to learn from strangers, and her course co-taught with renowned ethnographer Carol Stack emphasized the importance of weaving data through theory to tell bold stories about people's lived experiences. What a privilege to learn from these incredible teachers.

Along with the benefit of learning from my primary advisors, I had the support of brilliant teachers at Duke University, including William "Sandy" Darity, Sherman James, Adriane Lentz-Smith, Mary Hovsepian, and Michaeline Crichlow. Their guidance pushed me to expand my sociological lens to incorporate an interdisciplinary, global perspective on theory building and application. And the student-led race workshop provided a safe space in which to grow while learning how to build others up along the way. I would also like to acknowledge my colleagues at the Sheps Center for Health Services Research, who gave me the funding and space to write the book prospectus during my postdoctoral research fellowship supported by the National Institute of Mental Health.[1] Thank you to the American Institutes for Research for granting me a fellowship that included time to work toward completing this manuscript. And my amazing coworkers offered a steady stream of encouragement, read chapters, and helped brainstorm suggested titles. I am so grateful for such supportive colleagues.

Now for the people and places that made me who I am. Many communities and schools shaped my sociological lens. The communities include Shuqualak, Mississippi, where I spent summers listening to family stories, roaming from Big Mama's house to Mama Nani's house with cousins, and swatting mosquitos as the sun set; Humboldt Park and Sixty-Third and Western Avenue in Chicago, Illinois, where I passed time jumping double Dutch and playing hand games with cousins and neighbors; and Forest Park, Ohio, where my brother, Farris Jr., and I played kickball and Pokémon with school friends. The schools include A. N. Pritzker elementary and Washington Irving Elementary schools in Chicago, Illinois; Cameron Park Elementary, Winton Woods Middle School, and the Summit Country Day School in Cincinnati; my beloved alma mater, Davidson College, in North Carolina; and Charlotte Country Day School, where I got to teach fifth grade and learn from wonderful teachers who became wonderful friends. Each of these places taught me the tremendous value of empathy.

My parents, Farris Brookshire and Tonya McCoy Brookshire, were my first social scientists. My father is a proud US Air Force veteran and retired employee of the Department of Veterans Affairs. My mother works in administrative support at a medical office. Mom and Dad moved a shy and observant little girl through the world, showing her how to open up to others and listen to their experiences. Both of my parents could make friends with a tree if they stood next to it long enough! Their naturally friendly and open demeanors pushed me to be friendly and open—even when it was uncomfortable—and for that I am grateful. Thank you both for modeling the importance of talking with strangers and connecting other people's stories to our own. And thank you to my brother for living your truth without fear. This book would not be possible without a childhood foundation centered on the importance of shared humanity and authenticity.

I have brilliant and supportive friends who read chapters, give honest feedback, and push me to shine even when it makes me feel uncomfortable. Thank you to Felicia Arriaga, Austin Ashe, Rebecca Banks, Jessica Barron, Jean Beaman, Megan Browder, Felicia Browne, LaTisha Chapman, Elizabeth Hordge Freeman, Atiya Husain, Sarah Mayorga-Gallo, Adrienne Aiken Morgan, Danielle Purifoy, Victor Ray, Amy Reid, Alicia Reyes-Barrientez, Phia Salter Lee, Louise Seamster, Mary Square, Erin Stephens, SaunJuhi Verma, and Vanessa Young. I am so blessed to call each of these amazing people my dear friends. And my family at Baptist Grove Church kept me centered and spiritually grounded as I made my way through uncharted territory time and time again. At every step, they reminded me, "If He brings you to it, He will bring you through it."

My aunts Jasmine McCoy and Barbara Lawrence have told me with a matter-of-fact confidence—in whispers and in shouts—that I can do anything. Hearing this message from childhood through adulthood from people you love will make you start to believe it. If you are reading this, please tell someone that they can do anything. Cherese Childers-McKee, the sister I am so lucky to have, thank you for being a constant reminder of what it means to blend family and friendship. I am so grateful to have you in my life. To the McCoy family and the Brookshire family, thank you for keeping me honest, real, and grounded. To the Childers family in Salisbury, North Carolina, there are no words to express the peace and comfort your presence brings. Thank you doesn't seem like enough. To my children—Miles, Micah, and Maxwell—continue to seek justice and love mercy. You are my reason for speaking when I am afraid and for writing when I am unsure of what to say. You are my reason.

This book would not be possible without the grace, patience, and encouragement of my husband and life partner, Darryl Childers. He cared enough to ask me what I would research if I did not have a husband or children. He consistently reminded me of who I am outside of motherhood, and he was brave enough to help me follow through with what seemed like an impossible plan. When I first said I wanted to go back to the Dominican Republic for my research, my immediate thought was "That won't work with the kids." To which he responded, "Well, let's see if that's true." Darryl gave me the space I needed to get this project done. At crunch time, as the book moved toward the finish line and the anxiety was building, he calmly said, "Make a plan. We can find you more time." While I wrote, I left my little boys with the most amazing father, and the four of them cheered me on, assuaging any self-imposed guilt I may have felt. Darryl read chapter drafts with critical attention to detail, asking questions and pushing me to write with more clarity. Because of Darryl, I wrote a book, I am still sane, my children are happy and whole, and my life is filled with love and light.

Finally, and most important, I am eternally grateful to the people in the Dominican Republic who opened their hearts and told me their deepest personal stories. They boldly shared their experiences with clarity and insightfulness, all while questioning the system that consistently moves them to the margins. My hope is to place their voices front and center and shine a light on their hopes, fears, and dreams. We are one.

Note

[1] My postdoctoral appointment at the Sheps Center for Health Services Research was supported by NIMH grant T32-MH019117.

THE CARIBBEAN

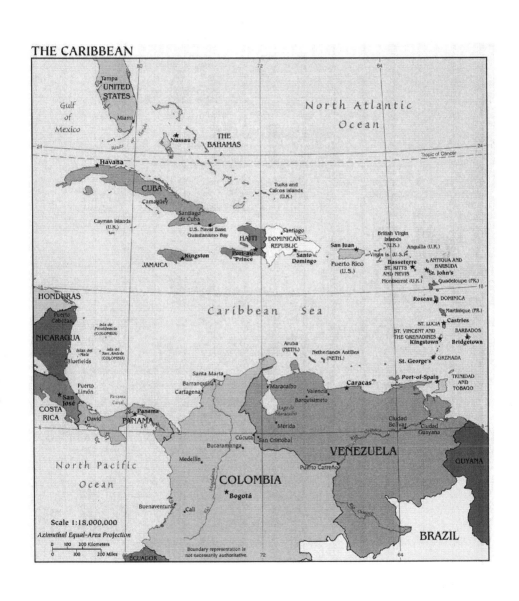

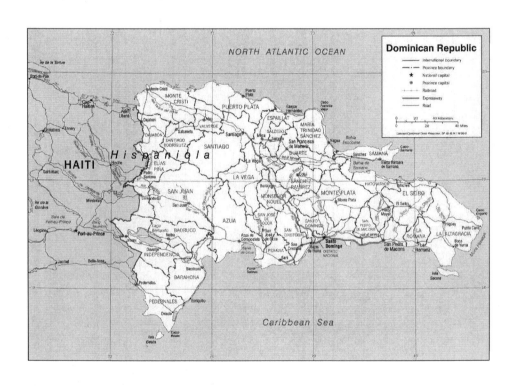

CHAPTER 1

The "Haitian Problem"

Krisla: "Haitians in the Dominican Republic Are Like Monkeys Trapped in a Cage"

> Haitians in the Dominican Republic are like monkeys trapped in a cage. They're given apples and bananas, and they think they're free—you understand? Even though they are in a cage, they feel like they're free. They play and jump, and they have their bananas, but their spirit is always trapped in the cage. Who else do you see living in these conditions like the Haitian? Or their children who live exactly the same way? They start to go to school until they get to a point where they can't finish because they don't have papers. Then they just stop there or get married—you understand? Then their children have children too. The same thing: They go to school until they get to a point where they are asked for papers. And the papers don't turn up, so they get married. That's what I mean when I say they are like the monkeys.

Krisla claps her hands for added emphasis on *trapped* as she connects the documentation constraints of people of Haitian descent to a larger, cyclical pattern that maintains generations of second-class citizens. "Haitians in the Dominican Republic are like monkeys *trapped* in a cage." Haitian parents and their Dominican-born children and grandchildren live in uncertainty and instability on the margins of Dominican society. Without birth certificates, Dominicans of Haitian descent have limited social integration. For example, the Dominican Ministry of Education allows children to matriculate through school even if they cannot present a birth certificate. Many schools, however, still require children to present documents upon enrollment. Further, if these children complete primary school, some school officials prevent them from taking the required national eighth-grade examinations if they cannot provide documentation.[1] Without completing the examinations, children cannot enter high school. Because of this pattern, many Dominicans of Haitian descent who do not have birth certificates drop out of school after eighth grade. This is one of many examples where the differences between policy and practice have a life-changing impact. Either children matriculate through high school or they drop out, get married, and continue the cycle, trapped in a social cage.

Krisla was born in Haiti and lived there most of her life. A seamstress, Krisla moved back and forth between Haiti and the Dominican Republic for years, only staying in the Dominican Republic for one or two months while she tried to sell the clothes she made. While Krisla was living in the Dominican Republic with another family member, her fourteen-year-old daughter became pregnant. Krisla moved from Haiti to the Dominican Republic to help her daughter with the baby.

The baby's father has a Dominican *cédula*, an identification card, but with recent changes to birthright-citizenship laws, his *cédula* has been suspended because his parents are Haitian migrants without legal residence.[2] Krisla says her daughter cannot register the baby's birth since she is a minor and will not have her own Dominican *cédula* until she turns eighteen. The baby's father suggests that his aunt and uncle register the child under their names. Krisla protests, saying she herself made that mistake in the past and it only complicates the situation. When her first son was born, Krisla was young, so she asked her mother to register her baby. "Now," Krisla says, "my son is successful, but he is my little brother, not my son. I don't want that for my daughter." At fifty-four years old, Krisla feels stuck in the Dominican Republic, unsure of what to do, until her grandchild gets his papers.

Policy responses to regulate immigrant populations often create unstable and unpredictable legal statuses, or "liminal legality," for affected groups. I provide a deeper discussion of liminal legality's key characteristics in chapter 3. A brief summary of the concept, however, can provide preliminary footholds to frame Krisla's complicated story. Liminal legality emphasizes the processes and systems by which government institutions create the gray areas of legality between what we call "documented" and "undocumented."[3] These binary categories are not specific enough to explain the varied experiences with documentation and legal status among immigrant families.[4] The father of Krisla's grandchild, for example, was born in the Dominican Republic and has a Dominican *cédula*. But since his *cédula* was suspended, he waits in limbo— neither documented nor undocumented—uncertain about whether he will be granted full citizenship in his home country.

For Krisla, liminal legality feels like being trapped in a cage. In the Dominican Republic, governmental and business organizations are complicit in maintaining a steady stream of workers without valid documentation, a readily exploitable labor force stuck in a cycle of vulnerability. Policy solutions that confer temporary legal statuses represent apples and bananas, but these solutions still preserve the cage around a subordinated group, maintaining their marginalization and limiting their social inclusion.

To add another layer of complexity to the way we understand documentation statuses, liminal legality happens within racialized social systems. A "racialized social system" perpetuates differential access to social and material resources based on race.[5] Racial contexts vary based on established local hierarchies in a given country. In the Dominican Republic, people of Haitian descent are the racial other that faces discrimination and social exclusion. Racial dynamics in the Dominican Republic are much more complex than I will discuss in this book. Such dynamics include both anti-Haitian discrimination and skin-color discrimination among Dominicans.[6] This book, however, focuses specifically on the social exclusion of people of Haitian descent. Where liminal legality and anti-Haitian racism converge, we find the stories and experiences of people of Haitian descent in the Dominican Republic.

Differences between Haitians and Dominicans include ethnic or cultural differences and practices. In this book, however, because participants use the language of racism to describe their experiences, I refer to systemic discrimination against people of Haitian descent as "anti-Haitian racism." One month after beginning this research, I held a group conversation with twelve people in a Dominican *batey*, a company town on a sugarcane plantation where sugar mill workers and their families live. As our discussion moved from discrimination to documentation, one participant said emphatically, "If a Haitian is born here, they are Haitian. If anyone else has a child here, they are Dominican." When I asked why, he responded, "Because they are racists." Several others nodded in agreement. I was struck by his use of the word "racist" and slightly surprised, since I was still learning how racism worked in this context. Over the course of my time in the country, however, people consistently used the term "racism" to articulate their opinions about how people of Haitian descent are treated in the Dominican Republic.

Following the lead of participants, I use "racism" to describe structural discrimination against people of Haitian descent. From a US racial lens, Haitians and Dominicans are categorically Black,[7] making it challenging for some to see how Black people could be racist against other Black people. Scholarship examining race and racism must, however, incorporate local hierarchies and interpretations. Stemming from their history of Spanish and French colonization, Dominican and Haitian populations include a range of skin colors, including people who might be categorized as white by US racial systems. In the Dominican Republic, however, people of Haitian descent face a swirling combination of racism and anti-immigrant sentiment. To apply a localized lens and distinguish anti-Haitian discrimination from skin-color discrimination among Dominicans, I use "anti-Haitian racism" to describe discrimination against people of Haitian descent.

Terms that describe populations matter. Political and media narratives intentionally conflate Haitian immigrants and Dominicans of Haitian descent to categorically classify Dominicans of Haitian descent as "not Dominican." For this reason, it is important that I define my use of descriptive terms for people of Haitian descent. Dominicans of Haitian descent are people born in the Dominican Republic to Haitian parents. Based on conversations with participants, either one or both parents may be Haitian. To add another layer of complexity, some Dominicans of Haitian descent in this study move back and forth between identifying as Dominican or identifying as Haitian, saying things like "Of course I'm Haitian. I can't deny my parents." The issue of self-identification is layered, and this book will not do it justice. For consistency, however, throughout the book, I use "Haitians" to refer to Haitian immigrants born in Haiti, "Dominicans of Haitian descent" to refer to people born in the Dominican Republic to Haitian parents, and "people of Haitian descent" when referring to both Dominicans of Haitian descent and Haitian immigrants.[8]

The "Haitian Problem"

Over decades, Haitian migrant workers were recruited to the Dominican Republic to perform agricultural labor under bilateral agreements between the Haitian and Dominican governments. The Dominican Republic needed a cheap labor source, and Haitians needed work. So in the 1970s and 1980s, the two governments agreed on a mutual exchange. Those policies have since lapsed, but the recruitment of Haitian workers continued. Human smugglers, the military, and border officials make promises, collect bribes, and confiscate documentation to funnel desperate Haitian workers—a vital labor source—to Dominican businesses.

After years of labor and living in the Dominican Republic, Haitian workers have created lives and had families in the country where they have worked. Since many were recruited without requiring proof of legal residence, they have had no official means of registering their Dominican-born children. So, following the lawful practice at the time, they used their work identification cards to get birth certificates for their children if they did not have a passport or visa. Today the Dominican government has invalidated the birth certificates for Dominicans of Haitian descent registered using work identification cards.[9] Even adults, like the father of Krisla's grandchild, have been affected by this change. At its core, "the Haitian problem"[10] resurfaces time and time again as the Dominican government continues to benefit from Haitian labor without incorporating the laborers into society.

In an action that codified the social exclusion of Dominicans of Haitian descent for generations, the Dominican Republic passed a new constitution in 2010 that increased conditionality on birthright citizenship. According to the new constitution, people born in the Dominican Republic are not Dominican citizens unless at least one of their parents can provide evidence of their own legal residence. Because Haitian migrant workers were recruited for labor regardless of whether they could provide evidence of their legal status, people of Haitian descent are the primary group affected by this change to birthright citizenship.

As if this were not enough to alter the life trajectory of people born since 2010, the Dominican government also initiated an audit of civil records to identify people who were "wrongfully" registered as Dominicans. They retroactively applied the 2010 constitution to suspend documents and strip citizenship from people whose births were registered in 1983, for example, based on a law that was passed in 2010. The government also created a Book of Foreigners for Dominicans of Haitian descent who could not document their parents' legality. The Book of Foreigners ensures that generations of babies of Haitian descent will be born into second-class citizenship. In subsequent sections, I describe this series of legal changes in greater detail. But this brief overview illustrates the breadth and depth of anti-Haitian racism evident in documentation policies. Without full citizenship, Dominicans of Haitian descent cannot complete their education, and they cannot vote. Government exclusion from both social-mobility pathways and political participation are ominous reminders that a Haitian labor source was never meant to be integrated into Dominican society.

In Someone Else's Country has three primary goals. The first is to discuss liminal legality in a context where both Haitian immigrants and Dominican-born persons are subject to policies that move them into precarious legal statuses. The second is to examine policy changes in the Dominican Republic to shed light on how legality operates within a racialized social system. Finally, I show how people of Haitian descent experience the policies that affect their lives. This is the first ethnographic account to examine the experiences of people of Haitian descent under new birthright-citizenship policies. The narratives and experiences shared in this book connect legality and racism while unpacking the ways that policies reproduce racial inequality.

Joseph: "It Was Me Who Took Care of You! You Should Feel Bad, Right?"

Joseph is a Haitian migrant who has lived and worked in Dominican *bateyes* for forty years. He and I sit on a makeshift wooden bench under a palm tree. His legs are crossed, and his arms are folded across his chest, his body protecting itself from this foreign encounter with a foreigner. I delve more deeply into Joseph's story in a subsequent chapter; however, a snapshot of his perspective illustrates how anti-Haitian racism and labor exploitation intersect.

During our interview, I can feel his heartache and frustration as Joseph describes what it feels like to be a problem. He repeatedly circles back to what Dominicans say about Haitians on the news. "They tell you 'You have no value; you have no country,'" he says. "All these words fall on the ears of the whole world, because, you know, we sit in front of the radio and we listen to what is happening in the world. . . . These things hurt!"

"The ones doing all the worst work are the Haitians," he continues. "So, for example, if a Cuban comes to this country, who do you think they are going to look for to find them land and raise their animals? Haitians! Who is taking care of the work for the big shots? Haitians! Everywhere you go, Haitians work."

Still, Joseph is confused about how he could work so hard and so long and be met with contempt on a global stage. "If I come to your house and you give me some of what you have, then afterward you talk bad about me? It was *me* who took care of *you*. You should feel bad, right? That's the problem."[11] This narrative reframes the "Haitian problem," shifting the perspective from the Dominican government to the Haitian people. The problem Joseph describes is that he took care of the Dominican Republic, but the Dominican Republic is avoiding its responsibility to take care of him in return. And instead of expressing remorse and taking steps to reconcile, the Dominican government makes Haitians feel like a burden on the economy that they maintain.

I understood that capitalism is about continually increasing the profit margin, but I kept asking myself: How does race factor into the equation? Joseph's illustrative perspective connects race and labor. Labor systems built on anti-Haitian racism justify exploitation by reinforcing the narrative that this is simply the kind of work Haitians do. This low-wage, undesirable work is Haitian work. Many people—both Dominicans and people of Haitian descent—describe Haitian labor as the most grueling labor in the country. And the beneficiaries, Dominican businesses, profit on the backs of Haitian workers while the government actively excludes people of Haitian descent from society.

Rosa: "Now I Can't Get Married Because You Are Haitian"

Rosa is a Dominican woman of Haitian descent and a hopeless romantic. One morning, Rosa and I sit on wooden chairs at a small, dark wooden table pushed against her living room wall. Her five-year-old daughter—often a playmate for my four-year-old son—waltzes in and out during our conversation, and Rosa shoos her off to play. At the start of our interview, I ask a question meant to build rapport and open conversation: "Can you tell me about the last time you had a really good day?" Rosa tells me a story about the time she went to a friend's wedding.

"Well, not long ago," Rosa says, "I had such a precious day. It's a good story." She laughs and continues.

> About three months ago, I had a beautiful day . . . because, really, I have always dreamed of having a wedding to celebrate my marriage. For me, a wedding is something beautiful and precious. Well, my cousin got married, and it was a marvelous day for me because I imagined that it was me getting married that day. I woke up early that day, happy. I organized everything I had to organize. I went to town to get their gift. I went to the salon, and I looked so pretty! Later, we went to the wedding, and it was something special. Really. I had a good time. I liked it because it has always been my dream!

Rosa chuckles softly, shaking her head. "And I hope that one day, I will celebrate my own wedding. God willing, maybe next year . . ."

We are deep into our conversation before I realize that Rosa and her husband are married in the community but not legally. They have not had a wedding, and they do not have an official marriage license. The topic arises when I ask about documentation: "Have you had any problems with documentation for yourself or for your kids?"

"Not really—not for my kids," Rosa replies. "They were born and registered the same day, thank God. And my father declared me and my sisters when we were born. And so . . . I mean . . . well, after this new law came out." Rosa looks down, shifting a little in her chair. "So, when I went to be married by law, and since my parents are foreigners, they declared me with a *ficha* [work identification card]. And that's given me a few . . . problems. I haven't been able to get married by law. Because of this, *no soy liberada* [I'm not free]."

An official marriage license has both material and social benefits. A marriage certificate allows women access to their husband's employer-provided health insurance. It also allows women to access their husband's pension payments that provide financial stability and support after he dies. Equally as painful as the exclusion from employer benefits are the interpersonal consequences of institutionalized social exclusion. Rosa describes intrafamilial tension with her parents and her husband. She and her husband had an argument when they realized they would be unable to get a marriage license. I asked Rosa a question about discrimination: "Have you ever heard a joke that made you feel offended?"

"Well," Rosa begins slowly, "my husband joked with me on the day that he and I were going to get married. When I got to the office, there was a problem . . . the one I was telling you about. My husband doesn't have this problem." Rosa fidgets, folding and unfolding her hands. "So, he started saying 'It's bad dealing with *el haitiano* [the Haitian]. Look, now I can't get married because you are Haitian.' It really made me feel bad. I said, 'Wow!' and I just stayed calm. But I felt bad, so I told him, 'Well, you're *congo*.'"

"What does that mean?" I ask.

"*Congo* means that someone is an immigrant that came from *allá* [Haiti; literally, 'there']. But he's not." She chuckles, a little uncomfortable. "I tried to . . . how do I explain this? I tried to *desahogarme* [blow off steam] by saying that to him. Besides, it's not my fault. It's my parents' fault for not getting their Dominican *cédula* after so many years here. And I told him, 'If I'm Haitian, you're *congo*.'" She chuckles again. "But I . . . really, I felt . . ." Rosa's voice trails off. She blames her parents for not having legal residence and feels hurt when her legal status drives a wedge between her and her husband. In the end, Rosa uses *congo*, a term reserved for Haitian immigrants, as a counterinsult—a last-ditch effort to repair her dignity shattered by a government that will not see her.

Liminal legality causes divisions within families, and its underpinning racism categorically lumps all people of Haitian descent as outsiders in someone else's country. Within families, communities, cities, and national boundaries, documentation policies built on anti-Haitian racism institutionalize second-class citizenship for people born in their own country.

Racism and Immigration: A Global Problem

Race and Labor

Racial hierarchies and labor exploitation work in tandem.[12] In this book, I am particularly interested in how racialized immigrant labor justifies corruption, inhumane living conditions, and unfair payment for undesirable (yet indispensable) work. These patterns are not unique to the Dominican Republic. The bracero program, for example, brought millions of Mexican workers to the United States under a bilateral contractual agreement between 1942 and 1964. Most braceros (manual laborers) filled an agricultural labor shortage in the United States economy. During this period, about two hundred thousand Mexican laborers came to the United States each year under the promise of work, a living wage, and a retirement savings plan. Upon arrival to work in the United States, braceros met a harsh reality: They worked and lived in unsanitary conditions and faced economic exploitation where employers withheld wages and used controlling measures to tether workers to the fields until the end of the harvest. Today agricultural workers in the United States still fight for improved labor conditions and a living wage.[13]

When groups originally meant to be a marginalized labor force step outside established boundaries, legal measures institutionalize social separation. In the 1920s, for example, Filipino farm workers were recruited to the United States for seasonal agricultural labor in California.[14] They endured deplorable working and living conditions while they fulfilled contracts to plant and harvest fruits, vegetables, and rice. As their numbers grew, Filipino workers faced racial discrimination from white Americans who accused them of stealing their jobs. Filipino farm workers were publicly framed in racist terms as uneducated, worthless, and prone to violence and crime. Mostly men, they were also seen as a threat to white women, and in 1933 the California government passed a law that retroactively invalidated all marriages between whites and nonwhites. In this case, racism against Filipino workers in the United States provoked a legal response to reinforce social separation of a population that would not stay in its government-intended place: the fields.

Despite their relatively small population within the Dominican Republic, people of Haitian descent are continually framed as a group out of place. Haitians comprise an estimated 80 percent of the total foreign-born population in the Dominican Republic. But relative to the broader population, Haitian immigrants comprise only 4.89 percent.[15] Likewise, Dominicans of Haitian descent comprise an estimated 91 percent of people who are native-born children of immigrants but only 2.7 percent of the Dominican Republic's total population. Haitians were historically recruited to work in sugarcane fields, and sugarcane labor was decidedly Haitian work.[16] But their labor has moved from isolated *bateyes* to more visible, urban spaces.[17] Construction sites, for example, employ Haitian migrant workers looking to earn a living and support their families. Their children, Dominicans of Haitian descent, are also veering outside their imagined boundaries. As they carve out a path to social mobility by trying to access higher-education opportunities, the government responds by passing laws that limit social integration and relegate Dominicans of Haitian descent to a social subclass. The inextricable connections between race, labor, and legality led me to explore the role of political power as an additional reason why racism and documentation policies converge.

Race and Legality

Across the globe, immigration policies that once protected vulnerable groups may be discontinued as immigrants are increasingly under attack. The current US government has taken a "tough on immigrants" stance that successfully rallied constituents who feel threatened by immigrants' presence in the country. And policies make no concessions for the people whose lives are upended as laws change. Yatta Kiazolu, for example, was born in Botswana to Liberian parents and has Liberian citizenship.[18] When she was six years old, her family moved to the United States. Since then, Kiazolu has lived in the United States under a temporary visa status. But at twenty-eight years old, in her final year of a PhD program, the US government is pushing to end the temporary visa program that has provided Kiazolu with legal residence all her life. Since Kiazolu has Liberian citizenship, an end to the program would mean that she would be deported to Liberia—a country where she has never lived. Immigration policies in the United States have a long history of incorporating racism by placing greater restrictions on immigrants from African and Latin American countries than on those from European countries.[19] Within racialized social systems, racism works to separate those deemed outside of the national imaginary.

The intersection of racism and anti-immigrant sentiment serves multiple political purposes. In many countries, a public stance against immigration is a rallying cry to unify a collective "us" against "them" to stimulate voter participation and maintain political power. Immigration debates have racial undertones that surface when they are politically useful. The United Kingdom's decision to leave the European Union—known as "Brexit"—was partially related to racial tension resulting from a growing immigrant population. The campaign to leave, led by a right-wing political party in the United Kingdom, was steeped in "racially charged animus toward immigrants."[20] Ultimately, campaigns to "put the 'Great' back into Great Britain" paralleled slogans in the United States promising to "Make American Great Again" by building a wall along the US–Mexico border to keep "the other" out. Both campaigns successfully entrenched a political line in the sand cemented by racism and anti-immigrant sentiment.

In other cases, racism and anti-immigrant sentiment intersect to create laws that control populations deemed undesirable. In India, for example, almost two million people may be stateless after being excluded from a national register of citizens in Assam, a state that borders the neighboring country of Bangladesh.[21] The vast majority of those affected are from the state's Bengali Muslim community, an ethnic-minority group in India. In 2013, India's Supreme Court initiated an update of their National Register of Citizens, a list of Indian citizens living in Assam. Nationalist groups in Assam have characterized Bengali Muslims as a cultural threat, but the government denies accusations that they are targeting a specific ethnic group, saying that they are simply complying with India's Supreme Court order to create a citizenship register for the state of Assam. People who were excluded from the register now must navigate financial and bureaucratic barriers to access legal statuses that protect them from deportation. In a context where illiteracy rates are high and clerical errors such as misspelled names on paperwork abound, hundreds of thousands of people must find electoral rolls, land records, bank accounts, government certificates, or other documents to prove their right to citizenship. Meanwhile, the Indian government is building mass detention camps to imprison those deemed illegal.

In countries across the globe, anti-immigrant sentiment and racism converge at the expense of immigrants from marginalized racial or ethnic backgrounds. In the Dominican Republic, this convergence serves two purposes. First, it replicates political power systems by solidifying "us" and "them" to cement the vision of a Dominican society without people of Haitian descent.

In addition, this second-class system institutionalized by the Dominican Constitution perpetuates the ability to control and monitor an undesirable, racially marginalized population.

Anti-Haitian Racism

Racism provides an ideological explanation for both labor exploitation and social divisions in the Dominican Republic. Racism perpetuates social divisions that justify why people of Haitian descent should be a source of cheap labor: "This kind of work is Haitian work." Racism also underscores differences between groups that substantiate sociopolitical divisions: "Because they are so different from Dominicans, the children of Haitians should not be given full citizenship." In this section, I provide an overview of historical and contemporary anti-Haitian racism to foreground a discussion of liminal legality among people of Haitian descent.

"Structural racism," broadly, refers to the complex systems that develop and maintain race-based hierarchies and inequality.[22] Structural racism results in differential access to opportunities and resources in government, education, and workplaces. At its core, structural racism is designed to ensure that power dynamics between racial groups remain imbalanced as one group maintains political, economic, and social control at the expense of groups deemed inferior.

Anti-Haitian racism[23] is systemic discrimination against people of Haitian descent. A form of structural racism, anti-Haitian racism is designed to maintain hierarchical systems that impede people of Haitian descent from political, economic, and social participation in the Dominican Republic. Anti-Haitian racism is rooted in the belief system that people of Haitian descent are inferior to other groups in the Dominican Republic.

Like alternative forms of racism in other countries, anti-Haitian racism is a political tool that supports elite groups as they preserve political power. It allows leaders to galvanize public support and maintain social control in the Dominican Republic while excluding people of Haitian descent from the national narrative. For example, just as the racial order in the United States socially positions Blacks and whites as polar opposites to maintain white supremacy,[24] Dominicans and Haitians have been portrayed as polar opposites within the ideology of anti-Haitian racism.[25] This positioning allows the Dominican elite to centralize political power around a common adversary: Haitian immigrants.

Historical Anti-Haitian Racism

A legacy of racist Spanish colonialism and cultural racism undergirds contemporary anti-Haitian racism. Hispaniola, the island shared by present-day Haiti and the Dominican Republic, was a Spanish colony that increased in geographic importance as the slave trade began to boom during the sixteenth century. By the middle of the 1500s, Santo Domingo was the main slave-import city for the region, and thousands of enslaved Africans were working in sugar mills and plantations.[26] In the second half of the seventeenth century, French settlers invaded Hispaniola and colonized the western part of the island, renaming the land "Saint-Domingue." The French brought thousands of enslaved people from Africa to their new colony to support a booming plantation system anchored on the production of sugar and coffee for the European market.

From 1791 to 1804, a thirteen-year slave revolt led by Toussaint L'Ouverture established Haiti as an independent nation. Fearing that the French would use Dominican territory to reconquer Haiti, the Haitian and Dominican sides of the island were unified under Haitian rule from 1822 to 1844. Contemporary narratives that reference the "Haitian invasion" in the Dominican Republic often invoke the fear that, if given too much power, people of Haitian descent will once again reunify the island, taking control of Hispaniola as they did over a century ago.

One of the most notorious leaders to solidify anti-Haitian racism as part of Dominican culture was Rafael Trujillo.[27] A brutally violent dictator, Trujillo used immigration policy and political propaganda to institutionalize anti-Haitian racism. Before becoming dictator, Trujillo had belonged to the Dominican National Guard, a military branch that had a virtual monopoly of power in the country in the 1920s. Part of what facilitated the Dominican National Guard's rise to power was the established presence and rule of the US military in the Dominican Republic between 1916 and 1924. During World War I, the United States feared that German forces might use the Dominican Republic as a base for attacks on US soil. As a defensive measure, over a highly controversial eight-year period, the United States disbanded Dominican local militia groups, centralized the Dominican National Guard, increased their weapons, and trained Dominican soldiers—including Trujillo.[28]

From 1930 to 1961, Trujillo used secret police and militarized rule to imprison, torture, and murder people who opposed his dictatorial reign. During the 1930s, economies across the globe felt the strain and desperation of the Great Depression. In the Dominican Republic, Haitian immigrants were the scapegoat for the country's economic instability. Although their labor contributed to the Dominican economy, Trujillo began a national agenda built on anti-Haitian racism. A central tenet of Trujillo's rule was to rid the country of Haitians and exclude them from the national narrative of Dominican identity. Addressing "the Haitian problem" would require a three-pronged approach: people, propaganda, and policy.

Trujillo's plan sought to rid the country of people of Haitian descent and reshape Dominican public identity. He initiated a national anti-Haitian campaign to create a widespread fear of Haitians, perpetuating the belief that they were not to be trusted.[29] School textbooks were full of distortions, exaggerations, and outright falsifications. A popular history textbook portrayed Haitians as apelike, while Dominicans were drawn to look like Spaniards.[30] During his rule, Trujillo planted and sowed seeds for growing anti-Haitian sentiment that culminated in the massacre of thousands of Haitians living in the Dominican Republic. Following the national anti-Haitian propaganda campaign, Trujillo ordered the murder of tens of thousands of Haitians at the border. In 1937, between fifteen thousand and twenty thousand Haitians and dark-skinned Dominicans were brutally murdered with machetes, bayonets, and clubs.[31]

Immigration policies during this era paralleled a national agenda of *blanqueamiento*, or "whitening." *Blanqueamiento* is both an ideology and a set of practices at the individual and national levels that whiten populations in the Latin American imaginary.[32] At the national level, many countries, including Argentina, Uruguay, Chile, and the Dominican Republic, enacted immigration policies that encouraged white immigrants and discouraged or excluded Black immigrants.[33] The Dominican government enacted immigration policies that imposed a tax on Black and Asian immigrants while gifting white immigrants with parcels of land in regions that the government established for agricultural development.[34] The history of colonialism, xenophobic dictatorial leadership, and discriminatory immigration policies provide a contextual foundation for understanding contemporary anti-Haitian racism in the Dominican Republic.

Contemporary Anti-Haitian Racism

The Dominican population includes people from many different countries. Chinese and West Indian immigrants in the Dominican Republic, for example, have integration experiences that are unique to their historical and political migration stories.[35] Haitian migrants and their families experience a particularly complex story of economic inclusion and social exclusion.[36] Verónica, a twenty-six-year-old Dominican woman of Haitian descent, describes what it feels like to be treated like an outsider in her own country. Malena, a Dominican research assistant of Haitian descent, asked Verónica about her experiences with racism.

"Do you think life is different for Blacks and whites?" Malena asks.

"Well, you don't need glasses to see what's right in front of you!" Malena and Verónica laugh. "I mean, because you see how we are in the Dominican Republic. There is a lot of preference between Blacks and whites."

"Where are they treated differently? In school? At work? In families?"

"Everywhere. *El blanquito* [the white person] is treated better."

"Have you ever experienced discrimination?" Malena asks.

"Yes," Verónica replies, as though the answer is obvious.

"Do you want to share an experience?"

"Well, sometimes, when you're walking in the street you hear, '*¡Mira a esa haitianita, esa prietica, esa tan fea! ¿Por qué no la mandan para su país? ¡Ellos sólo vienen para joder a nuestro país!*' [Look at that Haitian, that ugly dark-skinned woman! Why don't they send her back to her country? They just come here to fuck up our country!]"

"How do you feel when they say these things?" Malena asks.

"Horrible," Verónica replies. "Because it's not my fault."

Anti-Haitian racism and anti-Black racism are different, yet related, concepts. Anti-Black racism refers to discriminatory practices that advantage whiteness over Blackness.[37] In the Dominican Republic, for example, the range of categories between Black and white include *indio*, *indio claro*, *indio oscuro*, *trigueño*, and *moreno*.[38] Still, racism in Latin America negatively impacts people on the darker end of the racial spectrum. On almost every social indicator, those with dark skin in Latin America[39] do worse than their whiter counterparts. This includes having poorer health, well-being, education, and literacy.[40] In the labor market, darker-skinned Latin Americans earn lower wages than their lighter-skinned counterparts,[41] and social norms reinforce the privilege of whiteness. For example, employment opportunities in the tourism industry that require face-to-face interaction with customers are typically staffed by people with a whiter appearance, while darker-skinned employees work behind the scenes.[42]

Anti-Haitian racism, discrimination against people of Haitian descent, incorporates anti-Black racism. In the Dominican Republic, darker skin is associated with people of Haitian descent. People in La Tierra, the *batey* where this research was conducted, encounter discrimination related to both their skin color and their Haitian ethnicity, as in Verónica's anecdote. *Prietica*—the word she was called on the street, which is derived from *prieta/o*—describes very dark brown skin in the Dominican Republic. But the directive to go "back to her country" reminds Verónica that people see her as an outsider in the place where she was born. The anti-Haitian insults hurled at Verónica reinforce social boundaries of belonging for Dominicans of Haitian descent. It is as though she is living in someone else's country when, in fact, it is her own.

Francia is a Dominican woman who lives in La Tierra and views discrimination as part of the immigrant experience—especially for immigrants ascribed to lower racial categories in their new country.

"Some people say that the Dominican Republic is racist," I begin carefully, "and that they mistreat Haitians." Francia leans back in her chair.

"Look, I'm going to tell you the truth," Francia says. "The issue is that the people who come here, they are foreigners. And they are disrespected. If you're in a different country, you're going to be uncomfortable. Listen: If you are in your country and someone from here comes there, you'll disrespect them too! You'll say, 'Look at this damn Dominican! Coming here to fuck everything up!'"

Francia continues.

> I'll tell you, here in this country? We don't mistreat Haitians. The problem is that if they come here, they can't think that they are going to have the same life that we [Dominicans] have here. But they are not mistreated. If they were mistreated, then they wouldn't get the best positions and jobs. If you go to a store, the first cashier you see is a Haitian. Then you look and you realize that the manager is Haitian too! So where is the mistreatment? They are not barred from entering stores or banks. . . . Here they are not blocked from anything. I don't believe there is any racism here.

She stops and looks at me, reading my reaction.

I respond, "Some people say they are called a *maldito haitiano* [damned Haitian]. What do you think about that phrase?"

"It's the same as the phrase Dominicans hear when they go to Puerto Rico or New York," Francia replies. "They hear 'Fucking Dominican!'" She says the phrase in English. "That's just how it is."

As their labor moves from isolated *bateyes* to more public spaces, people of Haitian descent are more visible, sparking efforts to "control" the population.

Francia can see people of Haitian descent in stores and in leadership positions, which bolsters her argument that anti-Haitian racism does not exist. Yet when I offer examples of interpersonal discrimination against people of Haitian descent, Francia describes racism as a universal part of the immigrant experience: When immigrants move to another country, they are at the bottom of the racial hierarchy. Racism is to be expected.

Importantly, Francia's perspective mirrors that of the Dominican government: there is no anti-Haitian racism, and Haitians are everywhere. While Francia uses these two observations in tandem to illustrate the absence of racism, the Dominican government uses them to obscure discriminatory measures meant to push people of Haitian descent to the margins. As one person in La Tierra describes, politicians *tiran la piedra y esconden la mano* (throw a rock and hide their hand). The threat of Haitians in more visible social spaces sparks policy responses steeped in anti-Haitian racism. Yet the government hides behind the universality of immigration laws, even as such laws are applied in ways that target specific groups.[43]

Immigrants from marginalized racial or ethnic groups experience a form of racism that incorporates border control, social exclusion, and—in some cases—restricted political power.[44] Policies that provide documentation without full citizenship, as in the case of Dominicans of Haitian descent, create liminal legality. *In Someone Else's Country* highlights the experiences of people of Haitian descent to shed light on connections between racism and legality across the globe.

Liminal Legality in the Dominican Republic

A series of legal changes over a ten-year period affect contemporary legal status for people of Haitian descent in the Dominican Republic (figure 1.1). From 1929 until 2004, the Dominican Republic conferred birthright citizenship to anyone born on Dominican soil unless they were "in transit." Differences between policy and practice underscore the tensions that led to present-day discrimination codified into law.[45] In practice, many Dominican civil-registry offices refused to issue birth certificates to children of Haitian migrants. By the 1990s, these discriminatory practices were well documented.[46] In response, Dominican civil society mobilized, pressuring local civil registries to process applications in accordance with the law while influential dissenting voices pushed for the laws to change.

Until 2004, "in transit" referred to children of diplomats and children born to people who were residing in the country for ten days or less. In 2004, however, a new General Law on Migration (*la Ley General de Migración* No. 285-04) classified several new groups of people as "in transit."[47] The new groups included temporary foreign workers, migrants with expired residency visas, migrant workers brought into the country surreptitiously, and people who are unable to prove their lawful residence in the Dominican Republic. Since the primary population of migrant workers recruited for agricultural labor was Haitian, the new groups in transit included more Haitian

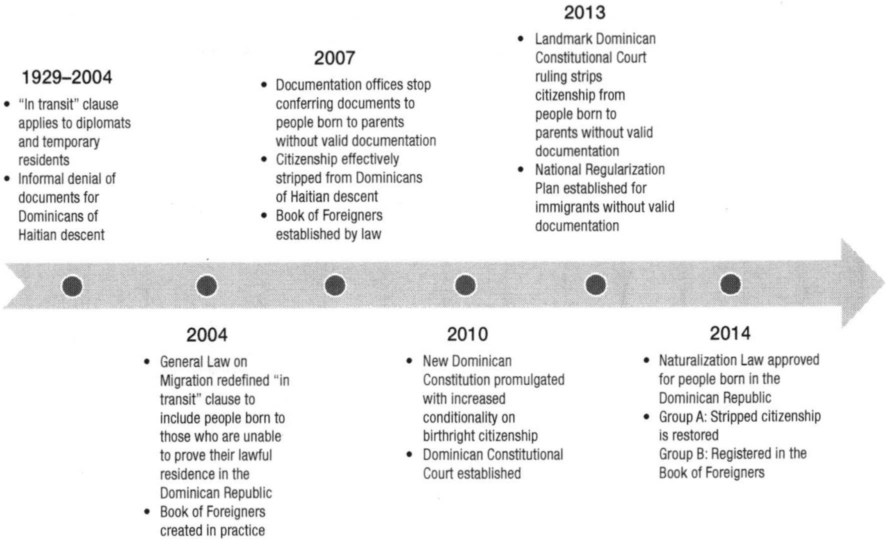

2013
- Landmark Dominican Constitutional Court ruling strips citizenship from people born to parents without valid documentation
- National Regularization Plan established for immigrants without valid documentation

2007
- Documentation offices stop conferring documents to people born to parents without valid documentation
- Citizenship effectively stripped from Dominicans of Haitian descent
- Book of Foreigners established by law

1929–2004
- "In transit" clause applies to diplomats and temporary residents
- Informal denial of documents for Dominicans of Haitian descent

2004
- General Law on Migration redefined "in transit" clause to include people born to those who are unable to prove their lawful residence in the Dominican Republic
- Book of Foreigners created in practice

2010
- New Dominican Constitution promulgated with increased conditionality on birthright citizenship
- Dominican Constitutional Court established

2014
- Naturalization Law approved for people born in the Dominican Republic
- Group A: Stripped citizenship is restored
  Group B: Registered in the Book of Foreigners

Figure 1.1. Timeline of legal changes related to documentation for people of Haitian descent in the Dominican Republic

Source: Trenita Childers

immigrants than any other group. Consequently, the new interpretation of the "in transit" clause effectively identified and denationalized Dominicans of Haitian descent. After the passage of the 2004 General Law on Migration, documentation offices ramped up the previously unofficial practice of denying birth certificates to children born of Haitian parents.

In 2007, as mandated by the 2004 General Law on Migration, the Central Electoral Board (CEB), the Dominican civil-registry office that provides documentation services, created a foreign registry, commonly known as the Book of Foreigners or "pink registers." The Book of Foreigners ensured that no children of Haitian migrants in transit would be mistakenly registered as Dominican nationals. When a child is born in a hospital in the Dominican Republic and the parents cannot prove their legal status with valid documentation, the child is issued a pink birth certificate. The child's parents must register the child in the Book of Foreigners using the pink birth certificate. Registration in the Book of Foreigners gives the child a document but does not confer full citizenship. For example, Dominicans of Haitian descent registered in the Book of Foreigners do not have voting rights. This broadscale disenfranchisement rooted in anti-Haitian racism ensures that generations of Dominicans of Haitian descent are excluded from civil society.

In the same year, the CEB also issued guidance known as Circular 17, or Resolution 12 (referred to as "Resolution 12" hereafter), which initiated the retroactive stripping of citizenship from Dominicans of Haitian descent. Under this guidance, civil-registry officers were instructed to stop conferring identity documents to "children of foreign parents who had received birth certificates under irregular circumstance[s]."[48] When interacting with various institutions, such as primary schools and universities, Dominicans must request their birth certificates from a civil-registry office. But following Resolution 12, many Dominicans of Haitian descent had their requests denied. Children and adults born long before the 2004 General Law on Migration had redefined people "in transit" suffered the consequences of the retroactive application of a law restricting birthright citizenship. As a result, thousands were pushed into statelessness, their legal status in limbo as officials audited their documents to determine their right to citizenship in their country of birth.

This change disproportionately affected Dominicans of Haitian descent. For example, the *ficha* is an identification card issued by a private Dominican employer—in most cases, a sugar mill. For decades, Haitian migrant workers were permitted to use the *ficha* to get birth certificates for their Dominican-born children if they could not provide other documentation, such as a valid Haitian passport. But documentation offices identify children and adults born to migrant workers with unauthorized legal status based in part on whether their parents used a *ficha* to register their births. An effort to "clean up" the national civil registry under increased conditionality on birthright citizenship, Resolution 12 effectively stripped citizenship from a group that was primarily Dominicans of Haitian descent.

Advocates in the Dominican Republic made clear the human-rights violations inherent in Resolution 12, which stripped citizenship along racial lines. In support, international human-rights organizations publicly denounced such discriminatory practices, especially as new interpretations of birthright citizenship under the 2004 General Law on Migration were not aligned with the definitions of citizenship outlined in the country's constitution. Rather than acknowledging the impact of unjust policies and practices, however, the Dominican government denounced any accusations of anti-Haitian racism and doubled down on discrimination by changing the country's constitution to align with the 2004 immigration law.

In 2010, the Dominican Republic passed a new constitution that mirrored the increased conditionality on birthright citizenship established by the General Law on Migration in 2004. According to the new constitution, birthright citizenship was no longer applicable to the children of "foreigners in transit or residing illegally in the Dominican territory."[49] This change to the constitution aligned the nation's governing document with previously applied policies and practices. The 2010 constitution also established the Dominican Constitutional Court (Tribunal Constitucional), whose thirteen judges were tasked with enforcing "constitutional justice." Their judicial authority would soon be tested using the legal case of a young Dominican woman of Haitian descent named Juliana Deguis Pierre.

In 2008, in accordance with the regulations of the audit ordered in 2007, the Central Electoral Board withheld Juliana's *cédula*. Juliana had been born in the Dominican Republic in 1984. Both of her parents lived and worked on a sugarcane plantation, and neither had legal residence in the country. Under the prevailing laws at the time of her birth, Juliana had been issued a birth certificate. In 2008, at twenty-four years old, she went to a documentation office to request a *cédula*, the national identification card. The staff not only denied her request but also nullified her birth certificate on the grounds that her parents both had Haitian last names. Juliana appealed her case, but the court rejected her appeal, saying that she had provided copies of her birth certificate when applying for her *cédula* instead of the original—which was being held by the Central Electoral Board.

As one of their first acts, the Dominican Constitutional Court picked up Juliana's case in 2013. But instead of deciding whether she was a victim of discrimination, the court ruled that Juliana did not have the right to birthright citizenship and that she never should have been granted a birth certificate to begin with. Further, the court ruled that all others in Juliana's situation—those born in the Dominican Republic to parents without legal residence—should never have been granted Dominican citizenship either and that their Dominican citizenship should be revoked. To correct these "errors," the court ordered another audit of civil records to identify persons registered as Dominicans between 1929 and 2007 under previous birthright-citizenship laws.[50] According to the court, those persons should have their Dominican documents nullified and, instead, be registered in the Book of Foreigners.

The Constitutional Court's landmark decision created chaos for those affected by the ruling while pushing three major political steps forward. The ruling (1) set legal precedent for denying Dominicans of Haitian descent their citizenship, (2) ordered an audit to strip citizenship from those "erroneously" registered as Dominicans, and (3) required that the Dominican government create a plan to regularize the status of migrants with unauthorized legal status within ninety days. The implications of the ruling are far-reaching, as they redefined interpretations of legality along racial lines while allowing the government to hide behind the guise of "universal" laws. In the face of international criticism, the Dominican government touted the sovereignty of the country's responsibility to construct national boundaries without international interference. Still, subsequent measures to regularize the legal status of Haitian migrant workers and Dominicans of Haitian descent without documentation would place bandages on the gaping wounds created by the Constitutional Court's ruling.

In November 2013, just two months after the ruling, President Danilo Medina issued a presidential decree stating that a regularization plan would be established. One month later, in December, the Dominican Republic established the National Regularization Plan for Foreigners with an irregular migration status (PNRE). The PNRE created a new framework for regularization that included temporary, permanent, and nonimmigrant classifications for people with unauthorized status residing in the Dominican Republic. The PNRE also outlined eligibility factors for the future regularization plan, such as length of stay in the country at a fixed address, ties to society, knowledge of spoken and written Spanish, children born in the Dominican Republic, and criminal record.[51] Importantly, however, the PNRE did not specify exactly how people would access this path to regularization, leaving them with a temporary and unstable legal status.

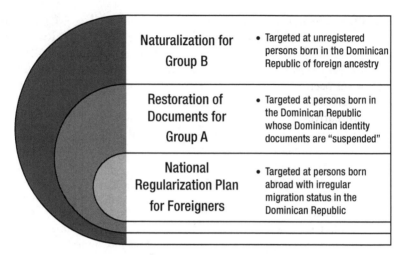

Figure 1.2. From mid-2014 up to the present, the Dominican government has been implementing these three parallel processes

Source: Bridget Wooding, "Haitian Immigrants and Their Descendants Born in the Dominican Republic," *Oxford Research Encyclopedia of Latin American History*, Oxford University Press, online publication January 2018, https://oxfordre.com/latinamericanhistory/view/10.1093/acrefore/9780199366439.001.0001/acrefore-9780199366439-e-474?rskey=PWgo27&result=188.

In 2014, eight months after the Constitutional Court's landmark ruling, the Dominican government enacted Naturalization Law 169-14 (Ley de Régimen Especial y Naturalización 169-14). Law 169-14 created a naturalization process for two groups born in the Dominican Republic (figure 1.2): Group A included the approximately fifty-five thousand Dominican-born people whose citizenship was stripped. Group B included Dominican-born people who had never acquired nationality documents either because they were born in rural areas and not in a hospital or because they left the hospital without documents amid administrative confusion about "pink papers" and the Book of Foreigners.

For those in Group A, Law 169-14 legally restored their Dominican nationality. In practice, however, five years after the ruling, only about half actually had their documents reinstated. Those in Group B, people whose births were never registered, were to naturalize through a procedure that required them to first declare themselves Haitian nationals and register in the Book of Foreigners—in spite of being born in the Dominican Republic—then complete an undefined naturalization process two years later. This process proved socially and politically complicated. Since they are living in the only country they have ever known, Dominicans of Haitian descent rejected the idea that they are foreigners. Further, there were several bureaucratic barriers to enrollment in the Book of Foreigners. Enrolling often required multiple trips to documentation offices and funds for transportation, making it difficult for families with limited resources to access. As a result, only 8,755 applications for Group B naturalization status were filed before the established deadline. It is difficult to quantify the population whose births were never registered. Some groups estimate that Group B is larger than Group A.[52] Conservative estimates place the Group B population at about fifty thousand people, suggesting that the vast majority of those affected remain stateless.[53] Further, five years after Law 169-14 was passed, no one in Group B had been naturalized because the naturalization process had not yet been established.

I cannot overstate the tremendous confusion associated with the sweeping government initiatives for multiple groups occurring in tandem. Dominican-born people in Groups A and B are trying to resolve their documentation issues, while Haitian migrants are trying to access the national regularization plan. Several groups receive information from documentation offices where officials conflate distinct groups with distinct needs. This conflation, sometimes intentional, reinforces the political narrative that all people of Haitian descent are foreigners, no matter where they were born.

In this book I shift the dominant lens away from governments by placing people of Haitian descent at the center. Their voices and their experiences unearth alternative ways to understand policy implications and accessibility. If you, the reader, are still confused after learning about government changes in Dominican birthright citizenship, one can only imagine how people of Haitian descent must feel trying to make sense of laws that have life-changing implications. If you still have questions after reading about the series of steps required to procure appropriate documentation under the national regularization plan or the naturalization law, then navigating these programs as a Haitian migrant who can read in neither Haitian Creole nor Spanish might seem impossible. As overwhelming as it was for me to make sense of these policy changes, it was even more daunting for the people impacted by these changes.

Policies, Presidents, and the People

The programs implemented by the Dominican government are confusing and inaccessible, creating a vast gulf between the policies and the people. Elice, for example, is a forty-five-year-old Haitian immigrant. She came to the Dominican Republic to reunite with her husband, who had left Haiti to work for a sugar mill. They had lived in separate countries for two years until Elice was able to immigrate with a Haitian passport. Elice has lived in the Dominican Republic for twenty-two years. Her passport has since expired, and her husband died eight years ago. Two of their four children, all born in the Dominican Republic, have different last names than their siblings.

"Two of my children have their correct birth certificates, but the other two don't," Elice explains.

> It was easier to register the older two, the ones that are nineteen and twenty years old, under Balaguer [Dominican president, 1986–1996]. After him, there was Leonel [President L. Fernández, 1996–2000], and it was much harder to register your kids. Now the older two are having problems getting their *cédulas*. They need them so they can go to university. One wants to do accounting, but I think he should do architecture. He draws very well. The younger two are twelve and fifteen years old. I have to fix their papers. When I went to the

office to try to register them, they told me that I couldn't register them because I didn't have my papers. So they told me to find Dominican parents and have them declare my children. So that's what I did. But now, it's like the children are not mine. It's like saying that the Dominican parents gave birth to my children. So now I can't prove that they are mine. I have been trying to find the Dominican parents so I can fix this, but I found the father and not the mother. As you know, these things go through the mothers. . . . The fathers can't do anything! So I'm trying to see what I can do.

Under a past political initiative, even though her passport was expired, Elice could register her two older children using her late husband's work-identification card. When her younger two children were born, that initiative was no longer an option. Like some Haitian immigrant parents without legal residence, Elice chose to register two of her children using someone else's last name—advice she received from the documentation office. Unfortunately, this choice has created long-term problems for those children. And the other two children who were legally registered using her late husband's work-identification card are affected by the national audit, which has suspended documentation for thousands of Dominicans of Haitian descent. As a result, Elice and all four of her children are trying to navigate a confusing and financially burdensome system to resolve their precarious legal statuses.

In addition to policy changes and confusing processes, clerical errors contribute to the bureaucratic chaos embedded in the gap between policies and the people. Because of low literacy among Haitian migrant workers, and since Spanish is their second language, it is not unusual for people to miss spelling errors on officially issued documentation. Some organizations that serve Haitian migrant communities take an ink pad with them so that people can use a thumb print if they cannot sign their names. With this in mind, interactions between Haitian migrants and Dominican documentation offices have ample opportunity for administrative errors.

When documentation offices notice inconsistencies in spelling across different documents as people enroll in registration programs, they require that people reconcile spelling errors before proceeding. For example, if someone's last name is "Pierre" on their birth certificate and "Piere" on their marriage license, they must consult a lawyer to have the spelling changed on one of the documents to ensure consistency across all paperwork as they enroll in the Book of Foreigners. This requirement adds an additional bureaucratic barrier. The time and financial resources necessary to resolving spelling errors often adds up to more than families can pay. In egregious cases, documentation officials may intentionally record names inaccurately.

In a context where policies change often, information about registration policies and programs travels primarily through word of mouth. Rumors are not always reliable, and scams emerge as the unscrupulous try to take advantage of a confusing situation. Although news outlets publicize instructions and deadlines for people to resolve their legal status, electricity outages are common across the country, and television is not consistently available in many homes. Some people took no action regarding their legal status because they had been unclear about what to do and, with good reason, unsure whom to trust. One Haitian immigrant told me that someone was selling a document with three flags on it: a Dominican flag, a Haitian flag, and a US flag. It costs US$80.00. He asked whether I had heard of it and whether it was legitimate. I had not; it was not. Because the process is so confusing, people have trouble sorting fact from fiction.

Many Dominicans of Haitian descent advocate for solutions that affirm belonging in their own country. Some who did not enroll in the Book of Foreigners firmly identify as Dominican, not as foreigners. Further, if they enroll in the Book of Foreigners, some suspect that they would be vulnerable to further marginalization under future governments that could be more restrictive than the current one. If Dominicans of Haitian descent are officially registered as foreigners, then they are easily identifiable through future bureaucratic processes that could push them even further onto the margins of Dominican society.

Chapter Overview

Scholarship at the nexus of race and immigration elicits nuanced understandings of both racism and the immigrant experience.[54] *In Someone Else's Country* employs a framework that emphasizes the material consequences of racial inequality while also incorporating the unique lived experiences associated with immigration. Such experiences contribute to broader conversations about legality, citizenship, and belonging.[55] Stories from people of Haitian descent in the Dominican Republic provide a case study that highlights these global thematic patterns.

In chapter 2, "*Batey* La Tierra," I describe the setting to familiarize readers with the broader social context of the Dominican Republic and the specific context of a Dominican *batey* called La Tierra. Chapter 2 also provides information about the people who live in La Tierra, including a description of families and social circles among Haitian immigrants, Dominicans of Haitian descent, and Dominicans who live in La Tierra. I also describe the community structure in the *batey*, including sugar mill labor roles, family structures, and gender norms associated with documentation.

Immigrants' legal status is shaped by the establishment of the law and targeted enforcement of existing laws. In chapter 3, "'Just a Baseball Game,'" I examine the established laws that created liminal legality among Haitian migrant workers. In this chapter, I center the voices of Haitian immigrants to show how they experience shifting policies and political interests. Migrant workers share stories of labor exploitation, including experiences with supervisors who withhold their earned pay. They also discuss lack of access to the pensions they were promised for decades of labor in the country. Chapter 3 also explains gender dynamics that create added vulnerability for Haitian women without legal residence. For example, without documentation, Haitian women cannot register the births of their Dominican-born children. Since women are typically responsible for getting children's documents, social norms produce liminal legality along gendered lines.

Chapter 4, "'We Are Not Free,'" discusses the experiences of the second generation. In this chapter, I examine the laws that created liminal legality among Dominicans of Haitian descent. Although they live in their country of birth, Dominicans of Haitian descent also experience liminal legality. They are subject to second-class citizenship that removes their voting rights and reclassifies them as foreigners in the only country they have ever known. The stories in this chapter reveal how increased conditionality on birthright citizenship impacts adults, children, and families as they hope for inclusion in their home country.

In chapter 5, "'They Are Rounding Up *Morenos!*'" I show how officials police documentation enforcement by coupling illegality and Haitian ethnicity. Enforcement practices use skin color, last name, and speech to identify people of Haitian descent. The chapter opens with a description of an attack against a Haitian man who was lynched in a public park. Following a discussion of anti-Haitian racism and public attempts to police boundaries, I explore how officials incorporate racial profiling to enforce documentation policies.

Chapter 6, "Racism, Resistance, and Reframing Illegality," concludes the book with a summary of how policies create liminal legality for both Haitian immigrants and Dominicans of Haitian descent. The conclusion also highlights the ways that civil society resists political efforts to maintain racial social divisions. Border regions across the world represent rich relationships and painful divisions. But they also provide an opportunity for nations to prioritize rules of engagement that center dignity and shared humanity.

In Someone Else's Country interrogates anti-Haitian racism as a critical element embedded within immigration policies that produce liminal legality among Haitian immigrants and Dominicans of Haitian descent. It shows how documentation policies are enforced in ways that incorporate racial profiling and exacerbate inequality among vulnerable populations. By addressing the nuanced ways that immigration policies incorporate race, *In Someone Else's Country* broadens international conversations about immigration, citizenship, and racism. The stories in this book amplify the voices of a wide range of people in a small community in the Dominican Republic to tell a universal story about borders and belonging. Narratives from Haitian immigrants and Dominicans of Haitian descent, from people who speak Spanish and those who speak Haitian Creole, from people who have valid passports and those who do not— each of these voices describes how policies produce liminal legality and harm the most disadvantaged.

Notes

[1] For an extensive study of documentation and education, see Khaled Alrabe et al., "Left Behind: How Statelessness in the Dominican Republic Limits Children's Access to Education," Georgetown Law Human Rights Institute, March 2014, https://www.law.georgetown.edu/human-rights-institute/wp-content/uploads/sites/7/2018/03/left-behind.pdf.

[2] I use the term "legal residence" throughout the book to refer to the legal ability of a person to reside in a given country. This is not to be confused with "lawful permanent residence," a specific legal status granted by governments to noncitizens.

[3] Cecilia Menjívar, "Liminal Legality: Salvadoran and Guatemalan Immigrants' Lives in the United States," *American Journal of Sociology* 111, no. 4 (2006): 999–1037 (text available online at https://www.researchgate.net/publication/249177038_Liminal_Legality_Salvadoran_and_Guatemalan_Immigrants'_Lives_in_the_United_States).

[4] For examples of legality among families, see Joanna Dreby, *Everyday Illegal: When Policies Undermine Immigrant Families* (Oakland: University of California Press, 2015), and Roberto G. Gonzales, *Lives in Limbo: Undocumented and Coming of Age in America* (Oakland: University of California Press, 2016).

[5] Eduardo Bonilla-Silva, "Rethinking Racism: Toward a Structural Interpretation," *American Sociological Review* 62, no. 3 (1997): 465–80 (text available online at https://sph.umd.edu/sites/default/files/files/Bonilla-Silva%201996%20Rethinking%20Racism%20Toward%20Structural%20Interpretation.pdf).

[6] See David Howard, *Coloring the Nation: Race and Ethnicity in the Dominican Republic* (Oxford: Signal Books, 2001), and Ernesto Sagás, *Race and Politics in the Dominican Republic* (Gainesville: University Press of Florida, 2000).

[7] *Black* is capitalized throughout the text when referencing a group of people. For a discussion of this stylistic choice, see David Lanham and Amy Liu, "Not Just a Typographical Change: Why Brookings Is Capitalizing Black," Brookings Institution, September 23, 2019, https://www.brookings.edu/research/brookingscapitalizesblack/.

[8] Ancestry in the Dominican Republic is heterogeneous; however, I use "Dominican" to reference people born in the Dominican Republic to parents and grandparents without Haitian ancestry. This allows discussion of the unique experiences of Dominicans of Haitian descent.

[9] For a discussion of the research on contemporary immigration and emigration in the Dominican Republic, see Organisation for Economic Co-operation and Development (OECD), "The Dominican Republic's Migration Landscape," in *Interrelations between Public Policies, Migration and Development in the Dominican Republic* (Paris: OECD Publishing, 2017), 37–55, https://read.oecd-ilibrary.org/development/interrelations-between-public-policies-migration-and-development-in-the-dominican-republic/the-dominican-republic-s-migration-landscape_9789264276826-6-en#page1.

[10] Eugenio D. Matibag and Teresa Downing-Matibag, "Sovereignty and Social Justice: The 'Haitian Problem' in the Dominican Republic," *Caribbean Quarterly* 57, no. 2 (2011): 92–117 (text available online at https://lib.dr.iastate.edu/cgi/viewcontent.cgi?referer=https://www.google.com/&httpsredir=1&article=1089&context=language_pubs).

[11] Emphasis mine.

[12] See Tanya Maria Golash-Boza, *Deported: Immigrant Policing, Disposable Labor, and Global Capitalism* (New York: New York University Press, 2015), and Moon-Ho Jung, *Coolies and Cane: Race, Labor, and Sugar in the Age of Emancipation* (Baltimore: Johns Hopkins University Press, 2009).

[13] See Noam Scheiber, "Why Wendy's Is Facing Campus Protests (It's about the Tomatoes)," *New York Times*, March 7, 2019, https://www.nytimes.com/2019/03/07/business/economy/wendys-farm-workers-tomatoes.html; see also Richard Marosi, "Hardship on Mexico's Farms, a Bounty for U.S. Tables," photo and vid. Don Bartletti, *Los Angeles Times*, December 7, 2014, https://graphics.latimes.com/product-of-mexico-camps/.

[14] Yến Lê Espiritu, *Asian American Women and Men: Labor, Laws, and Love*, 2nd ed. (Lanham, MD: Rowman & Littlefield, 2008).

[15] These and other population data provided by United Nations Department of Economic and Social Affairs (UNDESA), "International Migration Stock 2015," database, United Nations, 2015, http://www.un.org/en/development/desa/population/migration/data/estimates2/estimates15.shtml.

[16] Amelia Hintzen, "'A Veil of Legality': The Contested History of Anti-Haitian Ideology under the Trujillo Dictatorship," *New West Indian Guide/Nieuwe West-Indische Gids* 90, nos. 1–2 (2016): 28–54 (text available online at https://brill.com/view/journals/nwig/90/1-2/article-p28_2.xml?language=en).

[17] Although sugarcane labor is primarily Haitian, its economic significance is on the decline. Still, other agricultural products benefit from Haitian labor, including meat packaging and produce. Haitian labor is also extensive in the construction industry. See Allison J. Petrozziello,

Haitian Construction Workers in the Dominican Republic: An Exploratory Study on Indicators of Forced Labor (Washington, DC: US Department of Labor, Bureau of International Labor Affairs, 2012) (text available online at https://digitalcommons.ilr.cornell.edu/cgi/viewcontent.cgi?article=2813&context=key_workplace).

[18] Camila DeChalus, "PhD Student Faces Deportation to Liberia, Where She Has Never Lived," *Roll Call*, March 18, 2019, https://www.rollcall.com/news/facing-deportation-to-liberia-where-she-has-never-lived?fbclid=IwAR1OZjrjVCJP2I2W8RP582gThvvoAM2hfT0wUVvILICXN WkOD9hO1VSFCXk.

[19] For examples of how race, legality, and law intersect, see Mae M. Ngai, *Impossible Subjects: Illegal Aliens and the Making of Modern America*, updated ed. (Princeton, NJ: Princeton University Press, 2014); see also Ian F. Haney-López, *White by Law: The Legal Construction of Race* (New York: New York University Press, 1997).

[20] Leah Donnella, "Brexit: What's Race Got to Do with It?" NPR, *Code Switch*, June 25, 2016, https://www.npr.org/sections/codeswitch/2016/06/25/483362200/brexit-whats-race-got-to-do-with-it.

[21] Atul Dev, "India Is Testing the Bounds of Citizenship," *The Atlantic*, August 31, 2019, https://www.theatlantic.com/international/archive/2019/08/india-citizenship-assam-nrc/597208/.

[22] Bonilla-Silva, "Rethinking Racism." Structural racism has dire consequences for the most vulnerable populations. See, for example, Asad L. Asad and Matthew Clair, "Racialized Legal Status as a Social Determinant of Health," *Social Science and Medicine* 199 (2018): 19–28; Mary Bosworth, Alpa Parmar, and Yolanda Vázquez, eds., *Race, Criminal Justice, and Migration Control: Enforcing the Boundaries of Belonging* (Oxford: Oxford University Press, 2018); Tanya Golash-Boz, and Pierrette Hondagneu-Sotelo, "Latino Immigrant Men and the Deportation Crisis: A Gendered Racial Removal Program," *Latino Studies* 11, no. 3 (2013): 271–92 (text available online at https://www.researchgate.net/publication/263325706_Latino_Immigrant_Men_and_the_Deportation_Crisis_A_Gendered_Racial_Removal_Program); Louise Seamster and Jessica Welburn, "How a Racist System Has Poisoned the Water in Flint, Mich," *The Root*, January 9, 2016, https://www.theroot.com/how-a-racist-system-has-poisoned-the-water-in-flint-mi-1790853824; and Edna A. Viruell-Fuentes, "'It's a Lot of Work': Racialization Processes, Ethnic Identity Formations, and Their Health Implications," *Du Bois Review: Social Science Research on Race* 8, no. 1 (2011): 37–52.

[23] Some scholars refer to anti-Haitian racism as "anti-Haitianism" to emphasize the unique sociopolitical forces that contribute to discrimination against people of Haitian descent. I use the phrase "anti-Haitian racism" to connect anti-Haitian experiences to structural racism and global white supremacy.

[24] See Charles W. Mills, *The Racial Contract* (Ithaca, NY: Cornell University Press, 2014), and Michael Omi and Howard Winant, *Racial Formation in the United States* (London: Routledge, 2014).

[25] LaToya A. Tavernier, "The Stigma of Blackness: Anti-Haitianism in the Dominican Republic," *Socialism and Democracy* 22, no. 3 (2008): 96–104.

[26] For a comprehensive historical perspective, see Ernesto Sagás and Orlando Inoa, *The Dominican People: A Documentary History* (Princeton, NJ: Markus Wiener Publishers, 2003), and Frank Moya Pons, *The Dominican Republic: A National History* (Princeton, NJ: Markus Wiener Publishers, 2010).

[27] See Lauren Hutchinson Derby, *The Dictator's Seduction: Politics and the Popular Imagination in the Era of Trujillo* (Durham, NC: Duke University Press, 2009).

[28] See Alan McPherson, *The Invaded: How Latin Americans and Their Allies Fought and Ended U.S. Occupations* (New York: Oxford University Press, 2014).

[29] Kimberly Eison Simmons, *Reconstructing Racial Identity and the African Past in the Dominican Republic* (Gainesville: University Press of Florida, 2009).

[30] See Sagás, *Race and Politics*, and Sheridan Wigginton, "Character or Caricature: Representations of Blackness in Dominican Social Science Textbooks," *Race Ethnicity and Education* 8, no. 2 (2005): 191–211.

[31] See Robin L. H. Derby and Richard Lee Turits, "Historias de terror y los terrores de la historia: La masacre haitiana de 1937 en la República Dominicana," *Estudios Sociales* 26, no. 92 (1993): 65–76 (text available online at http://www.sscnet.ucla.edu/history/derby/derby_historiads_terror

.pdf), and Richard Lee Turits, "A World Destroyed, a Nation Imposed: The 1937 Haitian Massacre in the Dominican Republic," *Hispanic American Historical Review* 82, no. 3 (2002): 589–635.

[32] See Peter Wade, *Race and Ethnicity in Latin America*, 2nd ed. (London and New York: Pluto Press, 2010), and Ginetta E. B. Candelario, *Black Behind the Ears: Dominican Racial Identity from Museums to Beauty Shops* (Durham, NC: Duke University Press, 2007).

[33] For a rich discussion of how law creates racial divisions in Latin America, see Tanya Katerí Hernández, *Racial Subordination in Latin America: The Role of the State, Customary Law, and the New Civil Rights Response* (Cambridge: Cambridge University Press, 2013).

[34] See Marion A. Kaplan, *Dominican Haven: The Jewish Refugee Settlement in Sosúa, 1940–1945* (New York: Museum of Jewish Heritage, 2008), and Valentina Peguero, *Immigration and Politics in the Caribbean: Japanese and Other Immigrants in the Dominican Republic*, trans. Linda Crawford (Coconut Creek, FL: Caribbean Studies Press, 2008).

[35] See Edith Wen-Chu Chen, "'You Are Like Us, You Eat Plátanos': Chinese Dominicans, Race, Ethnicity, and Identity," *Afro-Hispanic Review* 27, no. 1 (2008): 23–40; Peguero, *Immigration and Politics*; and Samuel Martínez, "From Hidden Hand to Heavy Hand: Sugar, the State, and Migrant Labor in Haiti and the Dominican Republic," *Latin American Research Review* 34, no. 1 (1999): 57–84.

[36] Bridget Wooding and Richard David Moseley-Williams, *Needed but Unwanted: Haitian Immigrants and Their Descendants in the Dominican Republic* (London: Catholic Institute for International Relations, 2004).

[37] Racial categories in Latin America incorporate hair color and texture, skin color, eye color, and facial features. Although racial categories in the United States also include a range of phenotypical characteristics, race in the United States evolved based on "hypodescent." The foundation of the "one-drop" rule, hypodescent is the practice of assigning people of mixed ancestry to a "lower" racial category. According to hypodescent, people with any degree of African ancestry are classified as Black. "Hyperdescent" assigns people of mixed ancestry to "higher" racial categories, allowing more nuanced classifications for nonwhites.

[38] English translations of these categories would hold little meaning. But the categories range based on skin color, hair texture, eye color, and physical characteristics, including nose and lip shapes.

[39] In the United States, people with darker skin also do worse on social indicators, including income, education, employment, and housing. See, for example, Margaret Hunter, "The Persistent Problem of Colorism: Skin Tone, Status, and Inequality," *Sociology Compass* 1, no. 1 (2007): 237–54, and Linda M. Burton et al., "Critical Race Theories, Colorism, and the Decade's Research on Families of Color," *Journal of Marriage and Family* 72, no. 3 (2010): 440–59 (text available online at http://cds.web.unc.edu/files/2013/01/Burton-Bonilla-Silva-Ray-Buck elew-Hordge-Freeman-Decade-Review1.pdf).

[40] See George Reid Andrews, *Blackness in the White Nation: A History of Afro-Uruguay* (Chapel Hill: University of North Carolina Press, 2010); Tanya Maria Golash-Boza, *Yo Soy Negro: Blackness in Peru* (Gainesville: University Press of Florida, 2012); and Nora Lustig, Judith Morrison, and Adam Ratzlaff, "Splitting the Bill: Taxing and Spending to Close Ethnic and Racial Gaps in Latin America," Inter-American Development Bank, 2019, https://publications.iadb.org/ publications/english/document/Splitting_the_Bill_Taxing_and_Spending_to_Close_Ethnic_and_ Racial_Gaps_in_Latin_America.pdf.

[41] See Maria Cristina Morales, "The Ethnic Niche as an Economic Pathway for the Dark Skinned: Labor Market Incorporation of Latina/o Workers," *Hispanic Journal of Behavioral Sciences* 30, no. 3 (2008): 280–98, and Ariel E. Dulitzky, "A Region in Denial: Racial Discrimination and Racism in Latin America," in *Neither Enemies nor Friends: Latinos, Blacks, Afro-Latinos*, ed. Suzanne Oboler and Anani Dzidzienyo (New York: Springer, 2005), 39–59.

[42] Kia Lilly Caldwell, *Negras in Brazil: Re-envisioning Black Women, Citizenship, and the Politics of Identity* (New Brunswick, NJ: Rutgers University Press, 2007).

[43] Michele Wucker, "The Dominican Republic's Shameful Deportation Legacy," *Foreign Policy*, October 8, 2015, https://foreignpolicy.com/2015/10/08/dominican-republic-haiti-trujillo -immigration-deportation/.

[44] For additional examples describing the experiences of Afro-descendant immigrant groups, see Jean Beaman, *Citizen Outsider: Children of North African Immigrants in France* (Oakland:

University of California Press, 2017); Mary C. Waters, *Black Identities: West Indian Immigrant Dreams and American Realities* (Cambridge, MA: Harvard University Press, 2009); and José A. Cobas, Jorge Duany, and Joe R. Feagin, *How the United States Racializes Latinos: White Hegemony and Its Consequences* (New York: Routledge, 2009).

45 David Baluarte, "The Perpetuation of Childhood Statelessness in the Dominican Republic," *World's Stateless Children*, Institute on Statelessness and Inclusion, 2017, http://chil dren.worldsstateless.org/3/litigating-against-childhood-statelessness/the-perpetuation-of -childhood-statelessness-in-the-dominican-republic.html.

46 Human Rights Watch, "'Illegal People': Haitians and Dominico-Haitians in the Dominican Republic," April 2002, 14, no. 1 (b), https://www.hrw.org/reports/pdfs/d/domrep/domrep0402.pdf.

47 República Dominicana, Ley No. 285 de 2004 sobre migración [Dominican Republic], August 15, 2004 (text available online at https://www.refworld.org/docid/46d6e07c2.html).

48 Open Society Justice Initiative and the Center for Justice and International Law, "Submission to the Committee on the Elimination of Racial Discrimination: Review of the Dominican Republic," January 2013, https://tbinternet.ohchr.org/Treaties/CERD/Shared%20Documents/DOM/ INT_CERD_NGO_DOM_13708_E.pdf.

49 Constitución de la Republica Dominicana, January 26, 2010, art. 18[3] [Dom. Rep.].

50 The first time the "in transit" exception appears in the Dominican Constitution is in 1929.

51 República Dominicana, Decreto No. 327-13 de 2013, Plan nacional de regularización de extranjeros en situación migratoria irregular en la República Dominicana [Presidential decree 327-13 of 2013], Dominican Republic (text available online at http://www.scribd.com/doc/188044925/ Decreto-327-13).

52 Bridget Wooding, "Haitian Immigrants and Their Descendants Born in the Dominican Republic," *Oxford Research Encyclopedia of Latin American History*, Oxford University Press, online publication January 2018, https://oxfordre.com/latinamericanhistory/view/10.1093/acre fore/9780199366439.001.0001/acrefore-9780199366439-e-474?rskey=PWgo27&result=188.

53 Baluarte, "Perpetuation of Childhood Statelessness."

54 For examples of scholarship bridging immigration and race, see Rogelio Sáenz and Karen Manges Douglas, "A Call for the Racialization of Immigration Studies: On the Transition of Ethnic Immigrants to Racialized Immigrants," *Sociology of Race and Ethnicity* 1, no. 1 (2015): 166–80; Hana E. Brown, "Race, Legality, and the Social Policy Consequences of Anti-immigration Mobilization," *American Sociological Review* 78, no. 2 (2013): 290–314, https:// journals.sagepub.com/doi/10.1177/0003122413476712; Elizabeth Aranda and Elizabeth Vaquera, "Racism, the Immigration Enforcement Regime, and the Implications for Racial Inequality in the Lives of Undocumented Young Adults," *Sociology of Race and Ethnicity* 1, no. 1 (2015): 88–104 (text available online at https://www.academia.edu/11015509/Racism_the_ Immigration_Enforcement_Regime_and_the_Implications_for_Racial_Inequality_in_the_Lives_ of_Undocumented_Young_Adults); Vilna Bashi, "Globalized Anti-blackness: Transnationalizing Western Immigration Law, Policy, and Practice," *Ethnic and Racial Studies* 27, no. 4 (2004): 584–606; and Daniel Olmos, "Racialized Im/Migration and Autonomy of Migration Perspectives: New Directions and Opportunities," *Sociology Compass* 13, no. 9 (2019): e12729. For a critical examination of how this intersection manifests in the Dominican Republic, see Brendan Jamal Thornton and Diego I. Ubiera, "Caribbean Exceptions: The Problem of Race and Nation in Dominican Studies," *Latin American Research Review* 54, no. 2 (2019): 413–28, https://larr lasa.org/articles/10.25222/larr.346/.

55 See, for example, Irene Bloemraad, "Being American/Becoming American: Birthright Citizenship and Immigrants' Membership in the United States," special issue, *Who Belongs? Immigration, Citizenship, and the Constitution of Legality* 60 (2013): 55–84 (text available online at https:// sociology.berkeley.edu/sites/default/files/faculty/bloemraad/Bloemraad_Being_Becoming_Ameri can_2013.pdf), and Leo Ralph Chavez, *The Latino Threat: Constructing Immigrants, Citizens, and the Nation*, 2nd ed. (Stanford, CA: Stanford University Press, 2013).

CHAPTER 2

Batey La Tierra

When your flight lands at the Santo Domingo airport, applause and cheers of relief ring out when the plane's wheels touch the runway. If you arrive in August, you start to sweat immediately when you set foot outside and the hot, humid air meets your sticky face. If you arrive in January, perhaps you walk ten steps before your sweat glands fire up. "Don't fan yourself!" someone might say. "*Es ejercicio* [That's exercise]"—a warning to sit still in the heat lest you worsen your discomfort.

You make your way to a *guagua*, or a public bus, that weaves its way through the capital city. You sit shoulder to shoulder, hip to hip, as six or seven people squeeze into rows made for four passengers and hidden seats fold down into the aisles to miraculously fit two more people. Open windows let in a gentle morning breeze and the chaotic noise of the city. Horns honking. Motorcycle mufflers. And, of course, music. "*¡Algo, algo, algo grande viene a la tierra . . . predica . . . que todavía hay luuuuuzz!* [Knowing that something big is coming gives us hope!]"[1] The Antony Santos bachata blasts from a corner *colmado* [convenience store] at maximum volume. A man stands on the sidewalk singing along, his brows furrowed intently, hips swaying to the rhythmic melody.

"*Agárrame eso* [Hold this]," the passenger next to you might say, as they hand you a bag of mangoes, a sack of rice, or a baby. Or they might settle a sack tied with twine that holds a jittery rooster against your leg. Space is communal. Not mine. Not yours. It is just space.

When the bus stops, people hustle to sell you sweets, bottled water, chips, or other snacks for your ride. "*¡Tsssss! ¡¡¡Tsssssss!!!*" They hiss, shout, and tap your window to get your attention, hustling to make a few pesos. Passengers buy something they need or wag their fingers and look away to signal disinterest.

As you ride through city streets, the contrast between the bright green palm trees and the clear blue sky is breathtaking. The vivid colors on buildings—pink, yellow, blue, and orange—dance to the merengue tunes that float through the air. The bus chugs along as cars and motorcycles zigzag through traffic, navigating rules of the road that you have yet to identify. Since the country experiences sporadic power outages, traffic lights are functional only when there is electricity.

When you arrive at a neighborhood, you see a woman balancing a large *ponchera* on her head as she saunters along the road selling fruit. A *ponchera* is a large plastic basin often used for washing clothes, but women also use it to carry their merchandise. Their song-like cadence rings out, letting potential customers know what produce they have that day. "¡*Aaaaaaaguacate, guineeeeeeo*! ¡*Platanooo, a cinco pesos!*" Avocados, bananas, and plantains for sale, usually around the time people are preparing lunch—the largest meal of the day. Around noon, you notice a bit more activity as some people return home for lunch and the scent of *la bandera* fills the air. *La bandera*, "the flag," is the nickname for a typical Dominican meal—rice, beans, and meat. A *jugo natural*, maybe lime or passion fruit juice, completes the meal.

In the afternoon or early evening, the smack of dominoes hitting a wooden table might accompany talk of politics and baseball as people *compartir*, or spend time with family and friends. You swat at mosquitoes, laugh at jokes, and buy a *yaniqueque*, a fried dough snack, from a street vendor. You make plans to go to the car wash tomorrow, not for a car wash but because the car wash turns into a dance club after hours and people move all night to bachata, merengue, and salsa rhythms. A toddler brings you a mango from the neighbor's tree. A teen tells you about her new boyfriend. A *doña*, the lady of the house, offers to make hot chocolate. Today was a good day.

People in La Tierra

Research for this book is based on the experiences of people living in a Dominican *batey* community given the pseudonym "La Tierra." A *batey* is a company town on a sugarcane plantation originally established to house Haitian migrant workers. *La Tierra* translates as "the earth" or "the dirt." During a group discussion about anti-Haitian racism, one woman emphatically explained that there are no differences between any of us; when we die, we all go back to *la tierra*, no matter how much money we have and no matter our race. I chose La Tierra as the pseudonym for the community because of this discussion.

People in La Tierra live in perpetual instability. Their lives are rarely settled, and their days are rarely predictable. Women may plan to wash clothes in the morning, but if there is no electricity or if it rains, plans change. People may have money for food one day and not the next. They may have documents one day and lose them in a hurricane the next. During one of my visits to La Tierra, a church was torn down while onlookers *tsk-tsked* and shook their heads, hands folded across chests or planted on hips. Perpetual instability means they could have a church one day and not the next.

La Tierra is bustling with unusual activity when I arrive one morning. And a *thwack thwack* reverberates on the breeze, rustling through the palm trees. I wind my way between houses following the *thwacking* and *clanging* until I come upon a crowd of people standing near a slab of cement, guarding sacred keepsakes as their church is torn down.

The thwacking is the sound of hammering on wood and corrugated tin, called "zinc." Standing between two houses, I can see the church—a makeshift lean-to extension propped up against the back of another house. The frame of the church is made of thick, wooden planks. Sheets of rusted zinc create its door and roof. A few men who live in La Tierra hammer out the nails that attach the wooden frame.

A crowd is gathering now. This has become a spectacle. Kids are shooed out of the way to protect them from flying debris. To the right of the concrete slab that forms the floor of the church, the keepsakes that were once inside are now outside. Five women stand guarding a brightly colored bowl, decorations, and a white cloth with a hand-sewn scripture, "*Jehová es mi pastor. No me falta nada.* [The Lord is my shepherd. I shall not want.]"

A man wearing alligator boots, black sunglasses, a plaid dress shirt, and fitted jeans walks between the buildings near where we are standing. I have not seen him in La Tierra before, and I do not see him again after this day. Gator Boots joins two men in military-looking uniforms who hold long, black guns and wear black combat boots. After making small talk with Gator Boots—Yes, I'm married. No, I'm not interested in a Dominican husband—I ask him why the church is being torn down. "A commission from the United States is coming," he replies, "and this looks ugly." I do not know what commission he is referencing, and he does not elaborate.

Following a slow, rickety squeak, a loud crash echoes throughout La Tierra as the frame of the church falls and the roof collapses to the ground. The team of men knocks down all the wooden beams of the church and loads up the materials, separating the zinc pieces. The group sorts through the scraps to determine which pieces of zinc belong to the sugar mill and which do not.

People in La Tierra seem disappointed, yet resigned. We watch as people collect the church's belongings, disperse the wood and zinc that does not belong to the sugar mill, and move on. This is just another day in someone else's country, on someone else's land.

The next time I visit La Tierra on a Sunday, I walk past this church. About ten women sit in plastic chairs on the slab of concrete where the wood and zinc once provided shade. The women, wearing all white, fan themselves, singing a hymn and reading Bible scriptures.

Batey life is continually in flux. Limited resources, weather patterns, and unpredictable electricity create instability for people living in *bateyes*. At a structural level, however, employer-regulated life and labor dictates day-to-day freedoms.[2] The sugar mill owns both land and housing in a *batey*. Consequently, the mill governs not only people's work lives but also their home lives. The critical gaze of an international commission, for example, is enough to destroy a community's place of worship.

Despite instability and invasive company regulations, people are resilient. They forge ahead—having church on a cement slab without a roof—resisting the structural barriers that infiltrate their private lives. Although life is unpredictable, people carve out their own practices, customs, and rituals to bring stability to their lives. Each year, for example, the *batey* hosts a homecoming for friends and family members who have left to live or work elsewhere. Deferring daily struggles, people return to a welcoming community where dancing and celebration create and maintain collective connection.

Sugar Mills

The primary source of employment for people living in La Tierra is the sugar mill. Sugar mills, or *ingenios*, across the Dominican Republic can be government owned or privately owned. Public *ingenios* are run by the Dominican government, and private *ingenios* are run directly by sugarcane companies. Four major companies produce most of the sugar in the Dominican Republic: Central Romana Corporation, Ltd. (Central Romana), Consorcio Azucarero Central (CAC), Consorcio Azucarero de Empresas Industriales (CAEI), and the Consejo Estatal del Azúcar (CEA).[3] *Bateyes* were originally intended to provide temporary housing for the seasonal migrant workers employed by the sugar mills. Over time, however, sugar mills employed migrant workers throughout the year, and workers established long-term residence in *bateyes*.

Estimates vary, but approximately two hundred thousand people live in the 425 *bateyes* throughout the Dominican Republic.[4] Of these, about half belong to the State Sugar Council (CEA) and are run by the Dominican government. The remaining *bateyes* are privately owned and operated by independent sugarcane companies. In a given geographic region, *bateyes* are typically owned by the same company. For example, *bateyes* in the southern region of the country are primarily owned and governed by the CAC, and in the east most *bateyes* belong to Central Romana.

Central Romana is the primary producer of the country's sugar and the largest private employer in the Dominican Republic. Central Romana began when the South Puerto Rico Sugar Company bought twenty thousand acres of land in 1912. Five years later, the first Central Romana sugar mill was built. Today the Fanjul Corporation, a Cuba-based family business, owns Central Romana, and the business has expanded its traditional involvement in sugar to include livestock and meat processing, construction, and tourism.[5]

The CAC's roots trace back to the West India Sugar Finance Corporation headquartered in Connecticut, which established the Barahona Company in 1917. The Barahona Sugar Company would become today's Ingenio Barahona. After decades of business, Ingenio Barahona was leased by the CAC, a partnership between Dominican, French, and Canadian investors. Today the CAC is the largest employer in the southern region of the Dominican Republic.

The CAEI began in 1859 when the Vicini family, the wealthiest family in the Dominican Republic, created and began acquiring several *ingenios*, a project they continued over the next fifty years. Ingenio Cristóbal Colón, the only CAEI *ingenio* operating today, is the second-largest sugar producer in the Dominican Republic. The CAEI also cultivates and markets mangoes and pineapples and trades in livestock and construction.

The public *bateyes* run by the government belong to the CEA and stem from the rule of former Dominican dictator Rafael Leónidas Trujillo. Trujillo's government and personal financial endeavors were often intertwined. During his reign, between 1930 and 1961, he created three new mills and took ownership of nine privately owned mills that had previously been owned by foreigners. After Trujillo's assassination in 1961, his estate became property of the

Dominican state, and the government assumed ownership of the Trujillo family's twelve *ingenios*. In 1966, the CEA was created as the administrative body for the newly acquired *ingenios*, making the Dominican government the leading sugar producer in the country.

Today the Dominican economy is one of the fastest growing in the Caribbean, primarily fueled by tourism, remittances, textiles, and agriculture.[6] In contrast to previous decades, however, the sugar industry in the Dominican Republic is producing less sugar and creating fewer jobs than it has in the past, especially as mechanization of jobs increases.[7] In 1980, for example, the sugar industry represented 5 percent of the country's GDP. And in 2010, the sugar industry represented 0.9 percent of GDP. Still, cane cutters working in *bateyes* do the most challenging physical labor relative to other workers and are subject to harsh living conditions. To understand life in a Dominican *batey*, it is important to understand the leadership and labor structure in La Tierra.

Batey Labor Structure

Housing and Labor

People in La Tierra live under a matrix of governance structures, which includes mill ownership, land governance, and work supervision. Sugar mills created company-owned *bateyes* to house workers. Employees of various statuses live in La Tierra and work for the mill. In La Tierra, *batey* leadership includes a superintendent of cane cultivation, a *mayordomo*, and a *capataz de corte*. The superintendent of cane cultivation is the highest leadership position in La Tierra. He reports progress related to cane planting or harvest to the sugar mill. The *mayordomo* supervises the workers while they are in the fields. Superintendents and *mayordomos* are often responsible for multiple *bateyes* in a geographic region. The *ajustero*, an administrative role, distributes pay to cane cutters. In La Tierra, these positions are filled by Dominicans.

Three men in La Tierra work as *capataz de corte*, supervising small groups of cane cutters, dictating which sections are ready to be cut or burned in preparation for planting the next crop. Each team of four to ten workers moves from section to section in the sugarcane field. After the cane is cut, it is placed in wagons, either by the workers or by mechanical lifts. *Picadores* comprise the majority of *batey* workers, and they are at the lowest level of the labor hierarchy. They perform the most strenuous work, and receive the lowest pay in the industry. *Picadores* are responsible for cutting cane using machetes, and they may also perform other agricultural tasks, including planting and weeding. The vast majority of *picadores* in La Tierra are Haitian migrants, and some are Dominicans of Haitian descent.

All housing in a *batey* is owned by the sugar mill. Any worker changing companies must move to a different *batey*. Housing is assigned according to one's labor position in the *batey*. The superintendent and his family, for example, live in the largest house in La Tierra, and *picadores* typically live in one room in a shared house. Families in La Tierra live in an entire house, a shared house, a room in a house, or barracks. In shared houses, wood planks, cardboard, and

Photo 2.1. Sugarcane fields near a *batey*
Source: Trenita Childers

Photo 2.2. Example of *batey* housing made of cement
Source: Trenita Childers

Photo 2.3. Example of *batey* housing made of zinc or corrugated tin

Source: Trenita Childers

Photo 2.4. Example of barracks, or housing for seasonal migrants, in a *batey*

Source: Trenita Childers

Photo 2.5. Another example of barracks in a *batey*
Source: Trenita Childers

Photo 2.6. A resident entering a *batey* on a motorcycle
Source: Trenita Childers

Photo 2.7. Example of the community water source in a *batey*
Source: Trenita Childers

Photo 2.8. Example of a *colmado* in a Dominican *batey*
Source: Trenita Childers

sheets of zinc separate a small house into two distinct sections—the front of the house and the back. One family of two to six people may live in the front of the house, while a different family lives in the back. It is also common for one man or a small family to live in a single room in a house. One couple living in a single room in La Tierra had a small space that contained a bed, a small dresser, a refrigerator, and all their possessions. They strung a wire across the ceiling from corner to corner, creating a makeshift hovering closet space for their clothes.

In some *bateyes* I visited during my time in the country, I saw houses made of wood or zinc. These houses are less secure and more susceptible to flooding and damage during major storms. *Batey* housing may also have dirt floors, making it difficult to prevent damage from heavy rains. In contrast to other *bateyes*, each house in La Tierra is made of cement and has cement floors, providing added protection from inclement weather.

Forced Labor

International labor-rights organizations, human-rights advocates, and researchers have spotlighted the unfair treatment of sugarcane fieldworkers in the Dominican Republic.[8] Perhaps because of this attention, there may be negative consequences for workers who speak out against unjust living or working conditions. Before agreeing to speak with me, several workers in La Tierra clarified that I would not ask questions about the sugar mill. I assured them that the mills were not the focus of my research, and I did not ask questions related to their experiences working for specific mills. But to provide contextual information about *batey* labor, I reference findings from a 2010 study assessing forced-labor risks on Dominican *bateyes*.

Researchers from Verité,[9] an independent nonprofit organization, spoke with 740 workers living in bateyes across the Dominican Republic. Findings from the study highlight several indicators that workers are vulnerable to forced labor, including false promises about work, withholding and nonpayment of wages, and retention of identity documents. For example, *buscones*, or human smugglers, may deceive workers by withholding information about harsh working conditions. A common exploitative practice to control fieldworkers around the world, some *batey* supervisors can withhold cane cutters' wages or not pay them at all. In the past, employers have retained part of workers' wages to be paid to them at the end of the harvest season in the form of a bonus, or an incentive to work for the full harvest season. However, it is unclear whether this practice continues today. Since employers do not provide workers with detailed information regarding their conditions of employment, including payments and deductions, workers are vulnerable to the withholding and nonpayment of wages.

In addition to false promises about working conditions and the withholding of wages, the retention of identity documents makes workers more vulnerable to forced labor. When workers are recruited, they are often promised identification cards. This is also a stipulation of the Republic Act No. 285-04 on Migration, which requires that workers be provided with a "temporary worker card." But many never received the cards they were promised. Without identification cards, workers with no other form of documentation cannot prove their identity, leaving them at the mercy of sugar mill authorities. For example, if conditions at one mill are unbearable, workers without identification documents may be unable to seek work elsewhere. Further, since a company-issued identification card authorizes their presence in the country, those without a card are vulnerable to labor exploitation and deportation. Withholding documentation and the threat of deportation can be used to coerce workers to toil under labor conditions that they might otherwise leave.

Gender-Based Labor

Although some women cut sugarcane, most workers in La Tierra employed by the sugar mill are men. Men work for the mill in various positions, including planters, harvesters, technicians, or supervisors. The men in La Tierra work as cane cutters, security guards, machine operators, gas technicians, and mechanics. Some are also *chiriperos*—or people who look for odd jobs as they become available. A *chiripero* worker might plant seeds or cut grass with a machete as needed.

Few women in La Tierra worked in the formal economy, since formal employment requires transportation fare and childcare for those who are mothers. One woman, for example, worked as a bartender at a resort, and although her two small children spent the days with their grandmother, she sometimes struggled to find the bus fare for her two-hour ride to work each day. Most women in La Tierra work in the informal economy. Women often have a *negocio*, or a small business, selling goods to other community members or in the nearby city. In La Tierra, innovative women sold coffee packets, snacks, small bags of water, homemade peanut butter or bread, fruit, avocados, plantains, candy, handmade curtains or pillowcases, shoes or other goods purchased from a market in the city, charcoal for cooking, lottery tickets, and cell phone minutes. Some women also sold Avon products, women's underwear, or perfume using catalogues from various international companies. Those who want to learn a marketable skill, such as baking or sewing, might enroll in an educational workshop in the city. Local organizations often provide free short-term vocational classes that women take advantage of if they can find transportation fare and provide a copy of their *cédula*, the national identification card. Once they have acquired a skill, they can use it to earn money in the *batey*.

In addition to small-business endeavors, women may find domestic work in the city cooking, cleaning, and caring for children in homes with more financial resources. Many women in La Tierra, however, lament that the supply of domestic work outweighs the demand, making employment opportunities scarce. Domestic labor also makes women vulnerable to abuse. A few women in La Tierra shared stories about verbal or sexual abuse that they or someone they knew had experienced. One Dominican woman of Haitian descent explains, "My sister worked in a house, and one time the wife grabbed her and was saying horrible things to her. She insulted my sister saying, 'This damned Haitian!'

Sometimes you have to endure abuses from these people's children too. And sometimes the husbands want to be with the women working there. Look, a lot of things happen. Women must deal with a lot. It's not good."

From a vulnerable position, women strategically navigate such situations, maintaining their dignity while keeping their jobs. With a separate source of income, women have more flexibility and independence than if they were solely dependent on their partners' earnings. This is especially important for single mothers and women who are in abusive relationships. If they have access to valid documentation, women can create a small microlending business, or *sans*. Two Dominican women in La Tierra said they participated in a *sans*. One woman says, "I invented small businesses to make a little money. Once I borrowed money from the bank, and I was lending it, you know? Running a *sans*." Primarily run by women, the *sans* begins with one person who can get a loan from the bank. Alternatively, the *sans* leader might collect a small sum of money from a group of five or six women each month. Then, over the course of several months, each woman takes a turn receiving the larger sum of money generated by their collective contributions. One woman in La Tierra says that is how she bought her refrigerator. This cooperative economic strategy allows women in the community to support one another by achieving both individual and collective goals.

Living Conditions and Community Resources

Bateyes in the Dominican Republic vary widely in size, geographic location, and access to public resources, including transportation, water, and electricity. Variation in living conditions across *bateyes* also depends on which company owns the mill. Some companies have less regulatory oversight than others, which results in better or worse housing, for example. Despite their heterogeneity, *bateyes* are known to have some of the worst living and working conditions in the Dominican Republic.[10] Many *bateyes* in the Dominican Republic lack potable water, electricity, and waste disposal. Health problems such as tuberculosis, HIV/AIDS, and mosquito-borne illnesses including dengue and malaria are prevalent in *bateyes*, and few residents have adequate means of trash disposal, creating a major risk for environmental hazards. Residents often use nearby ravines or other public spaces to dispose of garbage, which poses health risks to residents, as waste attracts rats, roaches, and other vermin. Few houses in *bateyes* have plumbing, making human-waste disposal another environmental and health concern. In La Tierra, three of the seventy-five houses had indoor plumbing. Most families shared outdoor latrines. In *bateyes* without latrines, people expel human waste in nearby rivers, cane fields, or shallow ravines, contributing to high rates of infant mortality and diarrheal diseases.[11] In addition, discrimination contributes to poor mental health among people of Haitian descent living in *bateyes*.[12]

In La Tierra, a community pump provides water for about five hours in the morning. Each day, people take large plastic jugs and buckets to the pump to collect the day's water supply. In ten months, the water pump broke three times, leaving residents without water for up to a week each time while they waited for the mill to either fix the pump or send a mobile water tank. Since it is not potable, water from the pump is not drinking water; instead, people use it throughout the day for bathing and cleaning. People in La Tierra typically buy drinking water in a five-gallon container called a *botellón* or in small bags called *funditas*.

The Dominican Republic experiences unpredictable power outages across the country. At any time, the electricity could go out: while you are watching the news, waiting in your car at a stoplight that stops functioning, or picking up groceries at a nearby store. Major businesses and wealthier homes have backup generators that activate within minutes of a power outage. But since they cannot afford generators, people in La Tierra and other poor communities in the Dominican Republic manage without consistent electricity.

La Tierra has electricity for about ten nonconsecutive hours each day. The electricity is on for one to three hours at a time and then off for one to three hours. For example, when you wake up at 6 a.m., the electricity is on, but it goes out around 9:30 a.m. It might come back on around noon and then go out again at 4:00 p.m. During the night, oscillating fans start and stop, staving off hot, sticky nights with the unpredictable patterns of power outages.

People plan their daily activities around the availability of the electricity, or *la luz*. Sometimes people gather in a neighbor's home during the evening to catch snippets of *telenovelas* (soap operas) for an hour or two until *la luz* goes out and then spend the remainder of the night sitting by oil lamp or candle light. Refrigerators in La Tierra do not store much food, partly because people only have enough money to buy a day's supply of food, and partly because an excess of perishable goods would spoil when *la luz* goes out and the refrigerator stops running. Although most families in La Tierra wash clothes by hand, a few families have a small washing machine that has a churning mechanism on one side and a spin container on the other. The spin container wrings out as much water as possible, allowing the clothes to dry faster while they hang on a wire in the sun. Following the semipredictable pattern of electricity, women with these machines start the churning and the spinning as soon as *la luz* comes on in the morning, working to wash as much as they can before it goes out. After a couple of hours, someone will shout, "*¡Se fue la luz!*" alerting others that the electricity has gone out. Then women will continue washing by hand, hanging clean clothes on wires or fences, hoping that they dry before the rain rolls in.

Many in La Tierra compare the *batey* to others with worse living conditions. Although electricity in La Tierra is sporadic, people compare it with *bateyes* that have no electricity at all. Also, since La Tierra is located near a city, residents have access to employment opportunities and more reliable transportation than more geographically isolated *bateyes*. For example, one woman says, "I've lived in different *bateyes*. Before, I lived in a *batey* that was very uncomfortable. To leave, you had to go by foot. This *batey* was *más para adentro* [more inside, away from major cities]. You had to get a horse, because the *guaguas* . . . if it's just you alone, they won't take you anywhere. They leave you halfway to where you need to go. So, I would wait at someone's house and send children to get the horse. If I wanted to go see my family who lived nearby, it was difficult."

In addition to its geographic location, several resources in La Tierra create a social atmosphere in the *batey*. La Tierra has an elementary school, an outdoor basketball court, a baseball field, and several churches.[13] Because of these resources and its location near a main road, La Tierra sees people come and go regularly. It is not uncommon to see a group of teens from different *bateyes* playing basketball or baseball together. And churches host social events or prayer services, inviting people in surrounding *bateyes* to participate. Churches in La Tierra are an important source of material and social support. When someone is injured, unable to work, or otherwise in need, people look to the churches for food, clothes, and, sometimes, shelter as people pool their resources to help when they can.

La Tierra also has an elementary school that serves its own children as well as those from surrounding *bateyes*. The government provides the school with books and snacks for children from preschool through seventh grade. The school's director estimates that about 90 percent of students at the school are of Haitian descent. Some have had challenges related to documentation, but, regardless of whether children can provide birth certificates, she enrolls them. The director explains,

> If we can help children with anything, we help them. One teacher helped find money for transportation so that a student could go to Santo Domingo with his brothers and try to sort out their documentation issues. And she told them to let her know if they needed someone from the school to go with them. We would go. Then there was another child trying to go to high school, and they were making it hard for him to take the eighth-grade national exams. But we worked closely with him to help with those problems since he didn't have a birth certificate.

The school also provides a meeting space for government-sponsored adult-literacy classes. I spoke with two women in La Tierra who teach small groups of adults in the community how to read and write. They meet in the school one day each week.

Although living conditions in La Tierra are difficult, people familiar with the region stress that La Tierra is not a poor *batey* compared with other *bateyes* in the country. Problems associated with living conditions in *bateyes*, including food scarcity and illness, are worse for families living in more isolated *bateyes* with fewer resources. Still, in La Tierra I saw mothers give crying toddlers molasses to stave off hunger until they could rustle up rice from a neighbor. But because of the resources available in La Tierra, findings from this research underestimate the challenges associated with income and transportation barriers that limit access to government-sponsored documentation programs. Consequently, stories from La Tierra provide a best-case scenario of the ways that liminal legality impacts people of Haitian descent.

People and Families

Demographics in La Tierra

With the help of youth in the *batey*, I completed a community census to gain a systematic representation of the population in La Tierra. *Batey* La Tierra has 415 residents and seventy-five houses. About one-third of the population in the *batey* was born in Haiti, and two-thirds were born in the Dominican Republic (table 2.1).[14] Of the adults in the *batey*, 54 percent are men, and 46 percent are women.

Table 2.1. Demographic characteristics of La Tierra residents

Characteristic (*n* = 415)	Number	Percentage
Country of birth		
Haiti	133	32
Dominican Republic	282	68
Sex		
Male	224	54
Female	191	46

Fifty-five people completed one-on-one interviews. Of these, twenty-four were Haitian, twenty-one were Dominicans of Haitian descent, and ten were Dominican (table 2.2). Also, twenty-nine were men, and twenty-six were women. The average age of interviewees was forty; however, Haitian immigrants were older than Dominicans of Haitian descent. The average age of Haitian immigrants was fifty-nine, and the average age of Dominicans of Haitian descent was thirty-two. Most interviewees (65 percent) had not completed high school, and almost one in five had never attended school. Haitian immigrants had less education than those born in the Dominican Republic. Most of those who had never attended school were Haitian immigrants.[15]

Table 2.2. Sociodemographic profile of interviewees

Characteristic (*n* = 55)	Number	Percentage
Sex		
Male	29	53
Female	26	47
Age (years)		
18–24	10	18
25–54	26	47
55+	19	35
Country of birth		
Haiti	24	44
Dominican Republic	31	56

(continued)

Table 2.2. *Continued*

Characteristic (n = 55)	Number	Percentage
Ethnicity		
Haitian	24	44
Dominican of Haitian descent	21	38
Dominican	10	18
Language of interview		
Spanish	37	67
Haitian Creole	18	33
Education level		
no schooling	9	16
some elementary school	11	20
some middle school	16	29
some high school	15	27
some college	4	7
Documentation		
Haitian[1] (n = 24)		
none	8	33
birth certificate, no *cédula*	1	4
cédula	4	17
passport	3	12
ficha	9	37
Dominican of Haitian descent (n = 21)		
none	0	0
birth certificate, no *cédula*	2	9
cédula	18	86
passport	0	0
ficha	1	5
Dominican (n = 10)		
none	0	0
birth certificate, no *cédula*	0	0
cédula	10	100
passport	0	0
ficha	0	0

[1] Since one Haitian participant had both a *cédula* and a *ficha*, responses sum to 25.

Table 2.3. Occupations in La Tierra

Nationality	Age	Sex	Occupation
Dominico-Haitian	24	F	homemaker
Dominico-Haitian	26	F	homemaker
Dominico-Haitian	31	F	homemaker
Dominico-Haitian	33	F	not formally employed
Dominico-Haitian	29	M	mechanic*
Dominico-Haitian	54	F	homemaker
Dominico-Haitian	56	M	security guard
Dominico-Haitian	26	M	security guard*
Dominico-Haitian	45	F	homemaker
Dominico-Haitian	36	M	not formally employed
Dominico-Haitian	26	F	homemaker
Dominico-Haitian	23	M	not formally employed
Dominico-Haitian	18	M	high school student

Nationality	Age	Sex	Occupation
Dominico-Haitian	23	M	not formally employed
Dominico-Haitian	20	M	not formally employed
Dominico-Haitian	24	M	not formally employed
Dominico-Haitian	34	M	gas technician*
Dominico-Haitian	23	M	not formally employed
Dominico-Haitian	29	F	homemaker
Dominico-Haitian	22	M	not formally employed
Dominico-Haitian	69	M	*chiripero*
Dominico-Haitian	26	F	not formally employed
Dominican	27	F	medical student
Dominican	25	M	health promotor
Dominican	90	F	not formally employed
Dominican	56	F	homemaker
Dominican	47	M	machine operator*
Dominican	34	F	homemaker
Dominican	36	F	homemaker
Dominican	20	F	homemaker
Dominican	35	M	store manager
Dominican	48	F	school director
Dominican	21	F	homemaker
Haitian	65	M	security guard*
Haitian	71	M	*chiripero,* pastor
Haitian	65	F	not formally employed
Haitian	66	M	*chiripero,* pastor
Haitian	61	F	not formally employed
Haitian	51	M	security guard*
Haitian	68	M	retired cane cutter
Haitian	54	F	homemaker
Haitian	84	M	retired cane cutter
Haitian	65	M	cane cutter*
Haitian	80	M	cane cutter*
Haitian	34	M	cane cutter*
Haitian	59	F	homemaker
Haitian	81	M	retired cane cutter
Haitian	64	M	*chiripero**
Haitian	67	M	cane-cutting foreman*
Haitian	54	F	homemaker
Haitian	50	F	homemaker
Haitian	52	F	homemaker
Haitian	40	F	homemaker
Haitian	31	F	homemaker
Haitian	54	F	homemaker
Haitian	34	F	homemaker

Notes: "Homemaker" is a US-centric term that does not adequately describe the occupations of many women in the *batey*. The majority are responsible for household and child-care responsibilities, leaving little time for formal employment. Most women supplement their household's income with small earnings from odd jobs, including sewing, selling food or goods (e.g., baked goods, ice, charcoal, water, Avon, clothes), styling hair, or washing clothes for another family. The term "unemployed" is used here to designate those who expressed that they were looking for formal employment but found no opportunity available to them. An asterisk (*) indicates employment by the sugarcane company. A *chiripero* refers to a person who makes money here and there, doing odd jobs—usually manual labor or temporary agricultural labor.

Documentation status in La Tierra varies. Although some lacked documents due to robbery or natural disasters, sixteen out of twenty-four Haitian immigrants who completed an interview had some form of documentation, including a birth certificate, work identification card, or Haitian passport. In many cases, however, the document associated with legal status was expired. For example, some showed me an expired Haitian passport, saying that they use it for identification when necessary. Still, an expired passport does not reflect authorized legal status in the country, making them vulnerable to labor exploitation and deportation.

Of the Dominicans of Haitian descent who completed an interview, most had a Dominican *cédula*,[16] or national identification card. But because of changes to birthright-citizenship policies, many had difficulty using their *cédula* to register their children or obtain marriage certificates.

Families in La Tierra

To provide a clearer picture of people's lives in La Tierra, in this section I describe three families that I visited regularly during my time in the country for this research: one Haitian family, one Dominican family, and group of friends and family members who are Dominicans of Haitian descent. These families were the most engaged during my time in the *batey*. They often suggested other community members with whom I should speak or asked questions about my life or the United States as our conversations became opportunities for cultural exchange. Each of the following visits took place after I had been going to La Tierra for several months.

Fabienne and Mackenson

Fabienne is using a dull knife to scale sardines when I arrive at her house. After the small fish is clean, she runs the knife down its middle, pulls out its insides, and then tosses the slippery guts into a dented metal bowl. "Do you do this when you cook, Trini?"

"No," I say. "I've never gutted a fish."

"Well, here's how you do it." Fabienne explains, describing the importance of removing all the scales and getting the fish clean before cooking it. We talk easily about food and the best way to cook rice and beans. Fabienne sets a pot on a fire made of rocks and sticks because she does not have gas for an oven or charcoal for an *anafe* (a small outdoor stove). She and her husband, Mackenson, share a small room in one of the *batey* houses built for cane cutters.

Fabienne sits on the cement steps, stirring the pot of rice. "I'm tired a lot," she says, pointing to her belly. She smiles, excited and bashfully happy. "You can't tell yet, because I'm fat," she explains. "But it's there." She gets up to shoo away a hen and five fluffy yellow chicks heading toward her neighbor's yard. Fabienne has had two miscarriages. She lost one baby four months into her pregnancy, and she lost twins at seven months. "I haven't told Mackenson yet," she says, taking her seat in front of the pot. "So don't say anything." I look up and see Mackenson and two other young men approaching. The two men are Mackenson's cousins who live in a nearby *batey*. Mackenson sits in the doorway, nursing a stitched-up machete wound, and we chat while waiting for lunch.

An older man, Antoine, also lives in a room in the shared house. He looks to be about sixty-five years old. Antoine is not related to Fabienne by blood, but, he says, "We share a house; we are family." Antoine asks whether I can speak English. Then he says, "Can you do me a favor? Can you write some English words in this notebook?" I make a list of vocabulary words in Haitian Creole, Spanish, and English. He smiles, nodding pensively.

We sit together and talk for a while. "Ay, Trini!" Fabienne says. "You made me feel so happy. My heart is content," she clutches her chest. "When you are here, *me siento grande, grande* [I feel important]." She makes me promise to call her before I go back to the United States.

Fabienne was born in Haiti and has lived in the Dominican Republic for about fifteen years. During our recorded one-on-one interview, I learn that Fabienne's father died when she was young and that her mother died about ten years ago. Fabienne has ten brothers and sisters; some live in Haiti, and some live in the Dominican Republic. She also has a fourteen-year-old daughter who lives in Miami with her father and his sister. "I don't talk to them much," Fabienne says. During our regular visits, Fabienne rarely talks about her family, and she is visibly uncomfortable discussing them during our interview. Fabienne often redirects the conversation away from heartache and toward food and recipes. Once, when I ask about her experience living in the Dominican Republic, Fabienne responds, "I don't want to talk about that stuff. Sometimes you get sad, because you have family in different places. All countries have defects. They mistreat you. They do that to you. When you see things that happen in a country . . . I mean, I'm always thinking. And it's a shame. You feel it in your body. So much pain, so many tears, so much suffering. All these things happen, but God is great."

When she is finished cooking, Fabienne insists that I eat some of the rice and *guandules* that she has prepared. I oblige. The next time I stop by, I bring Fabienne and Mackenson banana bread. And Mackenson sends me home with a papaya.

Miriam

At Miriam's house, things are buzzing. Rosaury, Miriam's four-year-old granddaughter, is "cooking" something in a small plastic container: rice, water, juice, a cherry—anything she can find and stir. Her deep chocolate skin reflects the sunlight beaming into the kitchen from the back door. Her father is Haitian.[17] Two of Miriam's daughters are partnered with Haitian men. "¡*Mira*, Trini! [Look, Trini!]" Rosaury smiles a wide smile, revealing three rotting teeth, proud of her handiwork. Ashley, Rosaury's two-year-old sister, wanders into the kitchen, gives the plastic container a stir, and makes her way out the back door, holding on to the doorway to steady her balance.

Miriam and her daughter Amelia sit at the kitchen table cutting neon orange poster paper, called *cartulina*, into six-by-four-inch boxes with tops. Brightly colored scraps are scattered on the floor, and several sheets of *cartulina* sit propped against a porch beam. Amelia wears only a bright blue lacy bra and jeans, her pregnant belly bulging. She cuts her *cartulina* into a small box, carefully gluing the edges. She finishes one box and starts creating a cylinder. "How many boxes have you made?" Miriam asks. "*Uno*," Amelia responds, smiling. "One?! What?!" Miriam exclaims. "You know how many boxes I get out of one *cartulina*? Three!" Miriam laughs, playfully.

For Mother's Day, the school is hosting an event and giving mothers little gifts inside these colorful boxes. "*¡Tu presencia es el cielo para mí!* [Your presence is my heaven!]" Miriam sings a Christian pop song loudly, off-key, and on repeat as she shuffles about in the kitchen.

Micah, my eighteen-month-old son, is in La Tierra with me today. He clings to my leg for a little while then peels himself away to look for the chickens. Estefany, Miriam's two-year-old granddaughter, eyes Micah from a distance then makes her way to the backyard to join him and Ashley.

My eyes follow Micah, and I notice a few people in the backyard waiting to fill up jugs and buckets with water from the shed in Miriam's house. The backyard has a small, green wooden shed that also has a water pump. Miriam and her family often use it to wash clothes. Sometimes, when it is crowded at the public water pump, friends come to get water from here instead.

Miriam brags on her six children during our recorded one-on-one interview. "I have six kids, right?" she says.

> And I've never had to run after them. Never had to get anybody out of jail. They're not fighting in the streets. None of that. You know these problems happen sometimes, but I thank God, because I've never had to deal with any of that with my kids. My oldest is turning thirty-five, and the youngest is twenty-two, and I've never had to run after any of them. They turned out good, thank God. They are hard workers; they are studying and working, you see? Keila is studying medicine. Another finished high school, got married, had two kids, and is working in the factory. Another works at the health center. I thank God, you know?

Since her husband is the superintendent in La Tierra, Miriam lives in the largest house in the *batey*. It has three bedrooms and used to be home to nine family members: Miriam and her husband, four of their adult children, and their three grandchildren. But just a couple of months earlier, Miriam and her husband asked Amelia and her two children to move out to make room for Miriam's brother. Her brother had attempted suicide. He drank poison and was found convulsing in a ditch. He recovered but had no place to stay. So Miriam's daughter and grandchildren moved out, and her brother moved in.

Miriam finishes another bright orange box. "*¡Llegó la luz!* [The electricity is here!]" someone shouts. Miriam peers over her glasses at me. "Do you think Micah likes *jugo de guanabana con leche*?"

"I don't think he's ever had it," I say. She smiles and gets up from the table, heading to the counter to plug in the blender. She hums as she starts making the creamy fruit juice.

"*Ven, Trini. A aprender.* [Come and learn.]" Miriam beckons me to the counter.

Alexandra, Fior, and Mariana

As I make my way through La Tierra on a sunny afternoon, I see Alexandra sitting on the porch with Fior. Fior's hair is in plaits, large sections braided quickly, a temporary style while she waits for Alexandra to fix it. Alexandra and Fior are Dominican women of Haitian descent. Fior was raised by her Haitian grandmother, Luisah. Luisah is sixty-five years old, and her weathered skin and wrinkled face make her look ten years older. She sits just inside the doorway peeling dried husks from corncobs. The pastor's daughter, who lives in the city but visits regularly, is also on the porch, describing the contents of a three-by-three-foot box. Fior and Alexandra smell perfume samples and flip through an Avon catalogue. Fior hands me a sample to put on my wrists. There is an Avon office in the city. When people place orders, the pastor's daughter picks up the products and brings them to La Tierra. Fior hands me a different sample. "This one smells better," I tell her.

"*Modelando sin querer* [Modeling accidentally]," Fior mumbles as a woman stumbles in high heels along the rocky path, her hips swaying as she regains her balance. It still surprises me to see people leave the dusty *batey* in brightly colored, clean, and pressed clothing—the woman's bright green skirt and purple blouse a sharp contrast to the rocks and dirt supporting her stroll.

"¡*Trini!* ¡*Mira, Triiiniii!*" I look down the path to see Mariana and her one-year-old making their way to the porch. The little one is dusty, naked, and wailing. Mariana offers me up as a distraction. He eventually calms down and pushes a dented blue and silver truck through the dirt and rocks, still pouting. Mariana sits with us, picking up a perfume to smell. The four of us chat for a while. The sun is hot today. Scoot your chair over to get some shade. Then Mariana says something about a *yola*. "What's a *yola*?" I ask.

"It's a little boat that can take you to Puerto Rico. But it's dangerous to go that way. One time, a *yola* got stranded, and people were dying, so they had to eat each other." Mariana turns to Alexandra. "You know Señora Guzmán? ¿*La gorda?* [The fat lady?]" Alexandra nods. "They had to eat her thigh first." The women shake their heads solemnly. "There was only one survivor." Unsure of how to separate truth from embellishment, I have no idea what my reaction should be, so I shake my head too.

Always trying to figure out how to get ahead, Mariana has collected money on three different occasions to take a *yola* to Puerto Rico. A *yola* is a small, overcrowded, wooden boat that transports desperate passengers for the dangerous twenty-six-hour trip from the Dominican Republic to Puerto Rico. Each time she had the money, Mariana says something always came up. "God was protecting me," she says. "I know it's dangerous." People in *yolas* can die of hunger and dehydration, shark attacks, or drowning if they are forced to jump into the ocean to abandon a sinking ship.[18]

"*¿Y el libro, Trini? ¿Cómo va?* [How is the book going?]" Fior asks me, changing the subject. "It's going well," I say. "*Paso a paso* [Little by little]." A neighbor walks by, pausing for a moment to greet everyone; then she continues on her way. Mariana sighs and absently picks up another perfume, lost in thought.

Each visit to La Tierra left me with new questions and new discomforts. When I thought I understood, invariably I would learn something that challenged my understanding. In subsequent chapters, I describe how inadequate documentation programs affect the lives of people in La Tierra. Drawing on the voices of Haitian immigrants and Dominicans of Haitian descent, I show the challenges that people encounter when trying to access documentation within a system created for their exclusion. I present people's full personhood alongside their structural barriers to inclusion. People are more than their problems, but their problems need better solutions.

Notes

[1] Literal translation: "Something big is coming to the world. It means that there is still power."

[2] The *batey* may be considered a "total institution." A concept coined by sociologist Erving Goffman, a total institution is a place where people live and work, isolated from the larger society, leading a life formally administered under bureaucratic control.

[3] Consejo Estatal del Azúcar de la República Dominicana, "Historia del Consejo Estatal del Azúcar (CEA)," accessed February 3, 2020, http://www.cea.gob.do/index.php/sobre-nosotros/historia.

[4] Asociación Scalabriniana al Servicio de la Movilidad Humana (ASCALA), "Living Conditions in the Dominican Bateyes," August 17, 2015, https://ascala2.wordpress.com/2015/08/17/living-conditions-in-the-dominican-bateyes/.

[5] See Instituto Azucarero Dominicano (Inazucar), "Central Romana Corporation," 2017, https://www.inazucar.gov.do/index.php/ingenios/central-romana; Inazucar, *Informe Zafra Azucarera, 2017/2018* (Santo Domingo, DR: Inazucar, 2018), http://www.inazucar.gov.do/files/informes-za fra/2017-2018/INFORME_FINAL_DE_ZAFRA_2017-2018_-.pdf; Manuel Jimenez, "Dominican Government Gives Details of Naturalization Plan for 'Foreigners,'" Reuters, November 30, 2013, http://www.reuters.com/ article/2013/12/01/us-dominicanrepublic-citizenship-idUS-BRE9B000O20131201; and Miguelina Valenzuela, Cristina Rodríguez, and Carlos Despradel, *Un siglo de historia: Central Romana Corporation* (La Romana: Central Romana Corporation, Ltd., 2012), http://centralromana.com.do/Central_Romana_Un_Siglo_De_Historia/mobile/. The Central Romana Corporation also owns Casa de Campo, a major all-inclusive resort complex in La Romana.

[6] World Bank, "The World Bank in Dominican Republic: Overview," last updated September 25, 2019, https://www.worldbank.org/en/country/dominicanrepublic/overview.

[7] See Verité, "Research on Indicators of Forced Labor in the Supply Chain of Sugar in the Dominican Republic," 2012, https://www.verite.org/wp-content/uploads/2016/11/Research-on-Indicators-of-Forced-Labor-in-the-Dominican-Republic-Sugar-Sector_9.18.pdf, and Inazucar, *Informe Zafra Azucarera, 2017/2018*.

[8] See, for example, David Simmons, "Structural Violence as Social Practice: Haitian Agricultural Workers, Anti-Haitianism, and Health in the Dominican Republic," *Human Organization* 69, no. 1 (2010): 10–18; Samuel Martínez, "From Commoditizing to Commodifying Human Rights: Research on Forced Labor in Dominican Sugar Production," *Humanity: An*

International Journal of Human Rights, Humanitarianism, and Development 6, no. 3 (2015): 387–409; Bridget Wooding, "Haitian Immigrants and Their Descendants Born in the Dominican Republic," *Oxford Research Encyclopedia of Latin American History*, Oxford University Press, online publication January 2018; and documentary film *The Price of Sugar*, by William M. Haney, Peter Rhodes, Eric Grunebaum, Christopher Hartley, and Paul Newman (Waltham, MA: Uncommon Productions, 2007), DVD.

[9] Verité, "Research on Indicators of Forced Labor."

[10] See, for example, Simmons, "Structural Violence as Social Practice," and Global Health Data Exchange, "Dominican Republic Demographic and Health Survey 2013," Institute for Health Metrics and Evaluation, last modified January 29, 2020, http://ghdx.healthdata.org/record/dominican-republic-demographic-and-health-survey-2013.

[11] Hunter M. Keys et al., "Perceived Discrimination in *Bateyes* of the Dominican Republic: Results from the Everyday Discrimination Scale and Implications for Public Health Programs," *BMC Public Health* 19 (2019): 1513, https://bmcpublichealth.biomedcentral.com/articles/10.1186/s12889-019-7773-2; see also Simmons, "Structural Violence as Social Practice."

[12] See Hunter M. Keys et al., "Perceived Discrimination, Humiliation, and Mental Health: A Mixed-Methods Study among Haitian Migrants in the Dominican Republic," *Ethnicity and Health* 20, no. 3 (2015): 219–40; Keys et al., "Perceived Discrimination in *Bateyes*"; and Bonnie N. Kaiser et al., "Social Stressors, Social Support, and Mental Health among Haitian Migrants in the Dominican Republic," *Revista Panamericana de Salud Pública* 38, no. 2 (2015): 157–62 (text available online at https://www.scielosp.org/article/rpsp/2015.v38n2/157-162/).

[13] Most churches have a congregation that includes both Haitians and Dominicans of Haitian descent. Some churches have services entirely in Haitian Creole.

[14] To minimize apprehension during the community census, I did not ask whether people born in the Dominican Republic were of Haitian descent. I did ask about ethnicity during one-on-one interviews.

[15] See table 2.3 for a description of occupations among La Tierra residents who completed interviews.

[16] A *cédula* is a national identification card that allows Dominican citizens to work in the formal economy, attend university, and access services such as bank accounts and private health insurance.

[17] Miriam tells me that two of her daughters have children by Haitian men. When I ask one daughter, Keila, she explains that her boyfriend was born in the Dominican Republic and his parents were born in Haiti. But she and her mother both refer to her boyfriend as Haitian.

[18] I am unsure whether the story Mariana shares is true, but I did find news stories of the tragedies associated with *yola* voyages. See Associated Press, "Dominican Migrant: We Ate Flesh to Survive; A Small Group Turned to Cannibalism after Being Stranded in Mid-ocean," NBC News, November 4, 2008, http://www.nbcnews.com/id/27531105/ns/world_news-americas/t/dominican-migrant-we-ate-flesh-survive/#.XeKOApNKipo, and Associated Press, "Dominicans Saved from Sea Tell of Attacks and Deaths of Thirst," *New York Times*, August 12, 2004, https://www.nytimes.com/2004/08/12/world/dominicans-saved-from-sea-tell-of-attacks-and-deaths-of-thirst.html.

CHAPTER 3

"Just a Baseball Game"

Byen pre pa lakay.

Being close to home is not the same as being home.

—Haitian proverb

Bay kou bliye; pote mak sonje.

The giver of the blow forgets; the bearer of the scar remembers.[1]

—Haitian proverb

When I began this research, I wanted to understand how anti-Haitian racism affected people in La Tierra, especially as it relates to documentation policies. Admittedly a broad undertaking, I looked to participants to sharpen my focus and guide my thinking as I approached this topic. The primary concern for Haitian immigrants in La Tierra was that anti-Haitian racism barred them from accessing a stable legal status. They emphasized the roles of economic and political processes that brought them to the Dominican Republic and the structural barriers that excluded them and their families from social integration.

In this chapter, I draw on interviews and observations in La Tierra to share Haitian immigrants' experiences and show how their lives represent a poignant example of liminal legality. Financial barriers, heightened monitoring, and vulnerability to private and public actors characterize their precarious circumstances. By placing Haitian immigrants at the center, this chapter provides a deeper understanding of how shifting policies and political interests produce liminal legality and affect Haitian immigrants' daily lives.

The Politics of Exclusion: Policies that Impact Haitian Immigrants

The categories "documented" and "undocumented" are commonly used to describe immigrants' legal status. But these binary categories do not adequately describe the varied legal statuses that immigrants experience. In contrast to using binary categories, scholarship exploring "liminal legality" calls attention to the gray areas of legal status.[2] For example, people with documentation that allows them to work but that does not confer permanent residence live in liminal legality. People with legal statuses that are subject to policy renewal also live in liminal legality. If programs that confer a protected legal status are canceled, then people are pushed into illegality. People move into and out of illegality as policies change.

Political decisions shape and regulate immigrants' lives in profound ways, especially among those living in legal limbo. As political and business interests shift or converge, the lived consequences are real: People can either document their children or not. They are either subject to deportation or not. These decisions fluctuate based on private and public actors' interests. Public actors are organizations established by a nation's government, including public universities and political parties. Private actors are individual or collective participants in economic or social life not managed by the government. These include privately owned businesses. Private actors typically make decisions based on profit. In the Dominican Republic, Haitian immigrants are a critical labor source for both the private and the public actors. As the Dominican government excludes them from society while continuing to benefit from their labor, Haitian immigrants and their families struggle to make sense of changing policies—or wait in limbo until the laws change again.

Liminal legality describes the experiences of Haitian migrant workers in the Dominican Republic.[3] Lapsed bilateral labor policies between Haiti and the Dominican Republic, Dominican business interests, and inaccessible government-sponsored documentation programs contribute to precarious legal status among Haitian migrant workers. This chapter begins with a description of the policies that produce liminal legality for Haitian immigrants. I then use the narratives of Haitian immigrants themselves to show how the characteristics of liminal legality are reflected in their experiences.

Guest-Worker Programs and Haitian Migrant Labor

A common sentiment among Haitian immigrants in La Tierra is disappointment that the Dominican government has not held up its end of a bargain: Haitians were recruited to do some of the most backbreaking work in the country, and decades later, social integration remains elusive. Dominican businesses depend on Haitian migrant labor for production and profit. In the late nineteenth and early twentieth century, the sugarcane labor force was primarily Dominican.[4] Later in the early twentieth century, private sugarcane plantations recruited workers of African descent from surrounding English-speaking islands—locally known as *cocolos*, or less offensively *ingleses*—to work as cane cutters.[5]

The sugarcane labor force shifted from *ingleses* to Haitian immigrants during a period when the United States occupied Haiti and the Dominican Republic. From 1916 to 1924, the US military occupied and governed both countries. In 1919, the US–led government in the Dominican Republic issued executive orders to use Haitian labor to harvest sugarcane. With these executive orders from a country fraught with its own complications related to racialized labor,[6] a labor force initially comprised of Dominicans and *ingleses* was replaced by Haitians.[7]

Over the next thirty years, between the 1920s and the 1950s, as the Dominican government transitioned from US occupation to dictatorial rule, Haitians' presence in the country became increasingly linked to agricultural labor. Rafael Trujillo, whose violent dictatorship controlled the Dominican government from 1930 until 1961, made several policy decisions that reflect a persistent political enigma: the Dominican sugar industry needed the cheap, exploitable labor of Haitian migrant workers, but the government rejected their social integration.[8] This would come to be known as "the Haitian problem."[9]

Trujillo made several contradictory decisions during his rule that reflect the conundrum of "the Haitian problem." For example, the government sanctioned the brutal massacre of thousands of Haitians in 1937.[10] Then, a few years later, in 1942, Trujillo suspended the unofficial government-led recruitment of Haitian workers. Following this suspension, a decrease in the sugarcane labor force warranted a suitable response. To protect the sugar industry and address the need for agricultural laborers to work in the fields, Trujillo initiated a new system, wherein the Dominican government sent troops to recruit Haitian men from other areas of the Dominican Republic to work on the sugar plantations.[11]

But the worker shortage continued. So Trujillo entered into a bilateral agreement with the Haitian government. In 1952, the Haitian government signed an agreement with Trujillo to supply Haitian labor to Dominican sugar plantations.[12] According to the agreement, the Dominican Republic would pay the Haitian government between US$1 to 2 million annually. In exchange, Haiti would supply fifteen thousand workers who would be guaranteed wages, pension, transportation, housing, and medical insurance.

A recurring theme in this research, the difference between policy and practice is substantial. In practice, the contract-stipulated guarantees of adequate labor and living conditions were never verified. Haitian workers lived in company-owned *bateyes* on the sugarcane plantations. The *bateyes* were initially meant to be temporary communities established to accommodate an influx of migrant workers during the cane harvest; however, *bateyes* became permanent residences with some of the worst living conditions in the Dominican Republic, including limited access to clean water, limited electricity, and inadequate housing.

Ironically, although the regulations that protected Haitian workers were not verified, those that served business interests institutionalized a system of trafficking and exploitation that would last for decades to come. Under the agreement, workers were required to stay in the *bateyes* until the end of the harvest. Workers were also legally bound to the specific sugar mill for which they worked. This created new ways for either the mill or the Dominican government to coerce and exploit workers. For example, if a Haitian man could not prove his legal status, he could be arrested, accused of leaving his assigned mill, and sent to work at a sugar mill.[13] The bilateral agreement also delegated to companies the responsibility to ensure that workers returned to Haiti after their designated period of employment ended. With little oversight in the process, agricultural businesses continued to employ workers even after their contracts expired. Employing workers without evidence of valid documentation allowed companies to benefit from unauthorized labor and avoid the oversight of contractual obligations between businesses and workers.

Unregulated recruitment of Haitian workers persists today, regardless of whether migrant workers can provide documentation. In addition to spending time with people living in La Tierra, I interviewed human-rights advocates and legal scholars to gain a fuller picture of the situation facing people of Haitian descent in the Dominican Republic. One woman, a Dominican law professor, says, "There is a lot of money on both sides of the debate. Businesses, politicians, international organizations. Many people have money invested in this issue. And many stand to benefit economically from undocumented immigration. Haitians pay a lot of money—up to RD$5000 [about US$95]—to enter illegally. And police and military at the border pocket the money." The financial benefit of unregulated migration extends from the border to Dominican businesses. Many Haitian workers in La Tierra described instances of labor exploitation exacerbated by their lack of documentation. Employers, for example, stole earned wages from workers who had no avenue for advocacy because of their precarious legal status. Later in this chapter, Haitian migrant workers share these stories in their own words. Ultimately, liminal legality stemming from unregulated migration practices places Haitian immigrants at risk for human-rights and labor abuses.

The National Regularization Plan

After decades of unregulated migration benefiting Dominican businesses, the government initiated a plan to regularize the legal status of Haitian migrants without legal residence. In 2013, the Dominican Republic established the National Regularization Plan for Foreigners with Irregular Migration Status (Plan Nacional de Regularización de Extranjeros en Situación Migratoria Irregular). The PNRE, as it is known, created a new framework for regularization that included temporary, permanent, and nonimmigrant classifications. The PNRE also outlined eligibility factors for a more stable legal status, including length of stay in the country at a fixed address, ties to society, knowledge of spoken and written Spanish, and children born in the Dominican Republic.[14] But the PNRE had a critical omission: it did not specify exactly how people would access the promised path to a more stable legal status. This omission widened the temporal window of liminal legality for tens of thousands of Haitian immigrants.

For Haitian migrant workers, many of whom have limited literacy in both Spanish and Haitian Creole, the bureaucratic steps required to access documentation through the PNRE were insurmountable. Registration often required five or six visits to documentation offices. These trips and associated transportation costs were major barriers for Haitian migrant workers who barely earn enough for the day's meal. In addition to transportation funds, applicants must have money to pay taxes associated with legalizing and notarizing documents and to pay "tips" when trying to obtain certain documents. Such costs amount to an estimated 8,000 pesos (US$180) for each person applying for the PNRE.[15]

Further, weak computer systems and undertrained staff also made it difficult to enroll in the PNRE. Haitian migrants received conflicting information and confusing instructions at documentation offices. Some were told they could initiate the process while they continue gathering necessary documents. Others were told that they could not enroll until they received a valid Haitian passport, either by returning to Haiti or by visiting the Haitian embassy in the Dominican Republic. In support of the PNRE, Haiti initiated the Identification and Documentation of Haitian Immigrants Program to assist Haitian migrants who needed Haitian passports. Under this program, the Haitian government opened documentation centers in the Dominican Republic. But only five centers were set up under this plan, one of which opened only days before the PNRE's registration deadline.[16]

Even if Haitian migrants manage to enroll in the PNRE despite multiple barriers, their legality remains precarious, as there are still more steps and more documents to procure.[17] The PNRE offers temporary protection from deportation, and the enrollee's legal status must be renewed two years later. But as I write this book, six years after the PNRE was established, the Dominican government has yet to announce the protocol that would allow migrants to apply for a more stable, naturalized legal status.

Liminal Legality in Someone Else's Country

Haitian immigrants and their family members move in and out of authorized legal status based on the existing policies at any given time. When new policies warrant new documents, people scramble to collect the necessary paperwork, piecing together documents and scraping together pesos in a context where the rules change often. In this section, I describe how Haitian immigrants experience each of the primary characteristics of liminal legality: financial barriers to accessing more stable legal statuses, heightened monitoring and complex bureaucratic systems, and life circumstances left in the hands of self-interested Dominican businesses and government leaders. Haitian immigrants' voices illustrate the dire need for solutions that consider the people impacted by policies.

Financial Barriers

Emmanuel

Emmanuel insists that I sit in the cracked plastic chair while he sits on the ground. When the sun moves toward us, Emmanuel moves to the shade and stands, tall and slender, leaning against the concrete wall of the green house. He wears slacks held up by a thick black belt and a blue rope. Emmanuel is shirtless in the Caribbean heat, a ragged T-shirt draped over his shoulder. At one point in our conversation, Emmanuel describes his visible scars: A puncture wound with raised scar tissue—he was stabbed in an attempted robbery. A crooked line from below his belly button to just below his chest—he was hit by a car and could not work for eight months after the surgery. Since he does not have a wife and his adult children live in different parts of the country, he relied on community members to send him a meal when they could until he was working again.

In some *bateyes*, religious organizations have established eldercare facilities for aging Haitian men who have no familial support. There is no such facility in La Tierra. So, as in many other *bateyes*, women in the community informally adopt the *viejos* (old men). They send *viejos* a plate of food during lunch if there is a little extra. They listen while *viejos* sit in their yard on a plastic chair discussing politics or playing dominoes as they *compartir*, or spend time together. Since Emmanuel lives alone, he has forged ties with community members through one of the churches in the La Tierra. He supports the church by helping and participating when he can, and they support him by crowdsourcing food when he cannot work.

Emmanuel describes his family as *"pobre pero limpio"*—poor but clean, meaning they work hard for what they need without stealing. With only a third-grade education, Emmanuel has worked for the sugar mill since he was twenty-one years old. Although he is in the Dominican Republic because of "the situation," Haiti is his country. His blood.

"Do you feel connected to Haiti?" I ask.

"Of course! Haiti is my blood. It's my country. Why am I here? Because of the situation."

"How long has it been since you've gone to Haiti?"

"It's been a long time. Around twenty-five years." Then Emmanuel is silent. He shifts from one foot to the other, one hand resting on his hip, a shadow of longing across his brow.

"Could you tell me about the situation that brought you here?"

"The situation was . . . the situation . . ." Emmanuel struggles to find the words. After a moment, he continues: "It's like when you see that you are in a place and you're looking for some way to better your life. To see what else is out there. You look around, and something is missing. And later, you see something else that is missing. And you want to work. You want to have an opportunity in your life. The situation is hard, and you want to work . . ."

"Have you had any problems trying to get any documents?" I ask. I remind Emmanuel that a couple of days ago he showed me the paper that documents his preliminary enrollment in the PNRE.

"For now," Emmanuel says, "there's a Regularization Plan so that everyone has their documents. But right now, I have a problem."

"What is it?" I ask.

What is the problem I have? It's that you have to go to the Haitian embassy in the capital, get your passport, your birth certificate, a letter from Haiti. These things are sometimes a struggle to get. They say it's free, but for me, nothing is free. You have to look for seven witnesses, you have to go to the *junta de vecinos* [neighborhood association], you have to go see an *alcalde* [a community leader], you have to go to other places to look for papers. Spending 300 pesos here and 200 pesos there. A paper saying that you are not a delinquent or in trouble with the police for anything so that they can see that you are a person who lives free in the country. All of this is a problem.

"But you showed me the paper, so you've already received yours, right?" I ask, slightly confused.

"There are still more steps. You have to look for more things. You have to look for more things. You have to ask for a letter from the *empresa* [the sugar mill] that certifies that you work for them. Another example, if you bought *un traste* [major purchase, usually furniture or appliances purchased on credit] from a company, you have to show your receipt so they see that you are compliant or reliable, that you don't have any problems with the company. I mean, it's a lot of things, you understand?"

Emmanuel has a slip of paper to show that he has begun the process, but even after completing an initial step, he is nowhere near close to being registered. And at the time of our interview, the deadline to register was only months away. The Dominican government did extend the deadline, first by hours, then by months. But the threat of mass deportations loomed as people either scrambled to enroll in the PNRE or waited, unable to access crowded documentation offices.[18] Even those who had managed to complete the registration process were required to renew or change their immigration category two years later.[19] The money, time, and bureaucracy required to document and redocument their legal status proves insurmountable for workers like Emmanuel.

Like most Haitian sugar mill workers in La Tierra, Emmanuel left Haiti in search of better economic opportunities in the Dominican Republic.[20] But after decades of backbreaking labor, Emmanuel still struggles to make enough money to buy food each day.

"How much do you earn after one day of work?" I ask.

"When I've done a day, eight hours, of work, for now, they pay me 387 pesos [US$7.50]. But everything is expensive. Rice is 24 pesos [US$0.46], it's 6 pesos for the *sopita* [seasoning], oil is 60 pesos [US$1.15] per pound, beans are 40 pesos per pound, a pound of meat is 75 or 80 pesos [US$1.55], *la masa* [dough] is 100 or 120 pesos [US$2.30], a pound of fish will cost you a little more, around 187 pesos [US$3.60]."

"That adds up," I say.

"And we're not making anything. *Así mismo* [Exactly]. It's expensive," Emmanuel says.

In 2010, the National Wage Committee established the minimum wage for field workers in the sugar industry as 110 pesos (US$3) per day.[21] Since many laborers work seven days each week, the minimum weekly wage would be 770 pesos (US$21). In their national study examining labor among Haitian migrants working in the sugar industry, Verité—a nonprofit specializing in labor rights worldwide—reports that in their sample of 740 workers, 43 percent earned between 501 to 1,000 pesos (US$14 to $28) weekly, and 40 percent earned between 1,001 and 2,000 (US$28 to $55) pesos weekly. Emmanuel earns 387 pesos (US$7.50) in one day, more than the minimum wage. It is still not enough to meet his daily needs.

Emmanuel also endures physical pain, which makes it difficult for him to work in the sugarcane fields. But since he cannot access his pension payments, he works anyway. "If you're sick," he says, "you force yourself to go and work. I don't have anyone sending me money. Dead or alive, I have to go to work."

"My life is very difficult," Emmanuel explains. "I've been working for the company for forty-four years, since 1971. I have a pension request in at the company, some pension documents. The first Dominican peso I earned in the country, they took out three *centavos* [cents]. Forty-four years working up until now. In November of 2012, I applied for pension. Now, here we are on the twenty-third of January in 2015. That's two years traveling to the capital, and I have never been able to see results."

In La Tierra, several men described their eligibility for pensions that they never received—one of the stipulations of earlier bilateral guest-worker agreements. Many others are in Emmanuel's situation, still trying to access their promised pensions.[22] To accumulate earned pensions, agricultural companies withhold a portion of workers' earnings, which are returned to the worker upon retirement. The pension payment for workers is 5,000 pesos (US$97) per month. But thousands of Haitian workers have spent decades laboring in harsh conditions only to be denied their pension once they reach retirement age.[23] According to a local human-rights organization, Scalabrinianic Association for the Service of Human Mobility (Asociación Scalabriniana al Servicio de la Movilidad Humana—or ASCALA), an estimated eight thousand to ten thousand sugarcane workers are still waiting for their pensions.[24]

One explanation for denied pensions is that many Haitian workers are undereducated and struggle to navigate complex and unpredictable bureaucratic processes. Alternatively, some have spent the entirety of their work lives laboring without valid documentation, which means they cannot prove that they are eligible for pension. As a final complicating factor, pension payments are distributed through bank accounts. If a Haitian worker cannot provide a valid document, then they cannot open a bank account, making it impossible for them to receive pension payments after a lifetime of labor with a sugar mill. In these cases, businesses benefit from cheap labor for decades and have no obligation to support their laborers in their retirement.

Without his pension, Emmanuel works as a *chiripero*, or a person who depends on odd jobs as they become available. Less steady and more unpredictable than the seasonal agricultural work associated with sugarcane labor, work opportunities for a *chiripero* come and go. And Emmanuel's physical pain and mental anguish are ever present.

"I live with *la necesidad* [need]," Emmanuel explains. "I have a problem with my sight. It's a bad sickness, and it's what I have in my life. I don't have the money to do what I want to do, and now the pain. I don't have the money to buy the medicine that can take the pain away. There's an injection that you can get and right away, the pain goes away." He gestures wiping one hand across his body, signaling the magic of an injection that could erase his pain.

"There are days that I cannot go to work," Emmanuel continues. "There's a pain there." He points to his abdomen. "When I squeeze it there, I feel a ball, like that." He squeezes a round place on his abdomen that protrudes from his slender body. "I can't bend down or stand up. Really, at night I have to sleep with my head up so that I don't put my head like this." Emmanuel tilts his head to one side.

> Now I find that the only solution for my life so I can have rest is that pension. In a month sitting without eating, you die. Many times, that's why I go to work. Because things don't just hand themselves to you. Imagine! I go out in the name of God. This is how my life is. I have no help . . . I have no help. Who is sending me fifty pesos [US$1]? . . . Who is going to send me that? I'm struggling, struggling. To get half a peso. Not that it amounts to much, but hunger . . .

Emmanuel chuckles to himself, shaking his head slowly. "Imagine! Sometimes I lie down at night at one o'clock. And at two o'clock, I cannot sleep, thinking of not working. . . . It is taking me away. I think a lot." Emmanuel pauses.

"What do you think about?" I ask.

"Well, the situation and life," Emmanuel replies. "Sometimes I get up to work. I cannot go, but I must go. And later I will get older, and I won't be able to do anything. If I don't have that pension, what am I going to do? I'll die." He pauses for a moment and then says, "That's how I live."

Camille

Camille and her first husband were living in Haiti when he left in search of work in the Dominican Republic. They lived separately for a couple of years, and then Camille left Haiti to reunite with her husband. After some time, her first husband became very ill, and he died. Then Camille met another man who said he would take care of her. He invited Camille to live with him, and when she moved to the *batey*, she learned that he was married. So Camille lived in a house with him and his wife.

The English word "husband" does not accurately describe the partnerships between men and women in La Tierra. Some men and women live together and support one another but are not married by law. In these situations, men are a financial resource for women, and women take care of household responsibilities. In some cases, there is also a romantic relationship. In other cases, there is not. Because Camille is more comfortable describing her experience in Haitian Creole, she speaks with Malena, a Dominican research assistant of Haitian descent.

"I was with a man, and he died," Camille says. "The people who give me a hand when I'm in misery are strangers. I don't have family here. Now I'm with this man, and at first everything was fine, but now his wife and family hate me."

"Is the man who lives here your husband?" Malena asks.

"Mm-hm. You don't see him much though. He comes and goes."

"Who was the first wife? You?"

"No, he is married."

"But you're the wife?"

"No. I am the other woman. He came after me. I lived in another *batey*, and he came and found me there. But since I've been here, I have had the worst problems. I can't stay here."

Camille does not remember how long she has lived with her current partner. She was with him before Hurricane Georges, which had made landfall in 1998. At first, things were fine. He would go out to work in the sugarcane fields, and Camille would take him lunch. Sometimes, while she was at the fields, Camille helped him plant and chop sugarcane. He always made sure she had food to eat. "When he brought in a little money from working," she explains, "it wasn't money you could save. It was just for food. Just food."

On one of her trips to the fields, Camille was beaten and robbed.

"I was a thick, strong woman," Camille begins. "I planted with him. Harvested with him. If he was chopping, I was with him. In all kinds of work, I was with him. I worked like a donkey. But one time, a thief almost killed me when I was taking him food. He was working, and I went to take him food. And the thief smacked me and punched me. I had a little money. He took that and my shoes. I almost died taking him food. Since then, I stopped taking him food."

Camille is trapped in a situation where she has few options. She has no source of income, and the man who was supporting her barely provides a meal for her each day. Camille tries to sell packets of coffee to make a few pesos, but her earnings do not amount to much. "I used to sell coffee packets. Make 5 pesos [US$0.10] here and there when people could pay me. Or if they couldn't pay me right then, sometimes they paid me monthly. Because if I don't try to make my 5 pesos, what am I doing?"

"The misery won't allow me to leave," she says. "I want to go where my family is, but I haven't gone because I don't have the money for the trip. Now I'm looking to see if I can go where my family is, and I can't."

The term "misery"—or *la mize* in Haitian Creole—is commonly used to describe the suffering associated with extreme poverty and dire living conditions.[25] *La mize* has kept Camille in a dire situation, separate from her family. "If I say anything about happiness," Camille says, "it would be the greatest sin. Because I don't have happiness."

"Tell me, do you have a passport, an ID card, or a baptism certificate?" Malena asks.

"I don't have anything," Camille responds. "When I came here, I lost all my documents. I don't have even a little piece of paper. Nothing. I have to go take care of this issue with the papers, but I haven't been able to go."

"How did you lose your papers?"

"When the hurricane came. That's when I lost them. It came and broke the house apart."

"Have you tried to get your papers?"

"No. I haven't been able to go to Haiti. Because Haiti is where I must go to do my papers. If I can't go to Haiti . . ."

"What do you think about the situation?"

"Well, they say that they are going to deport people who don't have papers. When they find you, they will send you to Haiti. If they send me back, I would just like to be able to get my clothes."

During this portion of the conversation, the man Camille lives with enters the house. Malena quietly asks Camille whether she would like to move to a different place so they can continue their conversation in private. "No," Camille says. "We can stay here."

Camille lost her identification documents during Hurricane Georges, a category 4 storm that devastated the Caribbean more than twenty years ago now. In some circumstances, sugar mills were involved in connecting their workers to places where they could regularize their legal status. But these efforts were sparse. And since the focus was on migrant workers, the vast majority of whom are men, women were left with no concerted effort and no support for procuring documentation. Although Camille can apply for a Haitian passport at the Haitian embassy in Santo Domingo, she says she must go to Haiti to get her papers. Without the financial means to get to Haiti—or Santo Domingo—she lives with no way to prove her identity.

"I went . . . we went to get a paper," Camille continues, "but it doesn't work. I don't show it to people, because it doesn't work." Camille asks her husband to show Malena the papers she has. When he returns with the papers, Camille's husband says, "There are times when you are living with someone, and you try so that person get *un pedacito de papel* [a little piece of paper]. But then you see that you would have to spend 1000 pesos [US $20]. Here, any move you make is about money. And money is not easy to come by. Nothing is easy."

"This is a copy," he continues. "And when we went trying to present this, they told me it's a copy and they need the original. I said, I don't have it. Well, it wasn't me, because I sent her to the city with another person to support her. So, they said, This paper won't work. And it was 1000 pesos, just for a copy. They said you have to go to Haiti to look for the original."

"When you had papers," Malena asks, "did you feel different?"

"When you have papers," Camille says, "you can show them when you need to, everywhere you go. But now, since I've lost them, I am nobody."

Financial barriers to accessing a stable legal status are characteristic of a life lived in liminal legality. The funds required to pay for multiple trips to documentation offices or for the transportation fare associated with collecting documents from different sources are more than people in La Tierra can afford. In some cases, people look for cheaper options that will suffice; however, many are devastated to learn that they have wasted their money on useless alternatives.

Heightened Monitoring

Sylvestre

Sylvestre works as *capataz de corte*, or a cane-cutting foreman. In this role, Sylvestre supervises cane cutters as they clean the sugarcane stumps and smooth out the field every harvest. When the harvest ends, he says he "makes other moves to live." Sylvestre's work in Dominican sugarcane fields began in the late 1960s when he started to travel back and forth between Haiti and the Dominican Republic, moving with the seasonal work of the *zafra* [harvest]. "My first trip was in 1966. I was eighteen years old, so I was a big guy. It was after Hurricane Inez," he explains.

When Sylvestre came to the Dominican Republic to work in 1971, he settled in the country more permanently. "In '71, they were looking for people to go [to the Dominican Republic] in a truck," Sylvestre explains. "In Jacmel, I didn't have papers—no. I came *anba fil* [under the wire]. But everybody was here working. Since then, I haven't gone back [to Haiti]. I was working in '72, I met my wife in '73, and we had nine children."

Anba fil is a Haitian Creole phrase meaning "under the wire." It refers to migrants who enter the Dominican Republic without authorized documentation. In Sylvestre's description, "they were looking for people" to work in the Dominican Republic. And Sylvestre describes being recruited and transported to the Dominican Republic even though he did not have proof of legal documentation.

Human smugglers, called *buscones* in the Dominican Republic and *passeurs* in Haiti, are labor brokers who supply workers for the Dominican economy.[26] These smugglers form connections with the Haitian military and the Dominican border agents to bring buses of Haitian workers to Dominican businesses.[27] In these unregulated circumstances, many Haitian migrants do not have valid documentation, and some have their documents stolen by people promising to help them. Still others are vulnerable to robbery, violence, or life-threatening circumstances as they make the desperate journey to the Dominican Republic.[28]

"What kind of documentation do you have?" Malena asks.

"I had an immigration *cédula*," Sylvestre says.

"Did you lose it?"

"No," Sylvestre replies. "No, I didn't lose it. They collected everyone's. We turned them in, and they gave us Haitians . . . let me show you what they gave us. Look. They gave us this ID card. When we turned in our *cédulas*, they gave us this." He pulls out a laminated green card.

> The company gave us this and a paper that we use to collect our payments when we go to the office. But you can't just go anywhere with this. Only to the office to collect your payment. It's not worth anything anywhere else. You can't even buy a [cell] phone with this! Well, you used to be able to, but now they don't accept it. . . . Now they ask for a passport . . . or a *cédula*. During Balaguer's government, he ordered that all the *cédulas* be changed—just like now, when they changed out the old *cédulas* for new ones. So, I mean, they were changing the old *cédulas* for new ones, but when they changed the *cédulas* for us Haitians, they didn't give us a *cédula*. They didn't give us anything. The company gave us these old green pieces of paper that have absolutely no value! You can only use it to work for the sugar mill—that's it. That's what we have now.

The limited inclusion that Sylvestre describes by referencing the document that has "absolutely no value" is characteristic of life in liminal legality. People can have a form of documentation that allows them to work but bars access to any other form of social integration. For Sylvestre, the transition from more to less inclusion was the replacement of his *cédula* with the company-issued *ficha*, or work identification card, which is primarily used for interactions with the sugar mill.

Under the bilateral labor agreements between Haitian and Dominican governments in the 1950s, the Dominican government regulated Haitian workers' documentation. In 1986, following the collapse of a violent dictatorship in Haiti, interstate agreements regulating the flow of Haitian migrant laborers to the Dominican Republic lapsed. And regulation of migrant's documents shifted from the government to the sugar mills.

In many cases, depending on the country and its prevailing policies, migration permits and associated documentation are issued to the individual. But issuing migration permits to the sugar mills rather than to the migrants themselves gave sugar companies complete control over Haitian workers' movement within the Dominican Republic. With this shift, the limited oversight of Haitian migrants' labor rights virtually vanished. Sugar mills maintained control of workers' documents, creating a situation ripe for exploitation and labor abuses.[29]

Sylvestre describes having his Dominican *cédula* replaced with a company-issued *ficha*. Since Sylvestre entered the Dominican Republic *anba fil*, I am uncertain how he obtained a Dominican *cédula*. One possibility is that Sylvestre was one of the many Haitian workers issued a Dominican *cédula de cartón* during the 1990 presidential election.[30] During this period, the Balaguer[31] campaign included visits to *batey* communities. To manufacture new voters, the campaign issued Haitian workers a *cédula de cartón*, or an identification card made of paper rather than plastic. Until then, the voter-identification card and the national identification card were separate. In 1992, after the 1990 election, the national identification card was updated—likely a strategy to clean up the documentation mess created by underhanded campaign tactics. The new card was made of plastic, and it would be used both for identification and for voting, rather than having two separate documents for each purpose.[32] This approach would ensure that Haitian migrant workers were not mistakenly given the *real* right to vote—since their votes were fabricated during the previous election.

Once the *cédula de cartón* was nullified, Haitian workers' documentation remained an issue that would persist for Dominican presidents to come. In the early 1990s, when the government merged the voter-identification card and the national identification card, Balaguer—Trujillo's political protégé—also created an initiative to regularize the documentation status of Haitian migrant workers. Under the initiative, the sugar mill replaced workers' documents with a *ficha*, a work identification card primarily used for interactions with the sugar mill. The *ficha* gave workers limited temporary permission to remain in the Dominican Republic according to their employment contract. This period also included a wave of mass deportations and expulsions[33] to

Haiti as the Dominican military rounded up thousands of "Haitian-looking" people primarily from *bateyes*, loaded them onto buses and trucks, and transported them to the Haitian border.[34]

Meanwhile, Dominican business and government interests continued to converge at the expense of Haitian migrant workers. Under pressure from the International Monetary Fund, Balaguer applied several financial and labor reforms, setting the stage for privatization of sugar mills.[35] With increased privatization, the need for Haitian migrant labor to widen profit margins persisted, and the established system of unregulated migration from Haiti to the Dominican Republic continued.

"Okay, you're Haitian, and I'm talking with you in Haitian [Creole]," Sylvestre says to Malena.

> This country doesn't realize … after all the things Haitians have done? They should give us a paper that works. They say that [they] want to give us paper, but the truth is that they put too many obstacles and requirements. There are some big shots in the middle that want everyone in their own country. . . . But really, with the intelligence of the other countries and all the nations working together, they could bring us out of this darkness. And we would be better in the light. Now, if they give us a paper that works, that paper would bring us into the light.

Naomie

Naomie is sixty-one years old and has lived in Batey La Tierra for twenty-two years. She has eight children, and her eldest is thirty-nine years old. She lives in a house with one of her sons, his wife, and their three children. Naomie has lived with her son and his family since her husband got sick and died in her arms at the hospital eight years ago. Since then, she has relied on the financial support of her children while running a series of small businesses in the community to provide day-to-day income. Naomie used to make bread and sell slices, but now she buys sacks of *carbón* (charcoal) when a truck comes by and then sells small bags to women who need it. Many women use *carbón* for cooking.[36] During our conversation, a couple of women lean on a wood post along Naomie's wired fence to buy *carbón*. Naomie also has a small *conuco* (garden) where she grows corn, *auyama* (squash), and *batata* (sweet potato). Some is for cooking; the rest she sells. Naomie also runs a small business for her daughter: her daughter buys chicken from a nearby city, and Naomie sells it in the *batey*.[37] "Life is hard," Naomie says, "but you have to find a way to come out ahead."

Naomie is actively involved in the evangelical Christian church in La Tierra. "Sometimes I lead the service," Naomie says. "Or I might lead the devotional. I have always served in the church." She thanks God for her children, who take care of her. They give her money for food and unexpected expenses as they arise. If Naomie gets sick and needs medication, for example, she gives the prescription to her children, and they buy it for her.[38]

"My heart is content with my children, thank God," Naomie says. "There are some people who don't have children, and things are hard. So hard. A person might want to eat, but they are hungry because they don't have money. Sometimes people who are able give them a plate so they can eat."

"How does that make you feel?" Malena asks.

"Oh! I don't like it at all. Because I start to think, if I didn't have my children taking care of me, I would be living the same way."

"I came here because I had a brother who came here," Naomie says. "I was in Haiti with my parents, and my brother would leave and come back. I saw that people looked nice when they came back, and I liked the way they talked. So I said I wanted to go with him and learn to speak Spanish."

"Have you been back to Haiti?" Malena asks.

"I've made a few trips back and forth."

"How would you compare life in Haiti to life here in the Dominican Republic?"

"When you live in your own country, you live more peacefully, because when you're in someone else's country, they are always asking you for papers. Sometimes they give you problems about papers, and you want to get around, but you can't because you don't have papers. But in your country, it's not like that."

"Have you felt afraid to get around here?"

"Because of papers, they will grab you and send you to Haiti like animals!"

"Has that happened to you?"

Oh! If you just want to go to the city because maybe your family is there or you want to buy a little rice for your children, they will grab you and send you to Haiti! Girl! One time, I went shopping, and they grabbed me. It was God that made them let me go! I had just given birth, and I told them I had a one-month-old baby, and the guy in charge let me go. They even gave me *el pasaje* [the fare] to get back home. After that, I got my passport, and now when I go out, I take my passport.

Because she fears deportation, Naomie carries her expired Haitian passport when she goes to the city. She is trying to enroll in the PNRE, but she is still missing several documents: "Since they said they are giving papers, I went to the city. They told me that I have to have a paper from the *junta de vecinos* [neighborhood association], copies of *cédulas* for seven witnesses, you have to have a paper of good conduct, and all these papers cost money. There are people that don't have the money to do it."

She continues: "And two of my children still don't have papers. They still haven't been able to get them."

"Why not?"

"Their father didn't declare them with a *cédula*. Now for them to get a *cédula*, they have to go to the capital. One daughter who lives here has her own kids, and they are not declared because of problems with their father's papers."

"What do they tell her when she goes?"

"She went. They gave her a paper to take to the capital. And now they told her to wait three months to see if she can declare the kids."

"So you have children without papers and grandchildren without papers?"

"Yes. I have this little boy and this little girl who was crying earlier that still don't have papers. And I have two daughters that still don't have papers. One is not working, and the other works in a family's house. She can't work for a business because she doesn't have papers. Without a *cédula*, she can't work."

In Naomie's family, three generations live in liminal legality: Naomie herself, her children, and her grandchildren. Although she was born in Haiti, Naomie's Dominican-born children and grandchildren are pushed into second-class citizenship, their marginalization rooted in government efforts to keep labor in its place.

Vulnerability to Private and Public Actors' Decision-Making

Yves

Private actors, including agricultural businesses, make self-interested decisions at the expense of Haitian immigrants, especially those without legal residence. The first time I meet Yves, it is during a downpour. Dark clouds move across the sky, and within half an hour, the sky opens up, dropping buckets of rain. The downpour begins during my interview with Doña Josefa, a ninety-something-year-old Dominican woman who shares a house with two Haitian workers.

When the rain starts, one of the workers helps Doña Josefa inside. Trying to avoid sprays from the open window, she stands in a narrow corridor that is just wide enough for two people to stand shoulder to shoulder. Yves insists that I sit in the only chair in the house.

The wind blows fiercely, sending fat rain droplets into the house through the doorway. Luis, the other worker who lives there, closes the door a bit to keep the rain out. But then it is so dark that you can barely see your hand in front of your face. The electricity is out.

Yves opens the *persianas* (blinds) to let some light in through the window. He stands in the kitchen, eating rice from a metal bowl. He gestures the bowl toward me, offering me rice. "No, *pero gracias* [but thank you]," I say. He pretends to be offended and then smiles.

As I sit in my chair, I look around in the dim, tiny house. A sheet of corrugated tin closes off two, maybe three rooms. In the kitchen, pieces of wood of various sizes create a makeshift counter. The floor is about as wide as one person standing there. A broom made of twigs connected to a bigger stick leans against the wall.

We chat a little while we wait for the rain to let up. "How many planes did it take you to get here?" Luis asks.

"Two," I respond. "One from North Carolina to Miami. Then another from Miami to Santo Domingo."

"Are you British, like the *colocos*?"

"No, I am an American. My family is from the United States."

Yves listens, nodding occasionally, but he does not say much. The rain slows, and I peek outside at the river of rainwater gushing through the mud and rocks on the road. Doña Josefa offers to loan me her umbrella. "I have one in my purse," I say. "But I think I'll need a boat to get out of here!" We laugh, and as I step carefully between the rocks, mud, and a newly formed river, Luis guides me across. "No, don't go that way. There is less water if you go around." I nod gratefully and make my way out of the *batey* to catch the *guagua* and head home.

Yves smiles and nods each time I see him after that. I learn that he speaks very little Spanish, so he completes his interview in Haitian Creole with Malena.

Yves came to the Dominican Republic from Haiti in search of work. At the age of thirty-four, Yves is one of the younger immigrants in La Tierra. He has only been in the Dominican Republic for four years, in contrast to most of the others I speak with who have been in the Dominican Republic for forty years.

Yves left his family in Haiti, including his thirteen-year-old son, in search of work in the Dominican Republic. Yves has never been to school, but he would like to learn how to read and write. So he and a few other workers meet with a neighbor who teaches them the alphabet every now and then. "I'm holding my own in the class," he says. "I've learned to write my name."

"So, how are things going for you?" Malena asks.

"I'm okay, thank God," Yves replies. "Even though I got sick once, God healed me right away. I have never gotten sick here in this country. I've never seen a hospital bed. Even though I don't have money, I'm okay. I'm not in prison. Because there are people in prison that want to get out, but they can't. Others are in the hospital worried about going home, but they can't. I'm okay."

Yves was robbed one night when he fell asleep on the way home from the sugarcane fields. The thief stole his wallet, which included his money and his identification documents. Since the robbery, Yves can prove neither his identity nor his legal residence in the country. He has not been able to earn enough money to pay the fees and transportation costs necessary to get new documents.

"What papers do you have?" Malena asks.

"I don't have any papers," Yves responds. "I used to have an identification card, but I lost it."

"Where?"

"Cutting cane at night."

"You cut cane at night, too?"

"A long time ago, I did. But I don't anymore."

"What happened?"

"I was walking down the highway one Saturday, like today. Then I sat down to rest, and drowsiness passed over my eyes. When I got up, I checked my pockets and I said, 'I lost my wallet!' I looked around and never found it. I wish they had just taken the money, but my identification card was in there too."

Several people in La Tierra mentioned that robbery was commonplace. On days when they are paid, workers are targets for desperate people trying to make money quickly. Yves, either fortunately or unfortunately, did not realize he had been robbed until it was too late. He was not physically assaulted, but he had not had a chance to fight back before losing his wallet and his identification documents.

"After losing your identification card, has it been a problem for you?"

"Well, I know I have problems, you understand?" Yves replies.

When someone doesn't have even a little piece of paper in their hands, it's a problem. But I haven't gone to work here and been turned away. I mean, these little contract jobs that I'm telling you about, people do them with *cédulas* and without *cédulas*. You don't need a *cédula* for this kind of work. But if I had a document, I would look for better jobs where I could make a few more pesos. Here, there are places you can work anyway, but the work is worthless. The jobs don't have . . . these jobs . . . for example—a person who cuts cane, who pulls up cane, this is not worth any money.

The wage that Haitian laborers receive is barely enough to buy food for the day. And workers are too desperate to turn work down, even if they know they are being exploited.

"Some Dominicans treat Haitians badly because Haitians work for nothing," Yves continues.

And they shouldn't treat Haitians badly, because, look. You have that notebook in your hands, and I don't have one. What do I have to do? I have to work and save so I can by my own notebook. That's just how I am. But if I go somewhere looking for work and they give me 3,000 pesos for the work but the work is worth 20,000. . . . And I don't even have a little jar of *picantina* [seasonings]. I don't even have water to drink. I mean, you're going to give me 3,000 pesos to do this work. I have to take it. I don't have anything. Now you cut my head off because I did a 20,000-peso job for 3,000 pesos and it affects Dominicans? No. I'm in need. You understand?

Since the robbery, Yves is still able to find work, but because he has no documentation, supervisors take advantage of his desperation. He works at the mercy of employers who can either decide to pay him fairly for his labor or cheat him out of his earnings.[39]

"I'm not going to work in construction anymore, because I spent, like, two months in construction. After a pay period of two months, the trainer and the boss left with all my money."

"They left with just your money?"

They left with all the workers' money! They took it all! A Haitian woman gave me 150 pesos [US$3.00], and a man selling phone cards gave me 50 pesos [US$1.00]. I walked for part of the way, and there was a man in a truck who brought me here. That's how I got here from the other city where I was working. . . . But like I was saying, if I'm at one of these jobs, the little work we're doing isn't worth any money, you understand? We are working under these people. The price of these little jobs they send . . . [the city] takes a piece, [a larger *batey*] takes a piece, and when the administrator comes, he takes a piece. And on Saturday, he can report your work in someone else's name so that he can go collect for himself, taking money from the very people working in the *batey*. On Saturday, that guy is eating well in his house and you're not.

Deductions from workers' earnings are not uncommon. Although the Labor Code states that employers are obligated to provide workers with materials necessary for the work free of charge, in other studies, some workers report deductions for materials, including boots and a machete.[40] There is also little clarity about deductions related to pension. Employer representatives say that they do not make wage deductions for social security, but almost half of the workers surveyed in a national study of 740 workers at 49 Dominican *bateyes* believed that social-security deductions were pulled from their wages.[41] According to previous bilateral agreements between Haiti and the Dominican Republic, a pension program was one of the stipulations for contracted agricultural labor. Since those agreements have lapsed, however, it is unclear whether or how aging workers are able to financially support themselves when they are physically unable to work.

Unclear and unregulated wage deductions create confusion, but workers are also vulnerable to employers who steal their wages. Without documentation, Yves cannot earn a living wage working in the limited kinds jobs that he can get. Further, he describes experiences having his wages stolen by deceitful supervisors. Some supervisors routinely steal workers' pay. Yves explains,

> One time I was working at a sugar mill near Miches [a Dominican city], and the guy in charge up there was really bad. His name was Manuel. I mean, when I worked Saturdays, if I worked six days in the week, he would always take two of those days. You understand? He would take those two days that I worked for himself. I was not okay with that, so I had an argument with the guy, and I left. He is everyone's enemy up there. That's just what he does. You put in five days, and he takes one. It's an abuse, you understand? They want to keep you down, because they know that you don't have anywhere to run.

Vulnerability to the decision-making of private actors places Haitian immigrants at risk of labor exploitation. In the examples Yves describes, Haitian migrant workers accept low-paying jobs out of desperation. Even in the positions they can get, workers are subject to further corruption as supervisors cheat them out of earned wages without consequence. Unable to access programs that might provide documentation, Yves moves from place to place, working at the mercy of self-interested private actors.

Joseph

Public actors, including the Dominican and Haitian governments, also make decisions that push Haitian immigrants into liminal legality. Joseph is visibly uncomfortable as I read him the consent form for participation in this research. We sit on a wooden bench under a palm tree. His legs are crossed, and his arms are folded across his chest, his body protecting itself from this foreign encounter with a foreigner. Joseph is trembling slightly. He is wearing khaki slacks, a worn button-down white collared shirt with vertical and horizontal blue lines creating a faded plaid pattern, and a baseball cap that says "ICTOA Fighting Terrorism."

During our conversation, Joseph chuckles often. At first it is nervous laughter; then it is easy laughter as we get more comfortable with one other. At one point, he accidentally spits on me while he is talking, the saliva skipping past the place where a tooth used to be. He apologizes profusely, covering his mouth in embarrassment. "Oh, it's nothing," I say. "Just a little rain!" He throws his head back and laughs, tickled. Then he tells me about the two teeth he needs to get pulled because they have been hurting lately.

Joseph is the pastor of one of the five churches in La Tierra. He and his wife Estè live in housing attached to the Assembly of God church. When I ask how old he is, Joseph pauses thoughtfully and then says, "Let me see . . . I was born in 1943. Just put that down." He is seventy-one years old.

Joseph was born in Haiti and moved to the Dominican Republic in search of work when he was about thirty years old. While living in the Dominican Republic, he heard about the political violence of Haitian dictator François "Papa Doc" Duvalier. During his reign, Papa Doc declared himself president for life and established the Tonton Macoute—a militarized secret police unit that raped and murdered anyone with opposing political views. Often the Tonton Macoute left their victims' bodies on public display—hanging in trees as a warning to silence others.

"Duvalier and his group were strong in Haiti," Joseph says. "When he came to power, the people could not bear it. There was a lot of killing to free Haiti, but there were so many Macoute! They were always around. And you could not talk. *Uno no tiene boca para hablar* [You did not have a mouth to talk]." He buttons his lips with his thumb and forefinger. "If you are doing something and those people take you, they take all your things and sometimes the whole family, then they kill you and they kill them. It was grave."

The terror that Papa Doc invoked in Haiti spanned fourteen years, from 1957 until 1971. When Papa Doc died, his youngest and only son, Jean-Claude "Baby Doc," became a teenage dictator at the age of nineteen and continued his father's legacy of terror and corruption for fifteen more years, from 1971 until 1986.[42] These decades of violent governance created a perilous situation for thousands of Haitians who fled their homeland in search of peace and greater stability.

"When you hear that they are talking about you, it's not worth it to get upset," Joseph explains. "Because they're right: you're in their house. But we have been here for so many years! I've been here since 1973 when I came to the Dominican Republic. The ones doing all the worst work are the Haitians."

When I ask what documents he has, Joseph replies, "Wait a minute. Wait right here." He goes into the house and returns with a small, navy blue binder. Slowly and carefully, Joseph pulls out an old passport with a picture of him in his thirties. "An official told me I can use this if I need to," he says. Then he shows me his green *ficha*, saying he used this work identification card to register his children when they were born.

Next, Joseph shows me the half sheet of paper he received when he began the process of enrolling in the National Regularization Plan a couple of months prior to our conversation. "I signed up," he says. "They have a lot of requirements, but I signed up. But I'm still missing a few things. I still have to take some papers to the office."

"What are you missing?" I ask.

"The *brega* [challenge] is finding a paper for my studies. I studied in a Christian ministry here. A pastor has to find me a paper. And I need a certification of work from the company [the sugar mill]. And I might have to look for around seven witnesses, but I have a lot of people who know me. That's not hard. Let's see. What else is missing? Um . . . the good-conduct paper. I need that too." He pauses.

"Still, the paper we get will be worthless. What we want is to have a paper that has *validez* [validity]. We don't want a paper like the Dominicans. We don't want to be Dominican. We want a paper that has validity so we can have rights in the country. The Dominicans can have their Dominican documents, and we want to have a paper for immigrants—but with validity."

"Why do you think there are so many challenges in the process?" I ask.

"It's political," Joseph responds, matter-of-factly. "I mean, I asked myself the same thing. Where is all this coming from? And I can't understand it. There's someone who knows the reason why, but I don't. We can't understand the reasons behind this political stuff. Each time, they say, We need to give immigrants their papers. But then they don't want to. There's a group that doesn't want to, and I don't know why." Joseph pauses, crossing his legs and holding his chin in his hand.

"I don't know where this comes from. I asked someone once, and they told me it was because Haiti governed here years ago and they [Haitians] were mistreating people. They also told me that in the time of Trujillo, they [Dominicans] were killing a lot of Haitians. Maybe things like that . . ." Joseph's voice trails off.

Several people in La Tierra cite the historical memory of political tensions between Haiti and the Dominican Republic as an explanation for present-day anti-Haitian racism. The two countries were unified under Haitian leadership from 1822 to 1844. In conversations with people in La Tierra and with professionals in larger cities, many describe contemporary political measures to control people of Haitian descent as part of the persistent fear that people of Haitian descent will once again reunify the island.

"We are just a baseball game for the politicians to negotiate!" Joseph says with exasperation. "In Haiti, they know what's going on with us here. They know where we are." He frowns, his arms and legs uncrossed, then crossed again. "I mean, life is hard here in the Dominican Republic . . . but I blame my country too. On the one hand, they [the Dominican Republic] are right, because every country that has a president has a responsibility for its citizens, right? But the politicians here wanted to take Haiti down. So, really, both sides are to blame." Joseph stops speaking, pausing to watch the breeze rustle through the palm trees. When he looks back at me, I see heartache and frustration. Brows furrowed, he continues.

Sometimes you think and ask yourself, When will a government come that will allow you to live in peace? That will fix the problems in your country and let you live in peace? So, when you see what is happening—more pain. Pain here, pain there, pain here, pain there. I don't know if you understand that.... It could be that you live in someone else's country where you're mistreated with harsh words, and afterward, you feel hurt. So, you don't want to stay. And you want to leave their country, but then you turn on the news to see the same mistreatment in Haiti.

Joseph chuckles softly to himself, uneasy.

"This nation [the Dominican Republic] says a lot of silly things," he continues.

They tell you, "You have no value; you have no country." All these words fall on the ears of the whole world, because, you know, we sit in front of the radio and we listen to what is happening in the world. And when we hear these words, we must tie them up and throw them in the sea. These things hurt! Come on! If I come to your house and you give me some of what you have, then afterward you talk bad about me? It was me who took care of you. You should feel bad, right? That's the problem.

That's the problem. Haitian immigrants in the Dominican Republic are vulnerable to the self-interested decisions of public actors, including the Haitian and Dominican governments. Lapsed bilateral agreements between the two countries leave Haitian immigrants living in liminal legality after leaving their country in search of opportunities to improve their life circumstances. Instead of opportunity, Haitian immigrants have met with harsh living conditions, labor exploitation, and generations of statelessness for their children and grandchildren.

Joseph is frustrated and hurt by the public shame of anti-Haitian racism and the lack of acknowledgment that he is in the country because he was recruited for his labor. He worked and contributed to the Dominican economy, but now, after taking care of his responsibilities, Joseph is met with contempt before a global audience. The insults and the political baseball game are difficult to ignore, but, with few options, Joseph tries to "throw them in the sea" and move forward with his life.

Needed, yet Unwanted

Liminal legality includes financial barriers to a more stable legal status, heightened monitoring, and vulnerability to private and public actors' decision-making. The costs associated with gathering the documents required to enroll in the National Regularization Plan are too high for Haitian immigrants living in La Tierra. When people cannot afford the official processes to get documentation, they sometimes try a low-cost alternative, such as the promise of all the documents you need for 1,000 pesos. Rumors broadcast information about deals that sound promising to desperate ears. But these alternatives are often scams that leave victims feeling frustrated and confused about which efforts are trustworthy and which are not.

In addition to financial barriers, bureaucratic barriers prevent Haitian migrants in La Tierra from enrolling in the PNRE. Many have trouble pulling together the documents necessary: a paper of good conduct from the police department, letters from employers and places of education, a record of items in one's house, and a copy of the *cédulas* of seven witnesses. For a population with limited literacy and limited experience with institutions and bureaucracy, these steps and requirements are often insurmountable.

Haitian immigrants also experience heighted monitoring as they are continually subject to broader attempts to regulate their presence in the country. The Dominican government and the sugar mills transitioned Haitian migrant workers to *fichas*. The *ficha* is associated with employment at the sugar mill only and does not grant access to social or political participation beyond employment. This keeps Haitian migrant workers in a vulnerable social position and limits their ability to work for other employers. In this way, agricultural labor remains "Haitian labor."

Heightened monitoring and vulnerability to private and public actors' decision-making work in tandem to marginalize Haitian immigrants in the Dominican Republic. Governments and businesses collaborate for their own benefit at the expense of Haitian workers. For example, when it proved a convenient way to create voters, Haitian migrant workers were issued fake *cédulas* during a political campaign. When the Dominican government collaborated with sugar mills to move workers from the *cédula* to the *ficha*, it limited Haitian workers' social integration, ensuring that their inclusion remained temporary and strategic. The prevailing sentiment? They belong in the fields but not in society.

Government instability and lack of oversight also contribute to Haitian workers' marginalization. Bilateral agreements between Haiti and the Dominican Republic were established to benefit Dominican businesses and provide opportunities for Haitian workers. Although Haitian laborers found work, their living and working conditions were deplorable, and their labor is pervasively exploited by employers that undercut or steal workers' earned wages.

According to a Haitian proverb, *byen pre pa lakay*: being close to home is not the same as being home. Haitian immigrants in La Tierra left their homes in search of opportunities that might improve their lives and the lives of their children. But after working in the Dominican Republic for decades, they encounter marginalization for themselves and their children for generations to come. The proverb also has an alternative interpretation: it's not over until it's over—or, in other words, don't give up. The struggle continues as Haitian migrants and their families push against a system designed to exclude them. They organize, protest, collaborate, and resist to fight for the human rights they deserve.

Notes

1. For poetry and proverbs written in Haitian Creole, Jacques Pierre, *Omega*, pref. Josaphat-Robert Large (Gainesville, FL: Classic Editions, 2012).
2. See Menjívar, "Liminal Legality," and Jennifer M. Chacón, "Producing Liminal Legality," *Denver University Law Review* 92, no. 4 (2014): 709–67 (text available online at https://poseidon01.ssrn.com/delivery.php?ID=54102100211811512308410108702209208910902503201

0160321190840970760960960250660831060010601020050411110181160990670850
8312711204203400707600009606409408411500402703008401705710311611510109
91200060840640820891150250030160950720260960100250720030831160948&EXT=pdf).

3 Menjívar developed the concept of liminal legality based on the experiences of Salvadoran and Guatemalan immigrants in the United States, but it has been applied to the lived experiences of people across the globe, including migrant workers in Singapore, London, Russia, and Mexico. For examples, see Kara Cebulko, "Documented, Undocumented, and Liminally Legal: Legal Status during the Transition to Adulthood for 1.5–Generation Brazilian Immigrants," *The Sociological Quarterly* 55, no. 1 (2014): 143–67; Brenda S. A. Yeoh and Heng Leng Chee, "Migrant Wives, Migrant Workers, and the Negotiation of (Il)Legality in Singapore," in *Migrant Encounters: Intimate Labor, the State, and Mobility across Asia*, ed. Sara L. Friedman and Pardis Mahdavi (Philadelphia: University of Pennsylvania Press, 2015), 184–205; Cathy McIlwaine, "Legal Latins: Creating Webs and Practices of Immigration Status among Latin American Migrants in London," *Journal of Ethnic and Migration Studies* 41, no. 3 (2015): 493–511; Victor Agadjanian, Cecilia Menjívar, and Natalya Zotova, "Legality, Racialization, and Immigrants' Experience of Ethnoracial Harassment in Russia," *Social Problems* 64, no. 4 (2017): 558–76; and Tanya Basok and Martha L. Rojas Wiesner, "Precarious Legality: Regularizing Central American Migrants in Mexico," *Ethnic and Racial Studies* 41, no. 7 (2018): 1274–93.

4 For an analysis of power and systems that produced exploitation in the Caribbean sugar industry, see the classic anthropological work of Sidney Wilfred Mintz, *Sweetness and Power: The Place of Sugar in Modern History* (New York: Penguin, 1986).

5 *Ingleses* came from many islands, including Saint Kitts, Anguila, Antigua, and Saint Martin.

6 David R. Roediger and Elizabeth D. Esch, *The Production of Difference: Race and the Management of Labor in U.S. History* (New York: Oxford University Press, 2014).

7 See Wilfredo Lozano and Bridget Wooding, eds., *Los retos del desarrollo insular: Desarrollo sostenible, migraciones y derechos humanos en las relaciones domínico-haitianas en el siglo XXI* (Santo Domingo, DR: FLACSO and CIES, 2008), and Franc Báez Evertsz, *Braceros haitianos en la República Dominicana*, 2nd ed. (Santo Domingo, DR: Instituto Dominicano de Investigaciones Sociales, 1986).

8 Wooding and Moseley-Williams, *Needed but Unwanted.*

9 Matibag and Downing-Matibag, "Sovereignty and Social Justice."

10 In 1937, between fifteen thousand and twenty thousand Haitians and dark-skinned Dominicans were brutally murdered with machetes, bayonets, and clubs. For more information, see Turits, "A World Destroyed."

11 See Martínez, "From Hidden Hand to Heavy Hand"; Barbara L. Bernier, "Sugar Cane Slavery: Bateyes in the Dominican Republic," *New England Journal of International and Comparative Law* 9 (2003): 17, and Hintzen, "'A Veil of Legality.'"

12 Guest-worker programs for temporary migrants are not uncommon. Countries across the globe, including Brazil, Germany, the United States, and others, have implemented guest-worker programs to import cheap labor to maintain their agricultural economy. For example, the Bracero Program brought millions of Mexican workers to the United States under a bilateral contractual agreement between 1942 and 1964. Most braceros, or "manual laborers," filled an agricultural-labor shortage in the United States. During this period, about two hundred thousand Mexican laborers came to the United States each year under the promise of work, a living wage, and a savings plan. Agricultural companies deducted 10 percent of braceros' pay for savings accounts. Employers guaranteed that workers would receive these earnings at the end of their contracts. The harsh reality was that many braceros worked and lived in unsanitary conditions, faced economic exploitation, and never saw their deducted earnings.

13 Martínez, "From Hidden Hand to Heavy Hand."

14 República Dominicana, Decreto No. 327-13. For a description in English, see, for example, Jimenez, "Dominican Government Gives Details."

15 Wooding, "Haitian Immigrants and Their Descendants."

16 Ibid.

17 When the PNRE program's registration window closed in June 2015, fewer than five thousand migrants had been regularized as "residents," and an estimated 250,000 migrants were

regularized as "nonresidents." A nonresident status grants temporary exemption from deportation but confers no access to rights and social services.

[18] "Dominican Republic Extends Residency Deadline ahead of Mass Deportation," *Guardian*, June 17, 2015, https://www.theguardian.com/world/2015/jun/17/dominican-republic-deadline-residency-haiti.

[19] "Deadline for Foreigners to Seek Regularization Expired Sun," *Dominican Today*, August 27, 2018, https://dominicantoday.com/dr/local/2018/08/27/deadline-for-foreigners-to-seek-regularization-expired-sun/.

[20] In *Detain and Punish: Haitian Refugees and the Rise of the World's Largest Immigration Detention System* (Gainseville: University Press of Florida, 2018), Carl Lindskoog connects race and global power dynamics with the rise of the present day's immigration detention system in the United States. To maintain a relationship with the Haitian dictator in power, US leaders classified Haitian migrants fleeing political violence as "economic migrants" rather than as "refugees." This classification meant that the United States did not condemn political violence in Haiti, and it also restricted US aid to those seeking refuge in the United States.

[21] The conversions presented are those listed in the Verité report, "Research on Indicators of Forced Labor." Since conversion rates fluctuate, there may be inconsistency between conversions presented in the report and those presented throughout the book.

[22] Michelle Kanaar, "Dominican Republic: The Haitian Sugar Workers Denied Their Pensions," *Equal Times*, December 16, 2015, https://www.equaltimes.org/dominican-republic-the-haitian?lang=en#.XXeyKy5Kipo.

[23] Michelle Kanaar, "Dominican System Snarls Pensions for Haitian Workers," *Miami Herald*, October 21, 2015, https://www.miamiherald.com/news/nation-world/world/americas/haiti/article40778388.html.

[24] Michelle Kanaar, "Dominican System Snarls Pensions for Haitian Workers," *Miami Herald*, October 21, 2015, https://www.miamiherald.com/news/nation-world/world/americas/haiti/article40778388.html. Along with ASCALA, Dominican organizations, such as the Comisión Nacional de los Derechos Humanos (the National Human Rights Commission) and Movimiento de Mujeres Dominico-Haitianas (the Dominico-Haitian Women's Movement, known as MUDHA) have worked to improve the conditions of Haitian migrant workers.

[25] Paul Farmer, "On Suffering and Structural Violence: A View from Below," *Daedalus* 125, no. 1 (1996): 251–83 (text available online at http://www2.kobe-u.ac.jp/~alexroni/IPDreadings%202017/IPD%202017_10/On%20suffering%20and%20structural%20violence.pdf).

[26] Human trafficking and migrant smuggling are major businesses that create a global concern affecting many countries. Human trafficking is the unauthorized transport of vulnerable people—typically women, children, or undocumented persons—from one place to another for the purpose of forced labor. Typically, traffickers use force, fraud, or coercion to lure people and then transfer them to another city, region, or country for sexual exploitation or forced labor. Some people agree to work with traffickers because they are desperate and need help crossing international borders. But when they get to the receiving country, the traffickers take advantage of their lack of knowledge about the culture or their inability to speak the language. For example, traffickers may take victims' documents, threaten victims' families, or physically confine them, forcing them to work. It is difficult to generate reliable figures about the financial profits associated with human trafficking because of its underground and clandestine nature. But the International Labor Organization estimates that forced labor results in about $150 billion annually in illegal profits globally—and $12 billion in Latin America alone.

[27] Wooding and Moseley-Williams, *Needed but Unwanted*.

[28] See Diego Pesqueira, "Acusan 3 en caso mueren 24 haitianos perdieron la vida en tráfico ilegal," *Hoy*, January 12, 2006, https://hoy.com.do/acusan-3-en-caso-mueren-24-haitianos-perdieron-la-vida-en-trafico-ilegal-2/, and Jonathan M. Katz, "The Dominican Time Bomb," *New York Times*, July 2, 2015, https://www.nytimes.com/2015/07/02/magazine/the-dominican-time-bomb.html.

[29] Human Rights Watch, "'Illegal People.'"

[30] Natalia Riveros, *Estado de la cuestión de la población de los bateyes dominicanos en relación a la documentación* (Santo Domingo, DR: Observatorio Migrantes del Caribe, 2014).

[31] Joaquín Balaguer was a Dominican president who served three nonconsecutive terms: first from 1960 to 1962, again for a second term from 1966 to 1978, and again for a third and final term from 1986 to 1996.

[32] Eddy Olivares Ortega, "La cédula y su caducidad," *Acento*, January 17, 2015, https://acento .com.do/2015/opinion/8213611-la-cedula-y-su-caducidad/.

[33] "Deportation" refers to sending immigrants to their country of origin. "Expulsion" refers to casting people out of their own country of origin.

[34] Human Rights Watch, "'Illegal People.'"

[35] During this time, three major companies became fully privatized: La Corporación Dominicana de Empresas Estatales (Corde), La Corporación Dominicana de Electricidad (CDE), and the sugar-producing companies grouped under the conglomerate Consejo Estatal del Azúcar (CEA).

[36] Some women cook on a stove that uses a tank of petroleum gas. But gas can be expensive and hard to come by once it runs out. So many women cook on a *fogón*, a small outdoor fire hearth that uses *carbón* to create a flame.

[37] For more information about women's small businesses in the Dominican Republic, see Sherri Grasmuck and Rosario Espinal, "Market Success or Female Autonomy? Income, Ideology, and Empowerment among Microentrepreneurs in the Dominican Republic," *Gender and Society* 14, no. 2 (2000): 231–55.

[38] For data and information about how immigrants interact with healthcare systems for medical services in the Dominican Republic based on an analysis of the 2017 National Immigrant Survey (Spanish), see Fondo de Población de las Naciones Unidas (UNFPA), "El acceso de inmigrantes y descendientes a la salud y la protección social en la República Dominicana: Segunda Encuesta Nacional de Inmigrantes, ENI-2017," September 2018, https://dominicanrepublic.unfpa.org/ sites/default/files/pub-pdf/El%20acceso%20de%20inmigrantes%20y%20descendientes%20 a%20la%20salud%20y%20la%20protección%20social%20en%20la%20República%20 Dominicana.pdf.

[39] For information about Haitian workers' labor exploitation in other Dominican industries, see Petrozziello, *Haitian Construction Workers*.

[40] For more information about labor conditions in *bateyes* across the Dominican Republic, see Verité, "Research on Indicators of Forced Labor"; Martínez, "From Commoditizing to Commodifying Human Rights"; and Mark Curnutte, "Labor Dept. Finds Bitterness in Sugar Workers' Lives," *Cincinnati Enquirer*, published at *USA Today*, October 3, 2013, https://www.usatoday .com/story/news/nation/2013/10/03/sugar-workers-human-labor-rights/2919687/.

[41] Verité, "Research on Indicators of Forced Labor."

[42] Nathalie Baptiste and Foreign Policy in Focus, "Terror, Repression and Diaspora: The Baby Doc Legacy in Haiti," *The Nation*, October 23, 2014, https://www.thenation.com/article/ terror-repression-and-diaspora-baby-doc-legacy-haiti/.

CHAPTER 4

"We Are Not Free"

No voy a descansar, aunque me quede en el camino, porque yo sé que la lucha seguirá. Algún día, tarde o temprano, el Estado tendrá que reconocer a estas ciudadanas y ciudadanos que crecen aquí apátridas, sin nacionalidad, sin un nombre, para que sean incluidas en esta sociedad dominicana.

I will not rest, even if my life is cut short, because I know that the fight will continue. Someday, sooner or later, the State must recognize these citizens who grow up here stateless, without a nationality, without a name, and include them in this Dominican society.

—Sonia Pierre, activist and founder of Movimiento de Mujeres Dominico-Haitianas, Inc. (Movement of Dominican-Haitian Women, MUDHA)[1]

"I'm Dominican Like You"

On a bright, March day, I sit on a *guagua*—a public transportation bus—riding through the city of Santo Domingo. I tell a fellow passenger that I am looking for the Junta Central Electoral, or the Central Electoral Board (CEB), locally known as the *junta*. The *junta* is the Dominican civil-registry office that provides documentation services. As the *guagua* approaches a winding intersection, the passenger points to large yellow building. It would have been hard to miss. A black, metal gate surrounds the CEB building, and a large crowd of at least a hundred people sit, stand, sing, and shout on the sidewalk outside the gate.

The protest has been organized by Reconoci.do, a movement of Dominican youth and young adults of Haitian descent fighting to reclaim their right to nationality. Organizers hand out bread, water, and large umbrellas to block the sun and keep cool in the midday heat. This is day two of a three-day protest. The previous evening, they were arrested, held in jail for about an hour, then released. This morning, they continue their demonstration. And tomorrow, they will return.

Most people in the crowd wear black T-shirts with a message printed on back that reads, "*Soy de aquí* [I'm from here]. *Identidad para un future digno* [Identity for a future with dignity]." They carry signs that say, "*Soy dominicano como tú* [I'm Dominican like you]."

A few people from the Dominican press roam through the crowd, holding large cameras. Armed, uniformed police officers speak with protest leaders. People of all ages chant a call-and-response chorus that fills the air: "*¡Ey ya, ey ya, yo soy dominicano! ¡Yo soy dominicano!*" The sound of their voices, the megaphone, the metallic musical rhythm of the *güira*[2]—the scene is at once electrifying and emotional. I blink back tears and make my way through the crowd.

Unsure of what to do or where to go, I ask a man who appears to be in his thirties what brought him to the *junta* today. He replies, "I used to have a *cédula*. I had health insurance, and I was working. But now, I have nothing." The music transitions from fast to slow as a young woman sings a mellow, Christian pop song into the megaphone. "*Supe que me amabas. Lo entendí. Y supe que buscabas más de mí* [I knew you loved me. I understood. And I knew you were expecting more of me] . . ."

"But you still have your card, right?" I ask, not understanding what it means to have documents suspended.

"Yes," he replies. "But they've taken us out of the system." He shows me his *cédula*, the Dominican identification card, and explains, "See this?" he says, pointing to the card. "This is my *cédula*. When you type this number into the computer to find work or go to school, I used to be there. But now, if you type it in, I'm not there." He pulls a picture of his children from his wallet. "I have three children. Two are registered because they got birth certificates when my *cédula* was valid. But I haven't been able to register the third because of this law. What now?"

The man's voice is urgent, imploring me to see how his life has been upended by policies that have suspended his citizenship, pushing him into statelessness. Demonstrators sing, shout, and pace outside the black, metal gates of the *junta* building, demanding that the government hear their message: they, too, belong to the Dominican Republic.

An absurd display of anti-Haitian racism's extensive reach, Dominicans of Haitian descent experience liminal legality in their country of birth. A series of policy changes, including increased conditionality on birthright citizenship, results in tens of thousands of people denied full citizenship in the only country they have ever known. If they register in the Book of Foreigners, then Dominicans of Haitian descent affected by new laws can work, but they cannot vote. In this chapter, I summarize the laws that contribute to liminal legality for Dominicans of Haitian descent. Then I use the voices of those in the Dominican *batey* La Tierra to show how Dominicans of Haitian descent experience liminal legality and its political consequences in their own country.

The Politics of Belonging: Policies that Impact Dominicans of Haitian Descent

Liminal legality describes a gray area of legal status marked by continual instability and uncertainty. For example, people may have valid government-issued documents that confer limited legal rights, such as authorization to work, but they are not granted access to the benefits of full citizenship. Previous applications of liminal legality shed light on the experiences of immigrants across the globe. But considering the legal status of Dominicans of Haitian descent further widens the scope of those impacted by liminal legality to include people residing in their own country of birth.[3]

In the Dominican Republic, a series of policy changes pushes Dominicans of Haitian descent into liminal legality in their own country. Amendments to the nation's birthright-citizenship laws—including a constitutional ruling that stripped citizenship from thousands who already had it—a Book of Foreigners created for those who cannot prove their parents' authorized legal status, and a naturalization law with an undefined path to a more stable legal status all contribute to liminal legality among Dominicans of Haitian descent. By examining their experiences, we consider the plight of citizens who are pushed into liminal legality under the threat of expulsion while losing their right to vote.

Birth Certificates and *Cédulas*

In the Dominican Republic, people need three types of documentation to exercise fundamental rights including the right to attend school, to work, and to vote.[4] The three documents are the *certificado de nacido vivo*, the *acta de nacimiento*, and the *cédula de identidad*. The *certificado de nacido vivo* is a certificate of live birth, issued by a hospital or medical center where a child is born. Many families of Haitian descent leave the hospital without a certificate of live birth due to administrative oversight or outright discrimination against people of Haitian descent. Without a certificate of live birth, a child cannot get an *acta de nacimiento*.

The *acta de nacimiento* is an official birth certificate issued by local civil-registry offices. Within two months, families must obtain a birth certificate for their child, or they risk navigating an additional set of bureaucratic steps to procure documentation. After a child reaches two years of age without a birth certificate, individual civil registries can make their own requirements for obtaining one.[5] The birth certificate is the primary form of identification for children under the age of eighteen. The birth certificate is required when children and youth apply for a passport, matriculate through school, get married, or obtain health care. Children receive a birth certificate when parents provide the civil registry with both the child's certificate of live birth (received from the hospital) and their own personal identification document. If the parent is an immigrant, they must provide a valid passport from their country of origin. If the parent is Dominican, they can provide a *cédula de identidad*.

A *cédula de identidad*, or national identity card, also called a *cédula*, is the main form of personal identification for Dominican adults ages eighteen and older. People use the *cédula* for formal employment, opening a bank account, registering for social security, and voting. The *cédula* is also necessary in many areas of social participation, including signing up for temporary educational workshops, beginning a cell phone service, or making purchases on credit. The Central Electoral Board is the government agency responsible for issuing *cédulas*. To obtain a *cédula*, an individual must have birth certificate and be able to physically obtain that birth certificate from a documentation office.

Tens of thousands of Dominicans of Haitian descent have been unable to obtain their birth certificates from CEB offices across the country. When interacting with various institutions, such as primary schools and universities, Dominicans must request their birth certificates from a civil-registry office. But many Dominicans of Haitian descent have had their requests denied. Further, those who do not interact with such institutions may be unaware that their documents have been suspended. To further complicate the situation, many people born in the Dominican Republic never received a birth certificate, either because they live in rural areas and did not give birth in a hospital or because of administrative errors and discriminatory treatment at the hospital. Each of these layers creates an immensely complex situation in which those affected now advocate using both national and international platforms for appropriate documentation in their homeland.

A Civil-Registry Audit, a Book of Foreigners, and a Naturalization Law

For decades, if Haitian migrant workers did not have a valid Haitian passport, they could use a *ficha* to get birth certificates for their children born in the Dominican Republic. The *ficha* is an identification card issued by a private Dominican employer—in most cases, a sugar mill. Many Haitian migrants lawfully registered their Dominican-born children using the *ficha*. Today, under national civil-registry audits, officials use the *ficha* to identify children and adults born to migrant workers with unauthorized legal status. Once identified, their Dominican citizenship is subject to suspension until they can prove their parents' authorized legal status. In this way, birth registration using a *ficha* contributes to systematic discrimination and targeted surveillance of Dominicans of Haitian descent.

An extensive explanation and a time line of relevant policies can be found in the introduction chapter. To summarize and provide context for this chapter, I provide a brief outline here. In 2004, a new General Law on Migration (la Ley General de Migración No. 285-04) stipulated that Dominican-born children could only be eligible for citizenship if their parents could prove legal residence. Then, in 2007, the Central Electoral Board created a Foreign Registry, commonly known as the "Book of Foreigners" or "pink registers," to ensure that no children of Haitians without legal residence would be mistakenly classified as Dominican nationals. Following this process, when a child is born in a hospital, and the parents cannot prove their legal residence in the country, the child is issued a pink birth certificate and demarcated a noncitizen. By law, a Dominican child only needs one parent to provide evidence of Dominican nationality to receive Dominican citizenship. But Dominican children of Haitian descent are often given pink, foreigner birth certificates even when one or both parents have Dominican documents.[6] In some cases, this is a result of administrative confusion. In others, it is a result of discrimination against people of Haitian descent. Further, since the process was new and confusing, differentially applied, and often unregulated, some families—many of whom were poor, low literacy, or of Haitian descent—left the hospital with no papers at all, and the births were never registered.

During this time, the Central Electoral Board also began an audit of civil records to identify Dominicans of Haitian descent whose parents could not prove legal residence. The goal was to "correct" documents for Dominicans of Haitian descent by moving them from Dominican citizenship to the Book of Foreigners. This marked the beginning of a practice that stripped children, teens, and young adults of their previously conferred Dominican citizenship.

In 2010, a new Dominican Constitution incorporated distinctions in birthright citizenship established by the 2004 General Law on Migration.[7] Following this change to the country's constitution, any children born in the Dominican Republic after 2010 are not Dominican citizens unless at least one parent is a Dominican national or legal resident. This legislative act cemented race-based distinctions in citizenship.

In 2013, the Dominican Constitutional Court (Tribunal Constitucional) officially stripped citizenship from anyone born in the Dominican Republic to parents without legal residence dating back to 1929. To correct "errors," the court ordered another audit of civil records to identify persons registered as Dominicans between 1929 and 2007 under previous birthright-citizenship laws. According to the court, those persons should have their Dominican documents nullified and, instead, be registered in the Book of Foreigners. This landmark decision denied citizenship to thousands of Dominicans of Haitian and created chaos among those affected by the ruling.[8]

Public outcry against the ruling, both domestic and international, emphasized its discriminatory impact on Dominicans of Haitian descent. Dominican and Haitian public figures in the United States spoke out against the ruling and advocated for solutions that preserved human rights.[9] In response to public pressure, the Constitutional Court rescinded the retroactive application of amended birthright-citizenship policies. And in 2014, the Dominican government created Naturalization Law 169-14 (Ley de Naturalización 169-14), which legally restored citizenship for people with stripped citizenship. Six years later, however, tens of thousands of Dominicans of Haitian descent with stripped citizenship are still waiting for the policy's promises to materialize.[10]

Eight months after the Constitutional Court's landmark 2013 ruling, the Dominican government enacted Law 169-14 to solve the crisis that the ruling had created. Since the court's ruling had to be followed, this new law upheld the increased conditionality on birthright citizenship. To ensure that Dominicans of Haitian descent were not "erroneously" classified as Dominican, Law 169-14 established a new documentation process.

Law 169-14 applied to two groups of people born in the Dominican Republic (see figure 1.1 in chapter 1): Group A included the approximately fifty-five thousand Dominican-born people whose citizenship was stripped due to the Constitutional Court's ruling. Group B included Dominican-born people who had never acquired documents. Thousands of children born in the Dominican

Republic have no documents at all. Since many areas of the country are rural, children may have been born at home instead of at a hospital. And those who were born in a hospital may have left without certificates of live birth due to administrative errors related to confusion about issuing pink papers to Haitian parents who could not prove their lawful residence in the Dominican Republic.

To those in Group A, Law 169-14 legally restored Dominican nationality. But five years after the ruling, only about half actually had their documents reinstated. Dominicans of Haitian descent in Group B, those whose births were never registered, must declare themselves Haitian nationals and register in the Book of Foreigners. Registration in the Book of Foreigners provides documentation for people in Group B but not full citizenship. According to Law 169-14, those in Group B can complete a naturalization process two years after registering in the Book of Foreigners for a more stable legal status conferring naturalized citizenship. Five years after Law 169-14 was passed, because of an unclear process, no one in Group B had been naturalized, including those who registered before the deadline.[11]

Numerical estimates vary, but few people who are eligible to register in the Book of Foreigners have completed the process. This is likely related to several factors. First, the process is confusing. Dominican-born people in Groups A and B are trying to resolve their documentation issues in tandem with Haitian migrants enrolling in the National Regularization Plan. Several groups with distinct needs receive information from documentation offices where officials often conflate multiple groups into one. This conflation, sometimes intentional, reinforces the strategic and divisive political narrative that all people of Haitian descent are foreigners no matter where they were born.

Dominicans of Haitian descent live in liminal legality under policies that push them out of their country's national fabric. In subsequent sections, I share how Dominicans of Haitian descent in La Tierra experience the new laws, and I discuss the political implications of creating generations of people without a vote in their own country.

When Citizens Live in Liminal Legality

With increased conditionality on birthright citizenship, Dominicans of Haitian descent move into a state of liminal legality. Like Haitian immigrants, they too must scramble to collect paperwork, piecing together documents and scraping together pesos to prove that they belong in the place where they were born. A national audit to reclassify Dominicans of Haitian descent as foreigners demotes thousands of people to second-class citizenship. If their parents cannot provide valid documentation, Dominicans of Haitian descent must register in the Book of Foreigners under threat of expulsion to Haiti, a country they have never known.

Liminal legality has three primary characteristics. First, people living in liminal legality are often subject to financial barriers that hinder their ability to access legal statuses that could protect them from deportation. Dominicans of Haitian descent face financial barriers to proving their parents' legal status and must enroll in the Book of Foreigners. Second, governments monitor the continued ability to document one's presence in the country. Once appointed in the Book of Foreigners, Dominicans of Haitian descent must reenroll or verify their status every two years. Third, liminal legality leaves entire populations vulnerable to private and public entities that make decisions based on their own interests. The precarious legal status of those who register in the Book of Foreigners is subject to change as governments and businesses shift their priorities. The stories that follow illustrate the primary characteristics of liminal legality in the voices of Dominicans of Haitian descent in La Tierra.

Financial Barriers

Yeison

Yeison[12] sits on a makeshift wooden bench with three other young men. The group looks to be in their early twenties, and they are talking intently when I approach. "Hey, what are you guys up to?" I ask.

"Not much," one of the guys responds. "Just taking it easy."

I explain who I am and why I have been spending time in La Tierra. Then I say something like "Are any of you interested in talking with me?" A couple of the guys avert their eyes, run a hand over their head, and say nothing.

Yeison says, "Sure, okay."

Yeison is twenty-three years old and has the look of a person that Dominicans might call a *tiguere*. The word *tiguere*[13] is often used to describe young men who wear fashionably faded jeans, a black fitted T-shirt, and a baseball cap—as Yeison does. "You and the guys were just hanging out?" I ask.

"Yeah, you know," Yeison replies. "Just sitting with the guys. Talking about women, girlfriends. Stuff like that. Women always get jealous and try to pick fights."

"Well, let me scoot a little further away," I joke.

Yeison laughs. "Nah, don't worry about it. A man is a man no matter what."

When I ask about his family, Yeison says, "We're not perfect, but we're a beautiful family. It's the family God gave me." Yeison has eleven brothers and sisters, four on his mother's side and seven on his father's. Yeison is the youngest of all of his siblings. "We try to treat each other well. If there is food, we all eat. If not, we are all without it together."

Yeison's parents were both born in Haiti, and he has never met his father. "My father was here working a long time ago, cutting cane. My mother got pregnant with me, and after that, my father went to Haiti and never came back."

When we discuss documentation, I learn that Yeison has a Dominican birth certificate but has been unable to get a *cédula*. "Have you tried to get your *cédula*?" I ask.

"How do I explain this? Sometimes these people ..." Yeison pauses to gather his thoughts. He continues,

> When you get to the office to verify something, they say, "Look, you need to go to San Pedro or to the capital so they can give you this paper, because here,

we're not doing that." And sometimes, *uno no tiene movimiento de dinero* [you don't have money movement]. You can't move for nothing. And especially if you're not working and you don't have papers to work, you can't make moves to go anywhere. That's what's got me stuck. Every time they send me to the capital, I've never gone. I'll try to go this year, or maybe this month, to see what they'll tell me. But every time I go to the *junta, siempre la misma vaina* [it's always that same stuff]. This is why I'm fed up and I don't want to go to the office again.

Accessing the documentation processes is nearly impossible for Yeison. Sources estimate that gathering the necessary documents to begin the application process can cost up to 5,000 pesos [US$98] per applicant.[14] For a person who is barely scraping together enough money for food each day, this barrier is insurmountable.

In some *bateyes*, sugar mills have offered support to help register children and get birth certificates for those who do not have them. According to a report published by the Dominican Sugar Industry, sugar mills offered financial and logistical support for *batey* residents trying to register under Naturalization Law 169-14.[15] In La Tierra, however, when I asked whether there were any groups or organizations helping them with documentation, the answer, overwhelmingly, was no.

Yeison's primary concern is his ability to earn a living. "*Hombre es hombre, como quiera, donde sea y donde llegue* [A man is a man, no matter what]." Central to Yeison's manhood is his ability to work and provide for a family. Although he does not yet have a wife or children of his own, he wants to be able to give money to his mother and contribute to the financial stability of the household.

"The only work you can get without papers is in construction," Yeison explains. "If you don't have papers, you're not going to make anything. Without papers, I can't work. Wherever you go, you have to present a little piece of paper so you can work."

"How does the situation make you feel?" I ask.

I don't . . . I don't feel anything. How do I say this? In 2015, they say that they are going to send immigration for all the people that don't have their papers together and they are going to send them to Haiti. Me, on my part, I . . . I mean, it shouldn't be like that. How are they going to grab people, put them in a truck, and send them to Haiti? God knows where they will end up! For example, if you go to the United States, you know where you are because you're from there. But if they grabbed me and sent me to Haiti, imagine! They act like we're not the same people. We're the same people!

Without employment, Yeison cannot afford the financial costs associated with the steps required to register in the Book of Foreigners. Often, it takes repeated visits to multiple offices to resolve problems with documentation. These visits require money for transportation and any other requirements, such as paying to get photos taken or paying a lawyer who can navigate the complex process on your behalf. Yeison's documentation problems affect his ability to find work—and his inability to find work affects his documentation problems. The threat of expulsion looms in Yeison's mind, and he worries that he could be sent to a country he has never known.

Elisabeth

During her interview, Elisabeth's pain seeps through her words and into the spaces between her words. The frustration and heartache of living to survive each day is palpable. Malena, a Dominican interviewer of Haitian descent, begins their conversation by asking a few questions—her name, her age. Then, "How are you feeling?"

"I'm fine," Elisabeth replies.

"How are you feeling emotionally?" Malena clarifies, showing her a picture. The picture has five different faces, ranging from a smile to a frown to help people rate their physical and mental health. Elisabeth points to the number 1—a smiling face. Malena, sensing the difference between Elisabeth's selection and her mood, asks, "You feel like this? You're happy?"

"Sometimes you have a lot of problems in your head," Elisabeth explains.

"So, in your head, how do the problems make you feel?" Malena asks. "Do they make you feel embarrassed? Worried?"

"Sometimes it catches me and makes me want to run." Elisabeth says.

"Why?"

"I have too much stuff in my head."

"Like what, Elisabeth? If you're okay with telling me," Malena asks gently. Elisabeth says nothing.

Then, "I'm alone in my house. I don't have a husband. I always have to be looking for food for the kids."

"Because you're single?"

"Of course," Elisabeth replies. "I used to have a man. I lived with him in the house. We lived together. But there was a woman who, once she saw that he was treating me well . . . *esa no es mi gordura* [this isn't my normal weight]. I got skinny. Umm . . . she came and got between the two of us. Now they are *chulo y cuero* [thick as thieves]. And she took him for good. My husband was a tractor driver. She took him, and now I'm in misery. It doesn't matter if I have kids with him. He doesn't give me anything."

"How many kids do you have with him?" Malena asks.

"Three."

"Do you have kids with another man?"

"Yes."

"How many kids do you have in total?"

"Ten."

"Ten kids that you gave birth to or that you're raising?"

"I gave birth to them. My mother helps me with them. Sometimes I go look for clothes to wash in the city. I wash dishes. I go look for work in the school too. They give me *chiripa*, little things to do to make a few pesos, you know. I sweep the patio, dust, wipe the wall, clean the floors."

"And when you wash clothes in the city, about how much do you earn in a day?"

"They give me 200 pesos [US$4]. Maybe 300 pesos [US$6]."

To make ends meet, Elisabeth works in the informal economy, picking up odd jobs to earn a few pesos each day. Elisabeth also receives government assistance to provide food for her family. She uses a Solidarity Card to buy basic foods like rice, beans, and cooking oil.[16] Typically, eligible families receive 700 pesos [about $14 USD] to purchase food each month. Even with the assistance, Elisabeth struggles.

Elisabeth was born in the Dominican Republic, in *batey* La Tierra. At forty-five years old, she has lived in a *batey* all of her life. Now, she lives in another *batey* about fifteen minutes away from La Tierra but returns to see her mother every day since her father died. Elisabeth has a second-grade education. Her ten children range in age from twelve to twenty-seven years old. Some of her children live with her, and others live in a different *batey*. Her three younger children do not have birth certificates.

"There is a lot in the news about documentation," Malena says. "What do you think about it?"

"I don't know," Elisabeth replies. "I have three that are not registered."

"Where were they born?" Malena asks.

"Here," Elisabeth responds. "In town. They live with my nephew. I was going to register them, but they always told me I had to give them 800 pesos [$US16] to register the child," Elisabeth explains. "Eight hundred pesos. And after that, they said I had to give them 3,000 pesos [$US59]. Well, I don't have a husband. I don't have it."

"They said you had to give them 3,000 pesos for what?" Malena asks.

"To register the kids. And I don't have it."

"Do the kids go to school?"

"Yes, they go to school."

"Do they ask for papers?"

"Yes, of course."

"And what does the school say?"

"Umm . . . one time, I went to the school and the director told me that they would send help for the kids that don't have papers. But I never saw any help. It hasn't come. Supposedly, they sent help, but I told her I never saw it."

Some schools have programs that support parents trying to get documentation for their children. The goal of these programs is to encourage people to send their children to school. But if parents do not receive the promised support, then children without birth certificates often drop out during primary school. Elisabeth has a Dominican *cédula*. Still, she has been unable to register three of her children. Financial barriers partially explain her inability to register her children. Discrimination, however, also contributes to her family's liminal legality, as women of Haitian descent are often presumed illegal[17] and denied birth certificates for their Dominican-born children.

Dominican women of Haitian descent face a gender-based cycle of poverty and vulnerability that places them and their children at greater risk of liminal legality than men.[18] Unequal access to documentation for Dominican women of Haitian descent is rooted in historical migration patterns that led to the presence of Haitian women without legal residence in the Dominican Republic. For example, when groups of Haitian men migrated to the Dominican Republic to work in the sugarcane fields, border officials often turned a blind eye to the women who migrated with them, even if the women could not produce valid documentation. When women had children, their partners registered the children's births using the *ficha* if women had no form of documentation. If partners were not around, children's births remained unregistered. Alternatively, some Haitian women and young girls entered the Dominican Republic as human-trafficking victims. In these situations, documentation was often confiscated, leaving women with no means to register their Dominican-born children should they become pregnant.

Gendered social norms also contribute to the risk of liminal legality. Social norms impact documentation status from the time a child is born. Despite an existing policy that only one parent needs Dominican documentation to confer Dominican citizenship to a child, social practices in the Dominican Republic ignore Dominican fathers' rights and confer nationality based on the mother's documentation status at the time of a child's birth.[19] A mother who cannot provide adequate documentation may leave the hospital with the wrong documents for her baby or with none at all. These situations happen even when the child's father is Dominican and can legally use his documentation to register his child as Dominican.[20] This reliance on the mother's documentation status further contributes to the irregular documentation status of thousands of Dominicans of Haitian descent.

Even after a child is born, gendered social norms continue to influence documentation patterns. Women in the family are primarily responsible for registering children's births. The registration process requires both time and money. People must often take multiple trips to documentation offices. And the money required for transportation and any fees associated with obtaining the appropriate documents can be an insurmountable barrier for families facing food insecurity daily. Since some women do not have a steady source of income, they rely on male partners to cover the financial cost of registering children. Elisabeth, a single mother, has no male partner. She lists the associated expenses that she can remember, and since Elisabeth does not have a husband, she does not have the money.

Heightened Monitoring

Verónica

Verónica was born in La Tierra. About nine years ago, she moved to a small, nearby town where she now lives with her husband. Although they are not married by law, Verónica and her husband have what is called a "common-law" marriage: they live together in a long-term relationship but do not have the paperwork that makes their marriage official. Most of Verónica's family lives in the *batey*—her mother, father, sister, and nieces—so she visits La Tierra often to see her relatives. Another reason Verónica visits is to use her mother's sewing machine. To make a few pesos, Verónica sews sheets, curtains, and skirts. Then she sells them to women in the community or in the town where she lives.

Both of Verónica's parents are Haitian immigrants. She says her mother "didn't have any kind of document," so her father used his *ficha* to register her when she was born twenty-six years ago. When Verónica turned eighteen, she applied to get her *cédula*, and she was approved. But recently the government changed characteristics of the *cédula* and required that people apply for a new one. Verónica's request for the new *cédula* was denied.

Changes to the Dominican national identification card allow the government to closely monitor Dominicans of Haitian descent.[21] In the Dominican Republic, the Central Electoral Board began the process of transitioning to a new *cédula* in December 2014 when they announced that after January 10, 2015, the old *cédula* would no longer be valid. Officials claimed that a small change in the type of plastic used on the new *cédula* would make the card less liable to fraudulent use. So Dominicans needed to visit a CEB office to replace their old *cédula* with the new one by January 10, one month after the process was announced. Offices were overburdened by the influx of people. Lines wrapped around buildings, and sometimes offices ran out of supplies. One person went to get her new *cédula*, but the office ran out of plastic to laminate the ID cards, so she had to return another day.

The application process for the new *cédula* happened at the same time as the CEB's audit to identify people "incorrectly" registered as Dominicans. This timing provided the perfect opportunity for the government to reclassify a large segment of Dominicans of Haitian descent as foreigners. Unless people interacted with institutions and government offices, they would not know whether their documents were suspended. But by mandating a change in the *cédula* and requiring people to update their documents, everyone would have to face institutional scrutiny. Although people with stripped citizenship were supposed to have their documents reinstated, thousands like Verónica are still facing institutional barriers to documentation.

"There is a lot of talk about problems with documentation," Malena says. "What do you think about it?"

"It's really bad," Verónica replies. "I say that if a person is born in the Dominican Republic, they have to have their documents, just like anyone else. I mean, it doesn't matter that your parents might not be from the Dominican Republic. If you are born here. . . . For example, I was born here. I can't go to Haiti and look for documents because they aren't going to give them to me. I have to demand them here, where I was born."

"Have you had problems with your documentation?"

"Yes, I have a problem."

"What kind of problem?"

"Well, I have my *cédula*," Verónica begins. "But what's happening is . . . when I was born, my parents didn't have documents. My father declared me with a *ficha* back when they gave them to people who worked for the sugar mill. My mother didn't have any kind of document. I have my *cédula*, the old one. But what's happening is, I have to do some paperwork so that the *cédula* is legal. It has something to do with *liberación* [unblocking]. I have to send some papers to the capital so I can be unblocked, you understand?"

"Where did you hear that?"

"That's what they told me at the government office in the city. Because after a year and six months, this won't be valid because I'm not unblocked."

Verónica's reference to a "year and six months" is confusing. Her documentation and her legal status in the country have been suspended, likely as part of the civil registry's audit process. Since she already has identification documents, Verónica would belong to Group A, the approximately fifty-five thousand Dominican-born people whose citizenship was stripped. According to Law 169-14, people in Group A should have had their documents reinstated. And Verónica should be able to obtain a valid *cédula*.

However, since the process of addressing suspended documentation for Dominican-born persons coincides with the process for Haitian migrants to enrolling in the National Regularization Plan for Foreigners with an Irregular Migration Status (PNRE), there is ample opportunity for confusion and conflating the needs of distinct groups. According to the PNRE, Haitian migrants enrolling in the PNRE have a window of a year and six months to file for a naturalized legal status, during which they are granted immunity from deportations. Since Verónica is not a Haitian migrant, the PNRE does not apply to her. So either she is confused or the officials giving her this information are confused—or both. Ultimately, Verónica's application for a new *cédula* was denied, and she was funneled into a registration process for Haitian immigrants.[22]

"At least you have your *cédula*. But if they tell you in the future that your documents won't work, it would be like you wouldn't have anything," Malena says.

"It's like I wouldn't exist." Verónica replies. "Because a person without a document is not recognized by the authorities. My sister had the same problem that I have. She lives in Santiago, and she only had her birth certificate, and they didn't want to give her the *cédula*."

"So you both have to be unblocked," Malena says.

"That's right," Verónica replies. "We are prisoners. We are not free yet! Really! Because here we are, supposedly with a document, and unable to do anything."

"When you say 'We are prisoners because we're not free,' does it worry you?"

"Yes, it worries me a lot," Verónica says. "Because . . . for example, one day, God willing, I will have a baby. And I can't register him if I don't have documents."

Periods of heightened monitoring send tension and anxiety rippling through communities. Two processes—changes to birthright citizenship and the audit to reclassify Dominicans of Haitian descent as foreigners—have pushed

Dominicans of Haitian descent into the margins of society, even though they were once full citizens.[23] National updates to the *cédula* draw Dominicans of Haitian descent into documentation offices where they are denationalized and funneled into the Book of Foreigners, a definitive mechanism for monitoring their presence in the country.

Benito

Benito is sixty-nine years old and has spent his entire life living in a Dominican *batey*. He has four adult children, and he proudly says that they have all graduated from high school. The youngest, his daughter, is training to work in hospitality. Benito explains that she needs 2,800 pesos [US $55.40] to finish one of her classes, on top of money for transportation and food each day. He pulls out his money, frustrated. "Look, let me show you what I have so you can see that I'm not lying. I have 486 pesos [US $9.62]. That was my pay on Saturday for a week's work. I applied for my pension[24] a while ago, but it still hasn't come. I'm still waiting."

Benito spends most days looking for work he can do here and there, colloquially known as *chiripero*. He might plant seeds, cut grass with a machete, or perform odd jobs to earn a few pesos while he waits for his pension application to be processed.

Although he lives in his own country, Benito's situation is indistinguishable from that of Haitian immigrants in La Tierra—looking for odd jobs and waiting for his pension as he ages. Also like many Haitian immigrants, the only documentation that Benito has is a *ficha*, the company-issued document given to Haitian cane cutters.

"Have you had any problems with your documents?" Malena asks.

"Well, at first I had a *cédula*," Benito begins. "But the company took it and gave me a *ficha*. After that, they called me in, and they kept calling me. And when I went in, they told me, 'Never mind—someone called you by mistake.'"

"So the document you used to have was what they give cane cutters?"

"Um . . . the *cédula* I had was Dominican. They took it . . . well, it wasn't just mine that they took. They took everyone's, and now whether you're Haitian or Dominican, *es un tormento* [it's a mess]."

In 1990, President Balaguer announced a National Regularization Plan to address the lack of valid documentation among Haitian laborers. Balaguer, Trujillo's former speechwriter and political protégé, collected Haitian workers' documents and replaced them with the *ficha*, granting them authorized legal status tied to their labor at sugar mills.[25] During that process, Benito—a Dominican citizen by birth—had his Dominican *cédula* replaced along with the Haitian laborers. His description of the process reflects its chaos. First, he received multiple calls. Then the company told him that he was called by mistake. In the end, his Dominican *cédula* was replaced with a migrant worker's *ficha*.

Benito is affected by a confusing bureaucratic process that blends the needs of a heterogeneous population. Cane cutters include seasonal Haitian migrant workers, newly arrived Haitian immigrants, long-term Haitian immigrants, Dominicans of Haitian descent, and Dominicans who are not of Haitian descent. But often this diverse population is affected by sweeping policies that group them together. Further, the gatekeepers tasked with sorting between groups have neither the guidance nor the resources to appropriately apply new regulations, resulting in inaccurate classifications of people like Benito.

In addition to having his documentation reclassified, Benito has encountered immigration officials as they monitor Haitians' presence in the country. Many sugar mill workers travel to other cities if work in their area is slow. During a period when Benito was traveling in search of agricultural work, he was detained by immigration officials at a checkpoint.

"One time, immigration was picking up people in Bavaro." Benito begins. "I only had my marriage papers. That's it. I didn't have anything else. When they asked me for documents, I didn't know what they were talking about, because I had never met immigration. The truck stopped right here." He gestures to the space on the ground in front of him.

> They came to pick people up from here and take them away. So when I got in the truck, they said we had to wait for the chief. We waited and waited, and around 9 o'clock, I was hungry, so I said, "Come on! It's 9 o'clock, and it seems like the damn chief of immigration is not going to come!" Look, everybody started laughing. Then the guy told them, "Don't start laughing. You all see something? This *muchacho* [boy] doesn't want to go to jail. If he's asking that question, it's because he doesn't know the chief of migration. And you guys see me around. You know me. He doesn't."

Benito pauses for a moment.
"Did they let you go after that?" Malena asks.
"Not yet," Benito replies.

> We were in the front of the truck, and then the guy started arranging people in the back of the truck. I saw that the ones who had a passport, they had it in their hands. People who had any paper had it in their hands. So I took out the marriage paper, and when the guy looked at it, he said, "This is why I have problems with the police. They are sent to pick up illegal immigrants, and they brought me a Dominican." Then he told me to get down out of the truck. I told him I didn't know where I was, and he flagged down a *guagua* and asked the driver to give me a ride. Since then, *no me mando por nadie* [I don't go anywhere for anyone].

Police checkpoints are stationed throughout the Dominican Republic although they are more prevalent in some regions than others. Checkpoints are often marked by small wooden stands that block traffic and allow police to check passengers' documentation. On a public *guagua*, for example, the officer might board the vehicle and then individually check the documentation of each passenger on board.[26]

Photo 4.1. A military checkpoint on a Dominican road; at these checkpoints, vehicles are stopped, and passengers must provide evidence of documentation

Source: Trenita Childers

In the story Benito describes, it seems less like a stationed checkpoint. He and a group of workers were standing together on the side of the road when a truck pulled up in front of them and they were told to get in. Benito and others in the group were taken to another location where passengers in the truck were passed from the custody of police to immigration officials.[27]

Based on Benito's description of the other men's reactions, this kind of documentation check was probably routine in the area. But Benito, a Dominican citizen living in a different region of the country, had never had an interaction with immigration officials. He did not know that he should carry documentation with him. And he did not seem to know that he could have been sent to jail.

Again, Benito is mistakenly categorized as a Haitian laborer—this time by police and immigration officials. Benito's deep chocolate skin color and his sugarcane labor are markers of Haitian-ness, which associate him with "illegality" and place him on the brink of expulsion from his country. Without his Dominican *cédula*, which the sugar mill replaced with a *ficha*, the only document that Benito could use to prove his Dominican identity was his marriage license. Whether Benito carried it with him for such situations or whether it was purely coincidental, his marriage license saved him from going to jail. Fearful of future encounters with immigration, Benito decides not to travel outside his city again.

In La Tierra, I heard this story three times before hearing it from Benito himself. Others in the community laugh uncomfortably when they share it. They say things like "Remember when Lily's uncle almost got sent to Haiti? He got on a truck not knowing where it was going. They let him off, though. He didn't get far!" Stories like these become part of collective consciousness, reflecting the community's awareness that Dominicans of Haitian descent do not have the social freedom of movement associated with living in one's own country. Their freedom is restricted based on their ability to prove Dominican citizenship. And behind nervous chuckles looms the tangible possibility of expulsion to an unknown nation.

Vulnerability to Private and Public Actors' Decision-Making

Gerson

Gerson[28] has a contagious smile. He is an evangelical Christian who has the vocal cadence of a professional public speaker. We sit under a rustling palm tree in dusty plastic chairs discussing his family, his life, and his new *cédula*.

"So," I ask, "what did you do this morning?"

"Well, this morning I got up and I helped my mother with some chores around the house, you know? Later, I'll go out and find something to do." Gerson, his mother, and his father share the front half of a small house in La Tierra. Gerson has always lived in a *batey*, and he has lived in La Tierra since when he was seven years old. Gerson has twelve brothers and sisters. One lives in Haiti, and the remaining siblings live in different cities in the Dominican Republic. Gerson is the only one who lives with his parents.

Gerson and his family are very close. "People treat Haitians like they are the worst thing in life," Gerson says. "So that makes some people feel embarrassed of their parents. But for me, I don't feel that way. I feel proud. I thank God to know two kinds of people. I mean, I have as much Haitian blood as Dominican. I'm a mix of both nations, you understand? And I feel happy to come from both."

During our conversation, Gerson's responses are thoughtful and reflective. At twenty years old, he has finished high school, but he is not sure what he will do next. "Are you working?" I ask.

"Well, I hope to work," Gerson responds. "And later keep going with my studies. Right now, the economic situation is hard. I would do whatever work comes up!" He laughs.

I love to study, though. I really do. It motivates me a lot. Because whenever someone studies and explores, it is an opportunity to progress. It opens another world where you discover more things. With a deeper vision, you can get ahead. I mean, someone who studies can go further than another person who doesn't. That's why I like to study. I like to explore. And even though you want to get ahead a little more, you know how it goes with financial matters. Everything is about money, and you have to pay for education. But I'm waiting on God. We'll see.

Education is a source of personal fulfillment for Gerson and a potential path to upward mobility. Since Gerson's birth certificate was suspended during the civil-registry audit, he is fortunate that he was able to complete high school. The Dominican Ministry of Education allows children to continue their education even if they cannot present a valid birth certificate. But individual school leaders can choose to hinder or support children who do not have proper documentation. Many schools, for example, still require children to present documents upon enrollment. Further, even if these students can matriculate through primary school without a valid birth certificate, some school officials do not allow them to take the required national eighth-grade examinations if they cannot provide a birth certificate. Without completing these examinations, children cannot enter high school. Children's life circumstances are often contingent upon the kindness of individual teachers and school administrators who are willing to overlook missing documents or actively help children obtain them.[29]

It took Gerson two years to get his *cédula*, a process that typically takes months. Gerson says that when he turned eighteen years old, he applied to get his *cédula*. But because his parents are Haitian, his application process opened a two-year investigation to determine whether he was eligible for Dominican citizenship. When I ask why he was unable to get his *cédula* at age eighteen, Gerson replies,

> Well, I wanted to. And when I went to apply for my *cédula*, they told me I couldn't get it because my parents were immigrants in the country. But what saved us is that when my parents immigrated here, they immigrated legally. They carried a legal document. Their error was that they didn't update the document. Because they were given an old *cédula* before, in earlier times. But there came a time when they had to change it, but they didn't. It was a process that lasted around two years where they started to open an investigation. They looked to see if my parents were in the country legally and if they really had the documents they said they had. But after they investigated, it took a while. That's why I couldn't really get my *cédula* at eighteen years old. They gave it to me two years later, at twenty years old.

"Are you worried that they will take it away?" I ask.
"No." Gerson replies with confidence.

> No, because they unblocked me. That's why the process took two and a half years. First, they unblocked me. The unblocking means that I can now carry my documents legally without any problems. So it means my name doesn't have to be in the Book of Foreigners and that my parents were legally in the

country. They [the office] signed a liberation, which is a letter signed by the president of the Republic and also by the president of the Junta Central Electoral. It's a liberation saying that I can carry my documents legally. In other words, I don't have any problems. Now I don't have any fears about that. Those processes are finished.

Gerson wipes his hands together, back and forth, as if dusting away crumbs.

Early in our conversation, I ask Gerson a question meant to build rapport and generate conversation. I ask him to describe a good day. Gerson describes the day that he finally received his *cédula*.

"Well, the day that I loved, truthfully . . . the day that was very happy for me," Gerson begins, pauses to gather his thoughts, and then continues.

You know that with documentation, someone who has immigrant parents in the country . . . this was a problem for me. This was the cause of many closed doors for me. Because maybe if I had been able to get my documents earlier, perhaps now I would be working. Or maybe I would already be in a university. All of this was a *problemita*[30] for me. And all of this became a major process until finally they gave me my documents. But the day they gave them to me? Really, that was a very happy day for me, that God could give me that day . . .

Gerson smiles and looks at me.

Look, when I felt it in my hands, I really felt happy, content, so happy that now, finally, a door has opened for me. A greater opportunity in life. Because, you know, someone without documents? Really, it's a closed door for you. You don't have access to, for example, study, work, get paid, to have a bank account—none of this. But when you have a *cédula*, an identity is another opportunity to keep pushing ahead, you understand? Really, life was really different after that day. It was like a before and after in my life. Really, I felt so happy.

"What kinds of things were different for you after that day?" I ask.

"Well, now, it's a different reality than before," Gerson says, leaning back in his chair.

Before, when people came to the house to do interviews and ask us "Do you have a *cédula*?" I would feel like I was in trouble. Because you know that once you're eighteen years old, you should have your identification card that says you are of age. And so I was nineteen, then twenty years old, and I still didn't have my *cédula*. And so it was something . . . every time I went to the city or went outside the house, I always felt troubled, worried. I would ask myself, "Wow! What if immigration grabs me?" But now, after getting my *cédula*, it's like I was saying before: This has marked a before and after in my life. I feel more free. I feel more confident when I walk down the street, because now I know that I'm walking with my documents.

Given the series of political changes that have led to present documentation instability for Dominicans of Haitian descent, Gerson's security in his legal status is surprising. He describes a new freedom from the fear of expulsion to Haiti. But others in La Tierra are less trusting of the leaders who make decisions on their behalf. One person described politicians as people who "throw a rock and hide their hand." In other words, they intentionally act in ways that harm people and then pretend as though they were never involved. When I asked another person about a political billboard that appeared in La Tierra one day, nailed to a tree, she replied, "They came here lying and promising things they won't do to get people to vote for them." In spite of general political mistrust in La Tierra, with his *cédula* in hand, Gerson feels less vulnerable to the shifting sands of political interests. And for now, Gerson is free to walk down the street without fear.

Mariana

Mariana is a single mother to three young children who are ten, seven, and three years old. She and her children live in a small house with her mother and father. During our conversation, Mariana and I sit at a dark wooden table with just enough room for the two of us. The room is dim, lit only by sunlight that peeks in through the open doorway. When Mariana talks about her father, a retired cane cutter, a warm smile lights her eyes. "He is always there for me," she says. "We all take care of one another."

"When was the last time you had a beautiful day?" I ask, opening our interview. Mariana thinks for a brief moment and then smiles. "On Saturday," she replies.

"Can you tell me about it?" I ask.

"It was . . . how do I explain this?" Mariana pauses and then continues. "It is so beautiful to feel like you have someone who makes you feel good. That makes you feel loved in that moment." Her smile softens. "When that happened the other day, you wake up happy, still thinking about what happened that night." We both laugh.

"Well," I ask, in suspense. "What happened?"

"Right," Mariana laughs again, bashfully. "It was nice. Sometimes you forget about your problems for a moment. A friend . . . it had been a while since I felt happy like that. I mean . . . sometimes you smile so that people don't know what you're feeling on the inside. You laugh, but . . . you don't really feel it. But then there are days when you laugh with joy. You let go of what you have inside. That's how I felt on Saturday."

From the beginning of our conversation, Mariana makes it clear that she and her family are documented.

"How old are you?" I ask.

"Thirty-three," Mariana responds.

"What is your nationality?"

"My mother and father are Haitian," she responds. "But I was born here, and we have documents." Mariana's father used his work *ficha* to get birth certificates for his children when they were young. Even though she has a *cédula*, Mariana worries about being sent to Haiti.

"You were born here, and your parents have their roots *allá* ["there" in Haiti]. What is that like for you?" I ask.

"Exactly," Mariana says.

My dad, after he came from *allá*, he never returned. My mom too. She never went back. I think they've even forgotten *el camino* [the route]. All of us were born here, but we've never been there. Sometimes I talk with my dad, and he says, "Yes, I could go back, but you all can't. Because you don't know anything about life over there." So when they were fixing the documents of foreigners' children, I thought about that a lot. Because I don't know anything about Haiti. Nothing, nothing, nothing. Because I've never been. So, imagine: me walking and they grab me and send me to Haiti. Where am I going to go? I know a little Creole, but there are a lot of words in Creole that I don't know. Can you imagine? So I started to think, "My God. If I have to go to Haiti, how would I survive?" I said. They might throw me in a ditch or kill me or something! I don't even know where my parents came from, and I don't know any of that family over there. I thought about all of this. Thank God they're fixing it.

"You were worried about being sent to Haiti?" I ask.

"Exactly," Mariana replies. "Because they were saying that they would round up all the children of immigrants, and that had me worried. And I'm thinking, 'But if I have my papers, why am I worried?' How do I explain this to you?" Mariana takes a moment to think and then looks up at me. "This is a very racist country. They don't want anything to do with Haitians. For them, Haitians are like animals. Like a dog. They treat people from other countries fine, but the people they want nothing to do with are the Haitians. I don't know why," she says. "I don't know why. We all bleed the same blood. I don't understand it. It shouldn't be this way."

Anti-Haitian racism emphasizes differences between groups to justify sociopolitical divisions. From Mariana's perspective, *Haitians are like animals* in the eyes of Dominicans. An inherently inhumane ideology, racism entrenches divisions among people until those seen as *less than* are dehumanized. The narrative that "they" are so different from "us" is what ultimately fuels policies that carve Dominicans of Haitian descent out of their own country.

The threat of expulsion is a key facet of liminal legality. This threat leaves Mariana hyperaware that she is vulnerable to control, exclusion, and abuse by private actors serving their own interests. In the Dominican Republic, both citizens and noncitizens live with the worry that they will be sent away from their settled lives and removed from everything they know.

In 1999, the Dominican government initiated a mass-expulsion campaign targeting Haitians and Dominicans of Haitian descent. During this time, a coalition of nongovernmental organizations filed a case with the Inter-American Commission on Human Rights (IACHR) on behalf of twenty-eight Haitians and Dominicans of Haitian descent who were among the tens of thousands of people collectively sent to Haiti by Dominican immigration officials.[31] The Movement of Dominico-Haitian Women (Movimiento de Mujeres Dominico Haitianas, MUDHA) based in Santo Domingo, the Support Group for Refugees and Returnees (Groupe d'Appui au Rapatriés et Refugiés, GARR) based in Port-au-Prince, and the Center for Justice and International Law (CEJIL) and Columbia Law School's Human Rights Clinic, both based in the United States, were among the organizations filing the case. The group brought the case to the IACHR, challenging the mass expulsions and discriminatory treatment of Haitians and Dominicans of Haitian descent.[32]

In 2014, the IACHR ruled that the mass expulsions violated the human rights of people of Haitian descent, including their right to a nationality, the right to identity, the right to equality before the law, and the right to fair trial guarantees and judicial protection.[33] Just months after the IACHR's ruling, the Dominican Republic threatened to withdraw from the court, stating that the IACHR's ruling "constitutes a clear infringement of the sovereignty of the Dominican Republic."[34] Then, in 2017, Dominican officials reopened dialogue with the IAHCR to discuss a plan for the state to comply with the IACHR's recommendations to reduce human-rights violations.[35] Still, advocacy organizations worry that the Dominican Republic's reluctant engagement with the IACHR will deprive people of Haitian descent of a means to seek justice in international spheres, leaving them even more vulnerable to human-rights abuses as private actors change priorities at their expense.[36]

Mariana wants to trust the Dominican government to find solutions to the problem of providing documentation to those without it. But she still worries.

"I heard . . . I haven't seen it, but I heard that they were picking up people in the city," Mariana says.

"Near here?" I ask.

"Yes, right up there they came and took some people," Mariana says.

"A long time ago or more recently?" I ask.

"Recently," Mariana replies, a solemn look on her face.

While they were fixing papers, they were sending some people to Haiti. Some of those [Haitian immigrants] who hadn't been here long. Those who haven't been here long wanted to get papers, but those papers were for people who had been here a long time and had children here. And now, supposedly, they're at least fixing this for people who have never been declared. They're going to put them in the Book of Foreigners. But those who already had papers, they're going to stay that way, thank God! They're going to stay Dominicans. I will be able to vote and do whatever I need to.

"I've heard that some people who already had their *cédulas* have had them taken away," I say.

"Yes," Mariana says. "There were a lot who had theirs taken away. That's true."

"But not yours?" I ask.

"No. And people told me, 'Listen, if you go anyplace, don't bring your *cédula*.' And I asked why, and they said, 'Because they're taking them away.' But they can't take mine away because I'm Dominican. Even though my mother and father are Haitian, I'm Dominican. I was born here. This *cédula* is mine. It's not bought. It's not false."

Mariana has not yet interacted with an institution that might signal her *cédula*'s suspension.[37] Unless people try to apply for formal employment or enroll in university, for example, they may not realize that their legal status is uncertain. Since Mariana knows that she and her family followed the existing rules to register her birth, she has no reason to suspect that her Dominican citizenship could be taken away.

Still, Mariana has been warned not to carry her *cédula* to ensure that it does not get taken away. Some people in La Tierra avoided interactions with institutions precisely because of the idea that if you show up to documentation offices, they could nullify your legal status.[38] But if people are affected, their documents are suspended, whether they know it or not. Their interaction with an institution, however, opens an investigation and a complicated process to restore their legal status.

"Mariana," I ask. "Have you met anyone whose *cédula* was canceled?"
She begins a heavy sigh. "How do I explain this? . . ." she starts, slowly.

There was a girl I met on the *guagua*. She was crying when she got on, and I asked her, "What's wrong?" And she told me, "*La junta* took my *cédula* away." When I asked why, she said, "They told me it was because I'm Haitian and I can't have this *cédula*." So, I said, "How can that be? Were you were born here? Did your parents declare you?" And she said, "Yes, I was born here, and my parents declared me with a *ficha*." So I said, "Well, if you weren't declared with a false document, they shouldn't take it away." And this girl just kept crying. She was suffering a lot because she had to go to university; she was going to be a teacher. It was awful! And it just made me so sad, because I saw her suffering and I thought, "My God! Don't let this happen to me!" I mean, it hurts to see someone else who is suffering. Especially if you're in the same situation.

Mariana's voice wavers as she explains this interaction with the young woman on the *guagua*. The documentation situations of family members, friends, and even strangers remind Dominicans of Haitian descent that even if they are documented, they are still vulnerable.

The changes to birthright citizenship affect Dominicans of Haitian descent in many ways. Some have had their Dominican citizenship nullified and have subsequently been enrolled in a Book of Foreigners under the country where they were born. Others have had their documentation suspended and then endured years of auditing to prove their right to a valid Dominican *cédula*. Still others live in a state of constant instability, fearing that at any moment they, too, could lose citizenship in their home country.

"No Vota": Generations without a Political Voice

Dominicans of Haitian descent who are registered in the Book of Foreigners are unable to vote. Political power, specifically the right to vote, is a key characteristic of full citizenship. Political participation ensures that the voices of citizens from all backgrounds contribute to decisions about policies and practices that affect people's lives.[39] In racialized social systems, structural racism undergirds political systems. The anti-Haitian racism that pushes Dominicans of Haitian descent into liminal legality is the same racism that denies the right to vote for generations.

Andrés, a Dominican of Haitian descent in La Tierra, describes the political campaign of José Francisco Peña Gómez during our interview. Peña Gómez, also a Dominican of Haitian descent, was a presidential candidate whose 1994 presidential run was marred by violence and dirty politics. The campaign against Peña Gómez spewed racist and xenophobic attacks against him. He was depicted by news and media outlets as secretly planning to reunify Haiti and the Dominican Republic, a threat that stems from the period between 1822 and 1844 when the two countries were unified under Haitian rule. Commercials showed a map of Hispaniola, the island the two countries share, where a bright green Dominican Republic was gradually overtaken by dark brown Haiti, and political cartoons depicted Peña Gómez as a witch doctor. During his presidential race, some of Peña Gómez's supporters found that their names had been removed from the voting registry. And an investigation revealed that an estimated two hundred thousand people had been removed from voting polls.[40]

"There's something about Haitians . . ." Andrés begins, gathering his thoughts.

> They are racist against them. It's just like when José Francisco Peña Gómez was running for president here. He was a really good man and had a lot of support from Dominicans. But the legislators from here in the Dominican Republic stopped him from being president. He got the most votes, but they didn't let him become president. So what happened? They all got together and committed electoral fraud. They said a number of votes needed to be recounted, and they had a second round of voting. And in the second round, the council took away all the votes they gave to José Francisco Peña Gómez because he was Haitian. Some say that he was born here; others say he wasn't and that he came here when he was little. And they didn't let him be president. *Abusaron much de él* [They did him wrong]. Still today, there are people who love him. . . . Since forever they have been racist against Haitians.

Anti-Haitian racism is intricately tied to political participation. Government policies that exclude Dominicans of Haitian descent from social integration also exclude them from political participation. If Haitian parents cannot prove their own authorized legal status, then their Dominican-born children and grandchildren must register in the Book of Foreigners. With increased conditionality on birthright citizenship, Dominicans of Haitian descent born to parents without legal residence cannot vote. And this effect ripples across generations.

During a conversation I had with several Dominican scholars, one person stressed to me the importance of understanding the competing priorities of stakeholders weighing in on documentation in the Dominican Republic. After this conversation, I wrote,

> The role of organizations and political interests will be important. There are many NGOs, interest groups, activists, academics, and religious groups that have a say on documentation status and Haitian immigration. One Dominican

scholar said, "As far as politics, this seems to be an issue that politicians ignore unless it serves them." So who does it serve to deny the right to vote for tens of thousands of Dominicans of Haitian descent? And their children? And their children's children?

—Field notes, April 5, 2015

This haunting question stayed with me for years. In the end, those who benefit from denying Dominicans of Haitian descent the right to vote include politicians and other members of the public who maintain decision-making power in the country. Dominicans of Haitian descent comprise an estimated 10 percent of the country's population. But their vocal political activism as they push back against unjust policies poses a threat to nationalist constituents who violently defend a *patria* (motherland) that erases people of Haitian descent. As anti-Haitian nationalist rhetoric cycles in and out of the public sphere, politicians use their "crack down on Haitians" stance to garner public favor and win votes. Even people who are less conservative tread carefully to avoid being assigned the dreaded "pro-Haitian" label.

Today I spoke with a Dominican professor who commended President Medina for implementing the Nationalization Plan because it's a delicate topic. She says nobody wants to take sides because, on one hand you're labeled pro-Haitian, and on the other hand it's a human-rights violation. The "pro-Haitian" label must have serious consequences if it's worth risking human-rights violations for hundreds of thousands of people.

—Field notes, September 15, 2014

Politicians, organizations, and ordinary citizens run the risk of being labeled pro-Haitian. At one Dominican research organization, the leadership discussed how to carefully frame findings to mitigate perceptions that their work is pro-Haitian. During particularly tense political times, the organization removed the pictures of staff from their website to minimize the death threats they received.

In La Tierra, because of political mistrust, most people view political participation with mild indifference. Jeancarlos, a Dominican of Haitian descent, says his mother and his aunt enrolled him in the Book of Foreigners. Under Law 169-14, Jeancarlos would be in Group B, the group of Dominican-born people who had never acquired nationality documents. Jeancarlos explains, "This paper says that I'm in the Book of Foreigners. Let me show you. I have a copy here." He pulls a small paper from his wallet and unfolds it, showing it to me.

"So if they come here picking people up," I ask, "you can show them this?"

"Well, this isn't enough," Jeancarlos says. "You're supposed to take this paper and get a card. Once you have the card, you can work. Supposedly they'll give us a card, but it's still not here. It hasn't turned up yet."

"So if you get the card," I ask, "what will you be able to use it for?"

"You could use it to buy a house, or a *jeepeta* [an SUV]," Jeancarlos explains. "But you won't be able to use it to vote. You can't vote. The card will say 'No vote.'"

"Do you want the right to vote?" I ask.

"If I had a *cédula* to vote, I would vote. But if they give me a card so I can work, *amén* [Amen, fine with me]. Look, presidents and representatives come looking for people to vote for them. When they win, they forget about you. But you have to work hard and sweat so you can get yours . . . I mean, if I have my card so I can work? I'll be happy, you know? Then I will be legal here."

Dominican political forces have actively worked to remove people of Haitian descent—both Haitian-born and Dominican-born—from the country's collective consciousness. Attempts to politically disenfranchise Dominicans of Haitian descent, silencing their needs and their collective voices, returns to public debates decade after decade. The story of political candidate José Francisco Peña Gómez is one example of why many have little faith in the Dominican political system. So, instead of focusing on the ability to vote, Jeancarlos hopes for the ability to work while waiting until he is "legal."

Jeancarlos ties his legality to his ability to work. But Gloria, a Dominican woman of Haitian descent, ties her legality to her ability to vote. Gloria is fifty-four years old and has lived in a *batey* her entire life. "My *cédula* says I'm Dominican," Gloria explains. "But the politicians don't want to say that. They don't! I don't know why. Because when they are running for office, everyone born here who has their *cédula*, we go and vote for them. Why do we vote? Because we are Dominicans too. Because if our *cédula* said that we couldn't vote, then . . ." Gloria shrugs her shoulders. "Right? But it says that we can vote. You hear? So we are legal."

Legality for Dominicans of Haitian descent is connected to voting rights. Full citizenship includes the ability to have a political voice, even in a context of high political mistrust. Campaigns to address the "Haitian problem" evolve from one political cycle to the next. And if it is true that politicians largely ignore the issue of documentation for people of Haitian descent until it serves them, then the political gain in this era must be substantial.[41]

Intergenerational Second-Class Citizenship

Alexandra is energetic and charismatic, the center of her group of friends. Most days, she sits on a wooden bench or on a three-legged plastic chair trading news and gossip with a few young women who go to her church. Alexandra is the most vocal woman in the bunch and almost always wears a smile.

Since she and her friends are one of the groups I visit more regularly, Alexandra is one of the first people I interview. Alexandra sits with a friend who is shelling *guandules* to prepare the day's lunch. Alexandra's one-year-old son toddles around, first orbiting his mother's chair and then exploring the dirt and rocks a few feet away.

When I ask Alexandra to describe her family, she responds, "My parents are both from Haiti. We used to live in another *batey*, but we moved here a few years ago. One of my sisters lives here. Another sister lives up in Bavaro. Another sister is studying, and another is married. My grandmother lives over on the other side, and my father lives with another . . . I mean, he has another house. He doesn't live with my mother. They are separated."

"Careful! Don't fall!" Alexandra shouts as her toddler stumbles on the unpaved road. I ask Alexandra a few demographic questions: her age, education level, what languages she speaks. Then I ask, "How would you describe your nationality?"

"Dominico-Haitian, right?" she replies. "Because we are of Haitian descent." She seems slightly uncertain. And when we revisit the topic of nationality later in our conversation, Alexandra explains, "Well, I think that . . ." She pauses, scrunching her face while she gathers her thoughts. "I think that it should be that when a child is born in a country, he should be from that country. Right? Because if your parents are from the United States but *you* don't know the United States, you don't necessarily have to be from the United States, right?" I nod. "But they say that if a child's parents are Haitian and they are born anywhere, then they have to be from Haiti. *Obligao* [it's mandatory]."

"Is this only for people whose parents were born in Haiti?" I ask.

"That's all they talk about. Here, there are a lot of immigrants," Alexandra explains. "Not just Haitians, you understand? But they put us down the most. Look, this morning I was listening to the news, and they were talking about the immigrants, saying 'Haitians only . . .'" Alexandra pauses, perhaps choosing not to repeat a hurtful statement. "They don't want anything to do with Haitians, and I don't know why."

Dominican leaders and media outlets conflate Dominicans of Haitian descent and Haitian immigrants to emphasize the shift away from universal-birthright citizenship as social inclusion. This discursive approach reinforces their idea that Dominicans of Haitian descent are not Dominican and should not be included with other Dominicans born in the country. Not only does this tactic create confusion, but it also bolsters the intended narrative that Dominicans of Haitian descent were foreigners to begin with.

"You mentioned that you are Dominico-Haitian," I say.

"Domini—Well, I think that I'm Dominican." Alexandra replies. "But we'll see . . ."

When my conversation with Alexandra turns to documentation, I ask, "Have you had any problems with documentation?"

"Yes, I've had problems," she replies. "Because I . . . the problem is . . . I have my *cédula*, right? Well, I have my son, but I can't declare him because my parents are foreigners."

"But you have yours?" I ask.

"Yes. Here, that's what's happening," she explains. "Here, if you have documents and your parents are foreigners, they make it difficult to get documents for your child."

"But they haven't taken away yours?" I ask.

"They wanted to take it away, but the North Americans from the United Nations came and recorded what was happening. And they said that if they don't solve this, they wouldn't help the Dominican Republic anymore and that CARICOM wouldn't sell to the Dominican Republic. So for now, supposedly, they are . . . I mean, we filled out a paper the other day, so we'll see what they say. We'll see what results they give us so I can declare my son."

International organizations have publicized their objection to the constitutional ruling and its discriminatory effect on Dominicans of Haitian descent. The United Nations High Commissioner for Refugees (UNHCR) has expressed concern that the ruling will create a new population of tens of thousands of refugees if the Dominican government determines that unregistered Dominicans of Haitian descent should be expelled.[42]

The Caribbean Community (CARICOM) is an organization that promotes economic integration, foreign-policy coordination, human and social development, and security in the region. They, along with the Organization of the Americas (OAS) and Amnesty International, have advocated for solutions to the crisis that centers on the preservation of human rights, including the right to full citizenship.[43]

In response to domestic and international pressure, the constitutional ruling, which was initially retroactive, theoretically no longer affects people whose births were already registered. In practice, however, tens of thousands of Dominicans of Haitian descent are still waiting for their suspended citizenship to be reinstated. Alexandra, for example, is still waiting for her *cédula* to be valid so that she can register her son.

When I ask Alexandra how the situation makes her feel, she replies, "It makes me feel bad. If I told you I felt fine, it would be a lie, because this is a problem. I want my child to have his documents. I feel bad because the baby still doesn't have a document."

"Is there anything else you can do?" I ask.

"Well, now, we just wait," Alexandra replies. "We wait for them to decide what they are going to do . . . wait to see if they are going to give us the documents or not. Because they have canceled so many *cédulas*. I mean, sometimes you have the *cédula* in your hand, but it doesn't work. So we're still waiting. We'll see."

Generations of Dominicans of Haitian descent face an uncertain future in the country where they were born. Not only do they live in legal instability, but if they become newly designated foreigners in the Dominican Republic, then full participation in their country of birth is denied as well. Generations of adults and children of Haitian descent are excluded from social and political participation because of policies rooted in anti-Haitian racism. Alexandra and her family wait, in limbo, hoping that something will change.

Foreigners in Their Own Country[44]

Liminal legality impacts the lives of Dominicans of Haitian descent for generations to come. The Book of Foreigners does not provide an adequate solution for Dominicans of Haitian descent who identify as Dominicans, not foreigners. Further, once enrolled, people entered into the Book of Foreigners are still not provided a path to citizenship; rather, enrollment relegates Dominicans of Haitian descent into institutionalized marginalization. Though fraught with limitations, the Book of Foreigners grants temporary protection from expulsion to Haiti, a country Dominicans of Haitian descent have never known. Those who try to enroll encounter financial barriers to enrollment, and they are also subject to heightened monitoring. For example, changes to the *cédula* funnel people into documentation offices where Dominicans of Haitian descent face added scrutiny, suspended documents, and reclassification as foreigners in their homeland. Further, Dominicans of Haitian descent are also vulnerable to private and public actors' decision-making. When it benefits them, Dominican politicians take on the "Haitian problem," making promises to their constituents to win votes and maintain power. Consequently, Dominicans of Haitian descent are pawns in a high-stakes political chess game that leaves them stateless.

Similarly, the distinction between Dominicans of Haitian descent enrolled in the Book of Foreigners and those who are not creates a system that facilitates discrimination and targeted surveillance. The Book of Foreigners provides a form of documentation to those who did not previously have one. But the formalized lack of full citizenship that confers a separate legal status leaves people vulnerable to the preferences and practices of individuals and businesses that may discriminate based on their status as "foreigners." This opens the possibility for discrimination in hiring practices, for example, or in interactions with institutions, including banks and schools. In this way, the marginalization of Dominicans of Haitian descent compounds.

Despite these systemic challenges, Dominicans of Haitian descent work with both national and international organizations and allies to push back against anti-Haitian policies that move them to the margins of Dominican society. Political demonstrations, legal action, and public protests amplify their voices in an environment where they are actively being silenced. Although the situation is complex, many work tirelessly to ensure that Dominicans of Haitian descent attain the social integration they deserve.

A quotation from Sonia Pierre opens this chapter. A Dominican woman of Haitian descent, Pierre was an activist and the founder of MUDHA, Movimiento de Mujeres Dominico-Haitianas, Inc., or the Movement of Dominican-Haitian Women. She dedicated her life to improving the conditions of Dominicans of Haitian descent through public advocacy and community organizing. Using her voice and rallying others to use theirs, Sonia Pierre spoke out, drawing attention to injustices that separated discriminatory immigration policies in the Dominican Republic from international human-rights standards. She was a passionate voice for the people until 2011, when she passed away unexpectedly from a heart attack at forty-eight years old. But her inspirational legacy lives on in the songs and chants of young Dominicans of Haitian descent who demand recognition and full citizenship in the *patria* where they were born.

Notes

[1] "... even if my life is cut short" would be more literally translated as "even though I get stuck along the way."

This quotation is from an interview conducted with Sonia Pierre by Allison Petrozziello. See Movimiento de Mujeres Domenico-Haitianas, Inc. (MUDHA), "La líder: Sonia Pierre," MUDHA (website), accessed March 3, 2018, http://mudhaong.org/quienes-somos/la-lider-sonia-pierre/.

[2] The *güira* is a metallic Dominican percussion instrument played rhythmically with a stiff brush.

[3] See Chacón, "Producing Liminal Legality," for a critical discussion of how citizens experience the effects of liminal legality when governments regulate, monitor, and banish those living in liminal legality.

[4] Alrabe et al., "Left Behind."

[5] Ibid.

[6] See the OBMICA protocol for registering children of mixed families (Domingo Rincón and Natalia Riveros, *Facilitando el acceso al registro civil dominicano a descendientes de parejas mixtas: Protocolo para su acompañamiento legal* [Santa Domingo, DR: Centro para la Observación Migratoria y el Desarrollo Social en el Caribe (OBMICA), 2018], http://obmica.org/images/Publicaciones/Libros/Protocolo-2018-FINAL.pdf) and the accompanying video (http://obmica.org/index.php/parejas-mixtas/multimedia).

[7] Constitución de la Republica Dominicana, January 26, 2010, art. 18[3] [Dom. Rep.].

[8] For commentary on US opinion on the discriminatory ruling, see, for example, Jacqueline Charles, "U.S. Expresses 'Deep Concern' over Dominican Court Citizenship Ruling," *Miami Herald*, December 18, 2013, https://www.miamiherald.com/news/nation-world/world/americas/haiti/article1958632.html. The court ruling in Spanish can be found at https://web.archive.org/web/20150812200410/http://tribunalconstitucional.gob.do/sites/default/files/documentos/Sentencia%20TC%200168-13%20-%20C.pdf.

[9] See, for example, Richard André, "The Dominican Republic and Haiti: A Shared View from the Diaspora," a conversation with Edwidge Danticat and Junot Díaz, in "Higher Education and Competitiveness," *Americas Quarterly* 8, no. 3 (2014): 28–35, https://www.americasquarterly.org/content/dominican-republic-and-haiti-shared-view-diaspora.

[10] This information is based on personal communication with Bridget Wooding at the Caribbean Migrants Observatory (OBMICA) on July 26, 2019.

[11] The Office of the United Nations High Commissioner for Refugees (UNHCR) estimates that about 133,700 people were still affected by statelessness in the Dominican Republic after the June 2015 deadline. See United Nations High Commissioner for Refugees (UNHCR), Agencia de la ONU para los Refugiados (ACNUR), "Tendencias globales: Desplazamiento forzado en 2015; Forzados a huir" [Global trends: Forced displacement in 2015; Forced to flee], United Nations High Comissioner for Refugees (UNHCR/ACNUR), http://www.acnur.org/fileadmin/scripts/ doc.php?file=fileadmin/Documentos/Publicaciones/2016/10627, especially 61n16, which explains that there are 133,700 stateless persons, including only people born in the country both of whose parents were born outside the country. It does not include people born in the country having one parent born in the country and the other a Dominican national, in accordance with the 210,000 figure that was released previously.

[12] Pronounced like "Jason."

[13] The word *tiguere* is also used to refer to someone who is witty, cunning, or sharp.

[14] This is the estimated cost found in the Dominican Sugar Industry's 2016 report: Central Romana Corporation, Consorcio Azucarero Central, and Consorcio Azuceraro de Empresas Industriales, "Labor Conditions in the Dominican Sugar Industry: Moving Progress Forward," April 2016, https://static1.squarespace.com/static/57f5349f03596e786d9ae6f4/t/58a037263e00be6bfe5e5458/1486894889614/DSI+Update+2+04+16.pdf.

[15] Ibid.

[16] The Progressing with Solidarity Program is a food-security program that provides conditional cash transfers to families living in poverty. For more details, see Food and Nutrition Security Platform, "Progressing with Solidarity," accessed February 3, 2020, https://plataformacelac.org/en/programa/243.

[17] See chapter 5 for a deeper discussion of discrimination, illegality, and racial profiling.

[18] See Allison J. Petrozziello, Amelia Hintzen, and Juan Carlos González Díaz, *Género y el riesgo de apatridia para la población de ascendencia haitiana en los bateyes de la República Dominicana* (Santo Domingo, DR: OBMICA, 2014), and Allison J. Petrozziello, "(Re) Producing Statelessness Via Indirect Gender Discrimination: Descendants of Haitian Migrants in the Dominican Republic," *International Migration* 57, no. 1 (2019): 213–28.

[19] Ivet González, "Women of Haitian Descent Bear the Brunt of Dominican Migration Policy," Inter Press Service, February 5, 2016, http://www.ipsnews.net/2016/02/women-of-haitian-descent-bear-the-brunt-of-dominican-migration-policy/.

[20] Rincón and Riveros, *Facilitando el acceso*.

[21] It is not uncommon for governments to change something about their national identification card and then require people to apply for the new card if they want to access certain benefits. In the United States, for example, the federal government has moved forward with a new national ID card, the "Real ID." The new ID card will have a star on it, which easily separates people who provide extensive record of their documentation status from those who do not. The establishment of a new identification card in any country opens the bureaucratic process of identifying unwanted groups.

[22] On July 16, 2015, the Dominican Ministry of the Interior and the Police published a list of 376 people who had enrolled in the naturalization plan under Law 169-14 and been issued with residence permits. A week later, a new list was published, including a total of 620 people. However, most recently the ministry had included on the list of successful applicants the names of migrants who applied through the National Regularization Plan as well as those whose applications were made under Law 169-14. The lists are available at http://mip.gob.do/index.php/documentos-pnre. For more details, see Amnesty International, "'Without Papers, I Am No One': Stateless People in the Dominican Republic," 2015, https://www.amnestyusa.org/files/without-papers_stateless-people-dominican-republic.pdf.

[23] See Kristy A. Belton, "Rooted Displacement: The Paradox of Belonging among Stateless People," *Citizenship Studies* 19, no. 8 (2015): 907–21.

[24] See discussion in chapter 3 related to workers being denied applications for their pensions.

[25] Riveros, *Estado de la cuestión*.

[26] For another example of documentation-checkpoint procedures in the Dominican Republic, see Elena Guzmán, "Checkpoint Nation: In the Dominican Republic, Haitian Descendants Face Profiling and Scrutiny Deep within the Country's Borders," North American Congress on Latin America (NACLA), March 22, 2019, https://nacla.org/news/2019/03/22/checkpoint-nation.

[27] Experiences like these underscore the reality that heavily policed immigrant communities are more likely to come into contact with the criminal-justice system as enforcement priorities prioritize identifying people without documentation.

[28] Pronounced like "Harrison."

[29] Alrabe et al., "Left Behind."

[30] *Problemita* translates into English as "a little problem," but in the Dominican Republic the word is used to describe a major problem.

[31] The filed court case can be found at Inter-American Commission on Human Rights, Report No. 68/05, October 13, 2005, Organization of American States (website), http://cidh.org/annualrep/2005eng/DominicanRep.12271eng.htm.

[32] Laurel Fletcher and Timothy Miller, "New Perspectives on Old Patterns: Forced Migration of Haitians in the Dominican Republic," *Journal of Ethnic and Migration Studies* 30, no. 4 (2004): 659–79 (text available online at https://www.academia.edu/2632059/New_Perspectives_on_Old_Patterns_Forced_Migration_of_Haitians_in_the).

[33] See International Justice Resource Center, "In the Case of Dominican and Haitian People Expelled v. the Dominican Republic, IACTHR Finds Multitude of Human Rights Violations," October 28, 2014, https://ijrcenter.org/2014/10/28/in-the-case-of-dominican-and-haitian-people-expelled-v-the-dominican-republic-iacthr-finds-multitude-of-human-rights-violations/. The full ruling in Spanish can be found at http://corteidh.or.cr/docs/casos/articulos/seriec_282_esp.pdf.

[34] "Queman barrio haitiano," *Diario Libre*, October 30, 2008, https://www.diariolibre.com/actualidad/queman-barrio-haitiano-CODL175412.

[35] See Amnesty International, "Dominican Republic: Withdrawal from Top Regional Human Rights Court Would Put Rights at Risk," November 6, 2014, https://www.amnesty.org/en/lat est/news/2014/11/dominican-republic-withdrawal-top-regional-human-rights-court-would-put -rights-risk/, and Inter-American Commission on Human Rights (IACHR), "IACHR Welcomes Willingness of Dominican Republic to Comply with Recommendations," press release, Organization of American States (website), June 29, 2017, https://www.oas.org/en/iachr/media_center/ PReleases/2017/087.asp.

[36] For a broader discussion of countries' participation with the IACHR, see Ximena Soley and Silvia Steininger, "Parting Ways or Lashing Back? Withdrawals, Backlash and the Inter-American Court of Human Rights," special issue 2, "Resistance to International Courts," *Journal of International Journal of Law in Context* 14 (2018): 237–57.

[37] For a discussion of the importance of interactions with institutions, see, for example, Shannon Gleeson and Roberto G. Gonzales, "When Do Papers Matter? An Institutional Analysis of Undocumented Life in the United States," *International Migration* 50, no. 4 (2012): 1–19 (text available online at https://digitalcommons.ilr.cornell.edu/cgi/viewcontent.cgi?article= 2247&context=articles).

[38] In 2008, the UN Committee on the Elimination of Racial Discrimination (CERD) raised concerns that a circular from the Central Electoral Board resulted in the confiscation and destruction of documents when people of Haitian descent sought to obtain or renew documents. See United Nations Committee on the Elimination of Racial Discrimination, "Consideration of Reports Submitted by States Parties Under Article 9 of the Convention: Concluding Observations of the Committee on the Elimination of Racial Discrimination: Dominican Republic," United Nations, May 16, 2008 (text available online at https://www.refworld.org/publisher ,CERD,,DOM,4885cf9dd,0.html), and Open Society Justice Initiative and the Center for Justice and International Law, "Submission to the Committee."

[39] For a rich discussion of the connections between race, democracy, and policy in the US context, see Jamila Michener, *Fragmented Democracy: Medicaid, Federalism, and Unequal Politics* (Cambridge: Cambridge University Press, 2018).

[40] Sagás, *Race and Politics*, and Larry Rohter, "Jose Pena Gomez, 61, Rare Black Dominican Figure, Dies," *New York Times*, May 12, 1998, https://www.nytimes.com/1998/05/12/world/jose -pena-gomez-61-rare-black-dominican-figure-dies.html and https://nacla.org/article/dominican -elections-loser-take-all.

[41] Many believe that the Constitutional Court ruling resulted from internal strife between ex-president Leonel Fernández and current president Danilo Medina, both members of the same political party, the Dominican Liberation Party (Partido de la Liberación Dominicana, PLD). President Medina, a popular president, served his first presidential term from 2012 to 2016. Since Fernández considered running for a third presidential term, some contend that the ruling was an effort on behalf of Fernández supporters within the PLD to decrease Medina's popularity—or at least make the term challenging if Medina were to win the election.

[42] United Nations High Commissioner for Refugees (UNHCR), "Dominican Republic Urged Not to Deport Stateless Dominicans," June 19, 2015, https://www.unhcr.org/en-us/news/lat est/2015/6/5584221a6/dominican-republic-urged-deport-stateless-dominicans.html.

[43] See Amnesty International, "No Nationality, No Rights: Stateless People in the Dominican Republic," May 9, 2016, https://www.amnesty.org/en/latest/campaigns/2016/05/stateless-people-in-the-do minican-republic/, and Caribbean Community (CARICOM), "Crisis Related to Dominicans of Haitian Descent and Haitian Migrants in the Dominican Republic," October 13, 2015, https:// caricom.org/dominicans-of-haitian-descent-and-haitian-migrants-in-the-dominican-republi.

[44] For a rich and nuanced discussion of statelessness in the Caribbean, see Kristy A. Belton, *Statelessness in the Caribbean: The Paradox of Belonging in a Postnational World*. Philadelphia: University of Pennsylvania Press, 2017.

CHAPTER 5

"They Are Rounding Up *Morenos*!"

They say that we mistreat Haitians, but they have already invaded! Look, if you go to the public-health clinic, there are a lot of Haitians there. They have babies like rodents. And the services are bad for everyone! If I'm Dominican and you're Haitian and we go to public health, there are no beds. Not for you, and not for me.

—Schoolteacher

The other immigrants are fine. It's the Haitians! That little river separating our countries is nothing. They just walk across, and they're here. There are just too many!

—Taxi driver

When I was little, I was told that Haitians drink blood, kidnap children, practice brujería *[witchcraft], and turn people into zombies. Now people say they want to invade the country.*

—University professor

Tulile: A Public Lynching

In February 2015, a twenty-three-year-old Haitian man was found hanging from a tree in a public park in Santiago.[1] He was known in his community as Tulile. According to news reports, Tulile's lifeless body dangled from a tree, his hands and feet bound. He worked as a *limpiabotas*, shining shoes in the park for change. Earlier that week, a small group of Dominican nationalists who refer to themselves as "defenders of *la Patria*" had burned a Haitian flag and demanded the expulsion of all Haitians in the country. Some wore masks as they beat drums and shouted chants while stomping on the burning flag.

Two weeks after Tulile was lynched, thousands marched through the streets of Port-au-Prince in Haiti in counterprotest.[2] They marched to demand justice and improved human rights for people of Haitian descent living in the Dominican Republic. Haitians from all walks of life—professionals, musicians, adults, and children—walked together as they sang the Haitian national anthem, "*La Dessalinienne*."

When I visited La Tierra the day after Tulile was killed, some people in the *batey* had heard about the crime, and others had not. By then, I had been visiting the community regularly for about six months, and in that time I had spoken with three groups of people more often than others. One group was a Dominican family, another group included friends and family members who were Dominicans of Haitian descent, and the third group was a Haitian family. I purposefully asked each group about Tulile's death.

La Tierra is bustling with more activity than usual when I arrive. A community member recently passed away, and a *guagua* has come to take people to the funeral home. Others are scraping together 200 pesos (US $4.60) to make a copy of their *cédula* for a bartending/waitressing class. Mariana, one of the women interested in taking the class, stops to talk with me. She is a Dominican woman of Haitian descent. We sit together on a wooden bench, and two of her friends join us. After chatting about the class, I ask whether they have heard about the Haitian man found hanging in Santiago. They say no. Mariana couldn't watch the news last night because her antenna was not working.

Next, I visit the Dominican family. I am sitting in the kitchen with Miriam, the matriarch, and three of her adult children—Keila, Amelia, and Oscar. After a lull in our conversation about dating and relationships, I bring up the news story about Tulile by saying, "I heard something in the news about a man who was killed in Santiago." I pause. Miriam and Amelia nod their heads slowly.

After a period of silence, Amelia stops sweeping. "He killed a little girl," she says. "A nine-year-old."

"Oh," I respond, carefully measuring my reaction.

"He killed a little girl?" Keila asks, eyebrows raised.

"That's what I heard," Amelia says.

"*Bueeeeno* [Weeeellll] . . ." I respond. We change the subject, Amelia keeps sweeping, and I make my way out the door and head to Fabienne's house.

Fabienne is a Haitian immigrant who has lived in the Dominican Republic for ten years. She and her husband live in one room of a house. Her husband works as a cane cutter for the sugar mill. A neighbor is just leaving when I arrive and greet Fabienne with a kiss on the cheek. "Trini! I was just talking about you last night," she says, "but I didn't have minutes to call you."

"That's why I wanted to make sure I saw you today," I say with a smile. "So you wouldn't worry." Fabienne and I exchange pleasantries: The men are out working. The kids are fine, thank God.

"I'm so sorry, Trini, I don't have a snack for you or a chair for you to sit in," Fabienne says.

"Don't worry about it! I'm not staying, just passing by to say hello to you. . . . But I heard something on the news I wanted to ask you about. I heard that a Haitian man was killed and hanged in Santiago." Fabienne's eyes get wide and serious. She has heard about it, and she recounts the gruesome details of how his hands and feet were bound and how he was brutally beaten.

"They treated him like an animal! You don't do something like that to a *person*. And they burned the Haitian flag too! *¡Allá en Santiago, no quieren saber nada de haitianos!* [Over there in Santiago, they don't want to have anything to do with Haitians!]"

We are standing at her door, and Fabienne is one step above me. Then she lowers her voice and leans in closer to me. I wonder whether I am talking too loudly. She continues, her voice now at a whisper. "If it were because of a robbery, they might beat him up or kill him, but why would they tie his hands and feet and hang him from a tree?" Her arms and hands are open, pleading. Then she is wringing her hands. "You don't treat a person that way. There are Dominicans over there in Haiti, and they are not treated this way. We are all people! If you cut me, *yo boto sangre* [I bleed]. If you cut you or anyone else, they bleed. No matter what country they are from! You can't treat people this way." Fabienne wags her finger, eyebrows raised.

I shake my head but say nothing. Fabienne continues. "Look, if a Haitian had killed a Dominican, do you know what would have happened? I remember seeing in the news a Dominican raped a Haitian man's daughter, so the Haitian killed the Dominican. Do you know what happened? They killed fifty Haitians *and* burned his house down. Do you hear me? Fifty for one . . ."

People make sense of this brutal act of anti-Haitian racism using stories. Amelia's story adds speculative detail, providing a reason for Tulile's murder that is unrelated to race. Her story—that he may have killed a child[3]—shifts the focus away from systemic anti-Haitian racism and toward an individual's violent actions, which result in a violent response. Fabienne's story—"fifty for one"[4]—reinforces the social exclusion that Haitian immigrants experience living in the Dominican Republic. Her perspective underscores the core purpose of anti-Haitian racism: to devalue Haitian lives. The devaluation of Haitian lives compared with Dominican lives emerged among other Haitian immigrants in La Tierra. During a group conversation about anti-Haitian racism, one woman said, "These people see Haitians as trash! When a Haitian dies, they bury him like a horse! When you bury someone, you do it carefully, putting sticks on top, then rocks and dirt." She makes careful gestures with her hands. "But when a Haitian dies, they bury him like this . . ." She throws imaginary dirt into a hole sloppily, frowning, eyebrows furrowed. For Fabienne, Tulile was lynched because in the Dominican Republic, Haitian lives do not matter.

A lynching is a public display of boundary policing intended to keep a subjugated group in its place. Racial tensions escalate to violence as anti-Haitian legislation encourages nationalists, adding fuel to their fire. In 2009, six years before Tulile's murder, a Haitian man was lynched and beheaded by an angry mob in the capital city, Santo Domingo, while onlookers cheered.[5] Policies that create second-class citizenship for Dominicans of Haitian descent embolden people to enforce cultural boundaries using violence.

Anti-Haitian racism is central to documentation-policy enforcement in the Dominican Republic. When government policies reinforce social and political separation between Dominicans and people of Haitian descent, it endorses anti-Haitian racism and constructs illegality as inherently Haitian.[6] The creation and enforcement of immigration laws perpetuates liminal legality. Previous chapters discuss how documentation policies produce liminal legality for people of Haitian descent. In this chapter, I show how discriminatory enforcement uses racial profiling to police illegality.

Racializing Illegality

"Racialization" is a social process that confers racial identities and associated social and material resources based on the existing racial hierarchy in a given context.[7] Race and racism are not fixed phenomena; rather, they are socially constructed, changing with the prevailing local landscape. Oscar, for example, is a twenty-five-year-old Dominican man with skin the color of cinnamon. Although he lives in *batey* La Tierra, Oscar visits different regions of the Dominican Republic for work. When he travels, people assign his racial category based on the existing social and regional context. For example, in the Dominican Republic, in the eastern region of the country where most people have darker skin, Oscar may be called *indio*, a lighter-skin category. His ascribed racial category changes when he is in El Cibao, a region of the country where most people have lighter skin.

"Here [in La Tierra]," Oscar explains, "they call me *moreno*, or maybe *indio* or *trigueño*. But sometimes, in other places, they tell me that I'm Haitian. What happens is, if you are standing in a group of people with light skin, and you're the only one who is darker, they'll say you're Haitian. It has happened to me, especially when they see that I'm from a *batey*."

In this example, people call Oscar Haitian partly because his skin color is darker than those around him and partly because he lives in a *batey*. Just as the racialization process applies to people, so it applies to places.[8] A *batey* is a racialized place. It is primarily associated with people of Haitian descent; therefore, people who live there are thought of as Haitian regardless of how they self-identify.

Like people and places, illegality is also racialized.[9] Illegality is conferred a racial identity based on the existing racial hierarchy in a given context. In the United States, for example, black and brown immigrants—including those from Latin American or Caribbean countries—encounter racial profiling as authorities police illegality.[10] In the United Kingdom, visa requirements for citizens from Middle Eastern and African countries are stricter than the requirements for citizens from Western countries, and racial and ethnic characteristics are key factors in immigration-policy enforcement.[11] Passport raids target places that employ racial and ethnic minorities as authorities try to identify and arrest workers without valid documentation. In Australia, people from Arabic-speaking communities endure harassment related to suspected illegality. In each of these examples, policing illegality incorporates a racialization process that conflates illegality with specific racial or ethnic identities.

In the Dominican Republic, illegality is racialized as Haitian. Authorities use characteristics associated with Haitians, including having darker skin and a Haitian last name, to police suspected illegality. A public court case described in chapter 1 provides an example of how Haitian-ness and legality are intertwined. Juliana Deguis Pierre, a young Dominican woman of Haitian descent, was born in 1984 in the Dominican Republic to Haitian parents without legal residence. In 2008, Juliana applied for a *cédula*, the national-identification document in the Dominican Republic. But the Central Electoral Board (CEB), the government agency responsible for issuing *cédulas*, denied her application and suspended her birth certificate on the grounds that both of her parents had Haitian last names. As part of a broader advocacy approach, local organizations used strategic litigation[12] to file a lawsuit against the CEB for discrimination based on Juliana's skin color and last name.

In La Tierra, many people emphasized the connection between racialized illegality and anti-Haitian racism. In the following sections, Antonio, a Dominican of Haitian descent, references other immigrant groups in the Dominican Republic as evidence of racial profiling against people of Haitian descent. Gilberto, a Dominican, discusses illegality in tandem with historical and contemporary narratives of cultural differences between Haitians and Dominicans. Although Antonio and Gilberto articulate divergent opinions, both narratives underscore persisting racialized illegality.

"The Rules Are for Everyone, but More for the Hatitians"

During a focus-group discussion in La Tierra, we broach the topic of Haitian immigrants and documentation. Antonio, a vocal participant, makes a comment that stands out in the swirling discussion that moves from topic to topic in both Spanish and Haitian Creole. "If a Haitian is born here, they are Haitian," he says. "If anyone else has a child here, they are Dominican." When I ask why, he responds, "Because they are racists." Several people nod in agreement.

Antonio has deep brown skin is and racially identifies as *moreno*. He is a Dominican of Haitian descent, and his father is Haitian and his mother Dominican. Antonio's parents met at church and were married soon after. They had four children and spent fifty years together in the Dominican Republic. Antonio has been a fuel dispatcher for the sugar mill for seven years. When I arrange to speak with him one-on-one, I make sure to ask Antonio to elaborate on his perspective about anti-Haitian racism.

One sunny Saturday morning, Antonio and I sit on sturdy wooden chairs in his living room. His one-year-old son lays sleeping on his chest during most of our conversation, and his wife, Lily, is in and out—collecting clothes to wash, shooing their four-year-old daughter outside, and returning with rice from the *colmado*, a small shop in the *batey*.

Antonio cannot contain his frustration about feeling targeted by Dominican immigration policy based on his skin color and ethnicity. "They are rounding up *morenos*!" he says, using a term that refers to people with darker brown skin. "The rules are for everyone, but more for the Haitians. They don't bother other immigrants. The French are here. The Italians are here. The Chinese are taking the country for themselves! But Haitians are the ones getting attacked . . ."

Several others in La Tierra reference other immigrant groups in the country to describe the experiences of people of Haitian descent. Haitian immigrants comprise only 4.89 percent of the population in the Dominican Republic.[13] But of the immigrant groups in the country, Haitians are the largest. Chinese immigrants comprise less than 1 percent of the immigrant population in the country, but they are highly visible.[14] In Santo Domingo, for example, a bright yellow building houses the Institute for Chinese-Dominican Development, and Barrio Chino (Chinatown) spans several blocks. Although the rules are ostensibly for everyone, Antonio is frustrated that the true intended targets of changes in immigration policies are people of Haitian descent.

Racialized illegality undergirds a system that integrates indicators of Haitian ethnicity with the enforcement practices of immigration and documentation officials. For example, sugar mills issued Haitian workers with a *ficha*, or an identification card. Haitian migrant workers with no other form of identification could lawfully register their Dominican-born children's births using the *ficha*. Today, documentation offices are suspending documentation for people registered using the *ficha*. This process embeds racial profiling against people of Haitian descent into a system that racializes illegality as Haitian. For Antonio, although immigrants from many backgrounds live in the Dominican Republic, people of Haitian descent encounter systemic discrimination.

"I'm Not Racist, but They're Illegal"

Gilberto provides an alternative perspective that also illustrates racialized illegality. A machine operator for the sugar mill, Gilberto is one of about thirty Dominicans living in La Tierra, among the *batey*'s 415 residents. Gilberto and I sit in his backyard—one of the few yards in La Tierra enclosed by a fence.[15] Vertical wooden posts connected by barbed wire create a barrier between Gilberto's family and their neighbors of Haitian descent. During much of our conversation, Gilberto's body language is open. He leans back, the white plastic chair creaking, while we discuss depression and suicide. He uses his hands and arms to gesture emphatically when he talks about his extramarital affair with a woman he describes as promiscuous. But when Gilberto shifts the conversation to immigration, he leans in closely and lowers his voice.

"But we were going to talk about some things you can use for your book, right?" he begins, transitioning our discussion before I do. "Let's get to what you were going to ask me about immigration." He continues,

> Listen to me carefully: I am not racist. But the way I see it, if they are children of immigrants, just because they were born here does not mean they get Dominican nationality. They are illegals if their parents are illegals. For example, look—there are many Haitians who come here to give birth; then they stay. So they're illegal. You think just because they gave birth here that should make them a national [citizen]? Like I was saying, I'm not racist. There are Haitians here that I love more than some Dominicans. They grew up with me, you know? But because of their blood, they say they're Haitians. And I'm going to be honest, theirs is a very different culture.

"What do you mean by that?" I ask.

"Because they have their worship and we have ours," he tells me.

They have their culture, and we have ours. You know the vast majority of Haitians don't believe in God; they believe in the devil. They live in a totally different culture than ours. It's not that I don't respect them; I love them. I'm not racist, you understand? But they have to straighten out this issue so that they can come and go with their passport like people do in other countries. They can come and go with permission but not make a colony here. Because this part here, this *republica*? It cost a lot of blood to get it. A lot of bloodshed.

Despite his many protestations to the contrary, Gilberto's comments stem from decades of entrenched anti-Haitian racism. Historical and contemporary anti-Haitian ideology juxtaposes Haitians and Dominicans as fundamentally distinct groups. Haitian religious belief systems are deprecated and sensationalized during matter-of-fact discussions about cultural differences. Still, Gilberto's overarching narrative polices cultural and political boundaries. From 1822 to 1844, the island of Hispaniola was unified under Haitian governance. Today, people in La Tierra—like Gilberto—still reference a threat that people of Haitian descent could reunify the island and take political control of the Dominican Republic. As a result, people of Haitian descent are viewed as a population that must be closely managed and carefully controlled.

Through anti-Haitian documentation policies and racial profiling against people of Haitian descent, illegality is racialized as Haitian. In La Tierra, people discuss three primary ways that racial profiling is integral to policing illegality: First, people with dark skin are presumed Haitian and are, therefore, presumed illegal. Second, upon interaction with bureaucratic institutions, including documentation offices, those with a Haitian last name encounter added scrutiny. Third, people who speak Spanish with a Haitian Creole accent are presumed to be in the Dominican Republic illegally. These practices provide evidence that, in a context of heightened monitoring among immigrant groups, people of Haitian descent in the Dominican Republic are racially profiled. In the following sections, I further describe each element of racial profiling, using stories from people in La Tierra.

Skin Color: "They Want to Kick Out All of *los Prietos!*"

Skin color is the primary characteristic used to police illegality. At fifty-one years old, Josef has lived in the Dominican Republic almost his entire life, having immigrated here with his mother when he was an infant. Although he was born in Haiti, he identifies as Dominican. "*¡Claro!* [Of course!] I've spent fifty years here! I don't even know what color the dirt is in Haiti." Josef is the *alcalde* in La Tierra—which loosely translates as the "mayor," but generally speaking, the *alcalde* is a community leader. Many reach out to the *alcalde* in their community to provide a character witness as they enroll in the National Regularization Plan.

When we talk about the changes to birthright citizenship in the Dominican Republic, Josef says emphatically, "They want to kick out all of *los prietos!*"

The word *prieto* describes people with deep brown skin. For Josef, the entanglement between skin color and immigration enforcement is clear: the groups being rounded up or harassed by immigration officials are those with deep brown skin, like his own.

"I'm *un prieto*, and if they grabbed me, they don't ask, 'How long have you been in this country?' 'How long have you worked in this country?' No. They could just grab me and send me to Haiti. They are even burning Haitians' houses in El Cibao! Beating people up, throwing them in jail. Some people are dying *por su nación negro* [because of their Black nationality]."

In the Cibao region of the Dominican Republic, there are fewer people with dark skin than in the eastern or border regions of the country. Haitians with deep brown skin stand out among a whiter population and face discrimination or, in some cases, interpersonal violence.[16] Josef's reference to a "Black nationality" reflects patterns of national identity that coincide with racial categories. Just as illegality is racialized, nationality is also racialized. Although Haiti declared itself a Black nation upon liberation from French colonial rule, people in Haiti have varying shades of brown skin. And when I discussed connections between race and nationality with people in La Tierra, they often referenced Black Dominicans and white Haitians to show incongruences in presumed relationships between race and nation. During a group discussion, for example, one Dominican woman of Haitian descent says, "Being Black is not related to being Haitian. There are Dominicans who are *prieeeto pero muy prieto* [very dark skinned], and they don't even know where Haiti is!" Another Dominican woman of Haitian descent says, "Look, I know a woman who lives back there. And she is lighter than you. If she didn't speak, you wouldn't know that she is Haitian, because she's white. When she goes out in the city, *la toman como dominicana* [they think she's Dominican]." Because deep brown skin is associated with Haitians, those with lighter brown skin pass as Dominican.

Darker-skinned Dominicans and lighter-skinned Haitians complicate the relationship between skin color and nationality. Still, nationality and race are intertwined. Even as I discussed my own position in the Dominican racial hierarchy, the rules I thought I understood were often challenged. Once, for example, I was racially categorized as white because of my American nationality.

While I am talking with Jean, another guy rides up on a motorcycle—bright blue shirt, jeans, deep dark skin. He asks Jean, "What are you up to?" Jean responds, *"Aquí hablando con esa blanca* [I'm here talking with this white lady]." *"¿Blanca?"* I ask, pointing to my brown arms. *"¡Claro! Tú eres blanca, porque tú eres de allá* [Of course! You're white because you're from over there]." "Oh," I respond, completely confused. I know that people associate the United States with whiteness because they are often confused when I say I'm American. In their imaginary, Americans are not brown. But this is the first time I've been called white, and I am not sure what to make of it.

—Field notes, August 27, 2014

Although this is a rare instance of someone with my skin color being considered white in the Dominican Republic, the example illustrates the broader connections between racial categories and nationality. Similarly, Haitian nationality is associated with blackness.[17] Since illegality is racialized as Haitian and blackness is conflated with Haitian nationality, people with deep brown skin are subject to racial profiling. In his observations, Josef makes a poignant connection between skin color, immigration enforcement, and anti-Haitian racism. Having darker skin serves as a first-line screening tool for authorities policing illegality.

Samuel, a Dominican of Haitian descent, was born in the Dominican Republic to Haitian parents. He is fifty-six years old and has lived in *batey* La Tierra for twenty-five years. He self-identifies as Dominican and says he has his birth certificate and Dominican *cédula* to prove it. He has never been to another country. "Where would I go?" he asks.

Samuel's three-year-old granddaughter plays with an old, broken cell phone while he and I sit in plastic chairs on his front porch. He gently rubs her back when she leans her head on his knee, pigtails and barrettes resting on his leg.

Samuel is a security guard for the sugar mill. When I ask him to describe a good day, he explains that on a good day, his body is free from pain and his family has a little something to eat.

"Sometimes you start to think," he says.

Because you get to an age when . . . Let me tell you: if you don't have a roof, your own house, you don't have a small piece of land, your own property. And if you are living on someone else's property, sometimes you think: you are not going to leave anything to your family. And you think about all of that. Sometimes your house doesn't have a pound of rice, and you are thinking about a lot of things. Maybe your family is sick, and your wife doesn't have insurance. She comes home with a prescription, and I don't have anything to buy it with. I have to be thinking. Right?

When we discuss the increased conditionality on birthright-citizenship, Samuel says it is a major political issue.

"Why do you think the government is changing things?" I ask.

"Well, I don't know . . ." Samuel responds. "Because what they're doing is letting everyone see that they're racists. What they want to be is racist. Because they are the political party in power. We don't know why—only they know why they want to be racists."

"Racist against Black people or against Haitians?" I ask.

"Against Blacks," he replies.

Because, let me tell you something: Here, it's because of color. If they start to round up the Haitians but you're Dominican and *prieto* [very dark skinned], right away they'll say "You! Your documents!? Get in the truck!" Here, when you get to a place, because of your color, you are Haitian. But no, sir! You have to take out your documents and say, "Look! I'm Dominican." And if you don't walk around with documents, you're Haitian no matter what you say to them; no matter how nice you talk with them, you are Haitian. One time they picked up a bunch of Black Dominicans and sent them to Haiti! These were people who didn't know how to speak the Haitian language. But because they were Black . . .

Samuel's voice trails off, his eyebrows raised.

Illegality, blackness, and Haitian nationality converge in Samuel's description. Skin color is the first indicator of illegality because of its association with Haitian nationality. People with dark brown skin are vulnerable to harassment by immigration officials. Because of his deep, cocoa-colored skin, Samuel carries his papers with him to protect himself from expulsion from his home country.

Last Name: "She Couldn't Finish High School Because of Her Last Name"

In addition to skin color, officials police illegality by screening for Haitian last names. Because of divergent colonial histories, Haitian last names typically have French derivatives. In contrast, Dominican last names have Spanish derivatives. When people interact with public institutions—including hospitals, documentation offices, and school systems—last names are racialized proxies for Haitian-ness.

Sofía is a thirty-six-year-old Dominican woman who lives in La Tierra. She was born in a *batey* and has lived in a *batey* all her life. When we discuss birthright citizenship, Sofía connects last name and Haitian ethnicity, conflating Dominicans of Haitian descent and Haitian immigrants.

"Imagine! There are a lot of immigrants that were born here and haven't been able to get their *cédula*. They were born and raised here. I mean, they are Haitians, but they were born here and they can't get their *cédula*. So I think that's bad. Because many of them are intelligent, you know? So I think it's bad for the government."

"So if a person is born here, it's possible that they are not Dominican?" I ask.

"Yes. Look—it's because of last names like Pierre . . . Michel . . . those last names are for foreigners. So it's because of last name, you understand?"

Sofía describes Dominican nationality based on the origin of a person's last name. For Sofía, even if people were born in the Dominican Republic, a Haitian last name indicates foreignness. Further, she describes some Dominicans of Haitian descent as intelligent, which reveals beliefs about whether people deserve valid documentation based on what they can offer rather than basing immigration policy on fundamental human rights. Still, the connection between last name and foreignness reinforces practices that erect institutional barriers for people of Haitian descent.

People with Haitian last names are subject to heightened monitoring when they interact with institutions, including documentation offices, employers, and schools. Cecilio, a Dominican of Haitian descent, explains how last names can create barriers to education.

He and I sit at a square, wooden table in his living room. The electricity is out in La Tierra, so the front and back door are open to let the daylight in. Cecilio—more commonly known as "Teto"—wrings his hands as he tells me that his mother died from breast cancer one year ago. His leg bounces with nervous energy, creating a smacking sound as his flip-flop rhythmically hits the floor.

Teto has deep cocoa skin and a thoughtful gaze. His mother was born in the Dominican Republic, and his father was born in Haiti but raised in the Dominican Republic. Teto was an aspiring professional baseball player, but because of an injury, he changed directions. Since moving on from baseball, Teto has worked as a plumber, a security guard, a waiter, and a landscaper. He is also trying to learn English so he can be more competitive for jobs in hospitality and tourism.

Soon our conversation shifts toward documentation. When I ask Teto to share his thoughts about changes to birthright-citizenship laws, he explains that people with Haitian last names are having trouble getting their documents.

> Sometimes because of your last name, there can be problems. Because the last names from here and there [Haiti] are different. For example, my last name is Laurent on my father's side, and that's not very common here. On my mother's side, I'm Díaz, but that last name is very common here [in the Dominican Republic]. . . . It's like I said—I was born here, I have this last name, and I haven't had any problems yet. But I know people who have had to suspend their studies because of papers. . . . My brother's wife, she couldn't finish high school because of her last name. . . . So she's stuck, you understand? Until she can resolve this, she can't finish high school.

According to the law, people born in the Dominican Republic only need one Dominican parent to confer Dominican citizenship. Because of social norms, however, legal status is often conferred based on the mother's nationality. Since he has his mother's last name, a Dominican name, Cecilio has yet to encounter problems with his documentation.

Racialized illegality is policed using indicators of Haitian-ness, such as last name. When they interact with documentation offices, as in the case of Juliana Deguis Pierre, people with a Haitian last name can have their documentation suspended. With suspended documents, Dominicans of Haitian descent cannot work, vote, or complete school. Several people in La Tierra shared stories of people with suspended documentation who were forced to drop out of school as they were pushed into statelessness. These stories were often connected to having a Haitian last name, an indicator of illegality.

Speech: "You Just Have to Know How to Talk"

In addition to skin color and last name, racial profiling incorporates speech. Jean, a Haitian immigrant, describes how speech helps him pass as Dominican.

During my early visits to La Tierra, I was not always sure where to go. On one of these uncertain days, I sit on a rickety wooden bench across from the *colmado* [convenience store] and begin to write a description of the community. Just as I shift my seat to avoid a protruding nail, a man with weathered caramel skin slowly rides up on a motorcycle and stops next to me. He looks to be in his sixties, but I learn later that he is fifty-three years old. His name is Jean.

Jean wears a baseball cap, a faded red dress shirt with white plaid stripes, and jeans that carry the dust of the road. He is missing about four teeth and has a pinky fingernail that is much longer than all the rest. "*¿Pa' dónde tú va?* [Where are you going?]" he asks. I presume that he is a *motochonchista* [a motorcycle taxi driver] looking to rustle up some business, so I explain who I am and I tell him that I am in La Tierra to learn about the lives of Haitian immigrants in the Dominican Republic. He says, "Well, talk to me then!" So we talk.

Jean is a Haitian immigrant who is, in fact, a *motochonchista* in the community. Because there are few paved roads that lead to more isolated *bateyes*, often a motorcycle is the only means of transportation to get from one community to another. I tell him I will be having longer conversations with people, and he says I should make sure to find him.

One day when business is slow, Jean lounges on his dusty, black motorcycle, reclining on his back, a dingy white baseball cap covering his face. He peeks out from under the visor—probably wondering whether I am a customer—and then greets me with a warm smile. We exchange pleasantries. My family is doing well, thank God. Yes, we are always in the struggle. Of course, he can talk for a bit.

Jean starts to talk before I ask any questions. He was born *allá* (over there), in Haiti. His mother came to the Dominican Republic to earn money because she was struggling to feed her family in Haiti. Jean's mother worked in the Dominican Republic for a while; then she sent for her children to join her in the Dominican Republic. Jean was about eight years old when he moved to the Dominican Republic. At some point, I am unsure how or when, he was separated from his mother. "All my life," Jean says, "I've never had documents." He and his wife have five children. Since she is a Dominican of Haitian descent, his children are documented through her.

Soon we are talking about Haiti, and Jean tells me he has gone back a couple of times. "How do you make these trips if you don't have papers?" I ask.

"It's easy," he begins. Then he explains, narrating a hypothetical conversation between himself and the guards.

> They say, "You can't come through; you don't have documents. You have to pay more." I say, "Look, I have an emergency situation—I have to go see my family." They say, "Pay the money . . . 10,000 pesos." Then I say, "I have 300 pesos. I had more money, but I got robbed." I show them my work ID and explain about the money. It's a lie, but it's what you say. Then the guards talk to each other, trying to decide what to do, asking themselves, "Now, what are we going to do with this *moreno*?" After a while, they say, "Let him go; he's Dominican."

"They say you're Dominican?" I ask, confused.

"Yes," he answers matter-of-factly. "They say '*Él sabe hablar*' [He knows how to talk]. You just have to know how to talk."

Jean can enter and exit the country without valid documentation by knowing "how to talk." People without valid documentation often work and save money to pay higher entry fees than those with valid documentation, hoping to start a new life for their families in another country. The typical fee to enter the Dominican Republic at the border is about 300 pesos (about US$6), but people without valid documentation status pay 5,000 to 10,000 pesos (about US$100 to $200) to cross, sometimes as a bribe for police and immigration officials. But since he knows how to talk, Jean passes as Dominican. Knowing how to talk, in this case, is about knowing the right things to say and what stories to tell. Jean explains that he shows them his work identification card and tells them he was robbed because it is what you have to say.

Sometimes knowing how to talk is about a person's accent. Carolina, a Haitian immigrant, participated in a focus group about the experiences of people of Haitian descent in the Dominican Republic. During the group's discussion about immigration and documentation, Carolina explains that when you interact with immigration officials, they check to see whether you know how to talk.

"Before they deport you," she says, "they will interview you first to see if you know how to talk. It's an evaluation *a ver si te falla la lengua* [to see if your speech fails]. And they also ask about your family and your kids' birth certificates to see what your situation is."

Knowing how to talk involves a combination of knowing what to say and how to say it. When stopped by immigration officials, a person is asked questions to see whether their speech fails. The literal translation of the phrase is "to see if your tongue fails you." This reference to a failing tongue may incorporate the historical memory of a time when the Dominican military used the infamous "parsley test" to decipher Dominicans from Haitians during the Haitian massacre in 1937. Since Dominicans and Haitians share many phenotypical characteristics, such as skin color and facial features, government soldiers tried to draw a definitive line at the blurry Haiti–Dominican Republic border by demanding that captives say the Spanish word for parsley—*perejil*.[18] In Haitian Creole, a French-origin language, speakers have difficulty pronouncing the Spanish r. If captives could pronounce *perejil* correctly in Spanish, the soldiers let them live. If they pronounced it with a French accent, their trembling tongues tripping over the *r*, soldiers executed them.

Carolina's comment about speech that fails also refers to the content of the conversation. Similar to Jean's experience knowing *how* to talk, a person's responses related to their own documentation status and the status of their family members can be red flags for immigration officials trying to identify people without valid documentation. Both the content of a person's responses and their speaking accent can be used as indicators of illegality racialized as Haitian.

In some situations, the choice to remain silent can minimize complications associated with a tongue that might "fail you." Krisla was born and raised in Haiti and used to go back and forth between Haiti and the Dominican Republic, selling goods at the border. When asked whether Haitians and Dominicans are treated differently, Krisla describes how skin color and speech can make people blend in or stand out. She shares a story about how her choice to remain silent helped her avoid a confrontation between herself, a *guagua chofer* (bus driver), and an immigration official at a documentation checkpoint.

"Well, my daughter is light-skinned," she begins.

> And you see that you have people from a country of Blacks crossing into a country of whites: they're different. Because once, I got on a *guagua*, and I was sleeping. When the *guagua* was stopped, the police tapped me, but I was sleeping. I didn't say anything. So the *chofer* said, "Hmm—it's fine." You understand? I mean, because I was *de una forma normal* [in a normal way], you understand? I was traveling, but I didn't have my hair done, and I wasn't all dressed up, I didn't have myself done up. I was dressed normal. So the police saw me and said, "That one's not Haitian" . . . They saw by my demeanor—that I was a normal person on the Earth, you know? Actually, I laughed to myself because he let me pass and I won.

In some regions of the country, documentation checkpoints are common. At these checkpoints, vehicles are stopped, and passengers must provide evidence of documentation. For public-transportation vehicles, the *chofer* or the *cobrador* (fare collector) may interact with the officials on behalf of passengers. In the situation that Krisla describes, the *chofer* explains that she is not Haitian, and so the authorities do not push the issue.

Krisla's story begins as a conversation about skin color. She is a woman from a "country of Blacks" living in a "country of whites," but in many situations she and Dominicans around her all have skin color a similar shade of brown. Skin color is not what distinguished her from her fellow passengers on the *guagua*. Since both Dominicans and Haitians have brown skin, phenotypical characteristics are used alongside other markers of foreignness, such as style of dress and speech. Krisla attributes her ability to blend in to her style of dress. But she also chose to remain silent. Krisla speaks Spanish, but it is limited.[19] Since she pretends to be asleep, and chooses not to speak, Krisla is able to conceal any lilts in her French-accented Spanish. Like Jean, Krisla passes as Dominican.

Racial Profiling and Immigration Policies

In the Dominican Republic, illegality is racialized as Haitian. Accordingly, officials use indicators of Haitian-ness to identify people without valid documentation. Skin color is the primary means of racially profiling for illegality. Darker shades of brown skin are associated with Haitian national origin and, consequently, illegality. During periods of mass deportation and expulsion, dark-skinned Dominicans unable to prove their Dominican nationality were among the Haitian immigrants sent to Haiti. When Trujillo's government murdered thousands of people of Haitian descent to rid the country of Haitians, dark-skinned Dominicans mistaken for Haitians were also murdered. These examples and those shared by La Tierra residents underscore the inextricable link between illegality and deep brown skin.

The case of the Dominican Republic adds nuance to the way we understand racial profiling in a country where the population is primarily brown. Specifically, it shows how immigrants are racially profiled. In addition to skin color, last name and speech indicate Haitian nationality and illegality. In documentation offices, having a Haitian last name provides an acceptable justification for officials to suspend documentation. Further, those whose speech "fails" are subject to added scrutiny and institutional barriers, as their accent or explanations fall short of expectations of those who "belong" in the country. Such practices undermine the government's party line that documentation policies are universal and do not target Dominicans of Haitian descent. Using last name and speech as screening tools discloses the true intent of restrictive documentation policies: to move Dominicans of Haitian descent into second-class citizenship—or strip that citizenship altogether.

Because these laws are universal, they create the illusion of race neutrality.[20] But universal laws are not universally enforced.[21] Since people are products of racialized social systems, laws exclude and include in racially ordered terms.[22] Racial profiling systematically excludes people of Haitian descent from employment, education, political participation, and other social benefits associated with full citizenship. Government-sanctioned racial profiling, as evidenced by Juliana Deguis Pierre's court case, validates a nationalist vision of a Dominican Republic. Socially integrating people of Haitian descent poses a threat to a republic that excludes them from the fabric of Dominican social and cultural life. But narratives steeped in racism reinforce separation and inferiority, and they bolster violent responses from people who try to police illegality on their own.

Racial distinctions in how legality and citizenship are conferred violate common conceptions of egalitarianism and human equality. But anti-Haitian documentation policies and enforcement practices codify racialized illegality in the Dominican Republic. Dangerous descriptions emphasizing the urgency of border control, imagined intentions to reunify Hispaniola, and perceived population size provide examples of how anti-Haitian racism underpins conceptions of legality.[23] Incendiary statements about overburdened Dominican resources are coupled with anecdotes about Haitians' "violent nature" or cultural inferiority, covertly connecting racism and xenophobia. Yet the Dominican economy continues to benefit from their labor. The Dominican response, then, is an exclusionary immigration policy with a racially disparate impact. Anti-Haitian policies and racial profiling work in tandem to ostracize those deemed undesirable while maintaining the exploitable labor of an oppressed population.

Notes

[1] For related media articles, see Kenya Downs, "Haitian's Lynching Renews Protests against Dominican Citizenship Law," NPR, *Code Switch*, February 14, 2015, https://www.npr.org/sections/codeswitch/2015/02/14/384344141/haitians-lynching-renews-protests-against-dominican-citizenship-law; Maxwell Reyes, "Queman bandera haitiana en Santiago," *El Sol de Santiago*, February 11, 2015, https://elsoldesantiago.com/queman-bandera-haitiana-en-santiago/; and

"Apresan jóvenes por quemar bandera haitiana," *El Nacional*, February 13, 2015, https://elna cional.com.do/apresan-jovenes-por/.

[2] For a related article, see Jacqueline Charles, "Thousands March in Haiti over Dominican Racism," *Miami Herald*, February 25, 2015, https://www.miamiherald.com/news/nation-world/world/americas/haiti/article11180039.html.

[3] Official reports connect Tulile's attack to a gambling dispute, lending no support to the suspicion that he hurt a child. See "Dominican Republic Police Say Compatriots Lynched Haitian," *Dominican Today*, February 12, 2015. https://dominicantoday.com/dr/local/2015/2/12/Dominican-Republic-police-say-compatriots-lynched-Haitian/.

[4] For a related news article, see "Queman barrio haitiano," *Diario Libre*.

[5] For a related news article, see Mariela Rosario, "Lynching of Haitian Man Highlights Tension in Dominican Republic," *Latina*, May 11, 2009, http://www.latina.com/lifestyle/news-politics/lynching-haitian-man-highlights-tension-dominican-republic.

[6] Samuel Martínez and Bridget Wooding, "El antihaitianismo en la República Dominicana: ¿Un giro biopolítico?" *Migración y Desarrollo* 15, no. 28 (2017): 95–123 (text available online at https://www.redalyc.org/pdf/660/66053147004.pdf).

[7] Omi and Winant, *Racial Formation*.

[8] For example, see Victor Ray, "A Theory of Racialized Organizations," *American Sociological Review* 84, no. 1 (2019): 26–53.

[9] See, for example, Nicholas De Genova, *Working the Boundaries: Race, Space, and "Illegality" in Mexican Chicago* (Durham, NC: Duke University Press, 2005), and San Juanita García, "Racializing 'Illegality': An Intersectional Approach to Understanding How Mexican-Origin Women Navigate an Anti-immigrant Climate," *Sociology of Race and Ethnicity* 3, no. 4 (2017): 474–90.

[10] See, for example, Amada Armenta, "Racializing Crimmigration: Structural Racism, Colorblindness, and the Institutional Production of Immigrant Criminality," *Sociology of Race and Ethnicity* 3, no. 1 (2017): 82–95; see also Golash-Boza, *Deported*.

[11] From Mary Bosworth, Alpa Parmar, and Yolanda Vázquez, eds., *Race, Criminal Justice, and Migration Control: Enforcing the Boundaries of Belonging* (Oxford: Oxford University Press, 2018); see the volume's chapters by Ben Bowling and Sophie Westenra, "Racism, Immigration, and Policing," 61–77, and by Alpa Parmar, "Policing Belonging: Race and Nation in the UK," 108–24.

[12] Adam Weiss, "Strategic Litigation to Address Childhood Statelessness," World's Stateless Children (website), Institute on Statelessness and Inclusion, 2017, http://children.worldsstateless.org/3/litigating-against-childhood-statelessness/strategic-litigation-to-address-childhood-statelessness.html. And see chapter 1 for a more detailed discussion of the Deguis Pierre case.

[13] Oficina Nacional de Estadísticas (ONE), *Segunda encuesta nacional de inmigrantes [ENI-2017]: Versión resumida del informe general* (Santo Domingo, DR: ONE, 2018) (text available online at https://www.refworld.org.es/pdfid/5b1ef7a54.pdf).

[14] For more information about Chinese immigrants in the Dominican Republic, see Chen, "'You Are Like Us.'"

[15] For an example of how people maintain boundaries in multiethnic neighborhoods, see Sarah Mayorga-Gallo, *Behind the White Picket Fence: Power and Privilege in a Multiethnic Neighborhood* (Chapel Hill: University of North Carolina Press, 2014).

[16] For a related news article, see "Una organización denuncia hay 'ataques racistas' contra haitianos en la RD," *AlMomento.net*, June 18, 2019, https://almomento.net/una-organizacion-denuncia-hay-ataques-racistas-contra-haitianos-en-la-rd/.

[17] For a discussion on how the period of US occupation in the Dominican Republic (from 1916 to 1924) influenced local understandings of Blackness, see Micah Wright, "An Epidemic of Negrophobia: Blackness and the Legacy of the US Occupation of the Dominican Republic," special issue, "Dominican Black Studies," *The Black Scholar* 45, no. 2 (2015): 21–33. For additional discussion of blackness in the Dominican Republic, see also Silvio Torres-Saillant, "The Tribulations of Blackness: Stages in Dominican Racial Identity," *Latin American Perspectives* 25, no. 3 (1998): 126–46.

[18] See Turits, "A World Destroyed," and the documentary *Di Perejil* (Say parsley), directed and produced by Irene Rial Bou, Producciones Oya (Lanham, MD: National Film Network, 2006), DVD.

[19] Krisla's interview for this research was completed in Haitian Creole because she was more comfortable in that language than with Spanish.

[20] David Theo Goldberg, _The Racial State_ (Malden, MA: Blackwell Publishing, 2002).

[21] Louise Boon-Kuo, "Visible Policing Subjects and Low Visibility Policing in Australia: Migration and Race in Australia," in _Race, Criminal Justice, and Migration Control: Enforcing the Boundaries of Belonging_, ed. Mary Bosworth, Alpa Parmar, and Yolanda Vázquez (Oxford: Oxford University Press, 2018), 93–107.

[22] Critical race theorists emphasize the intersections between laws, legal categories, and racial hierarchies. See, for example, Kimberlé Crenshaw et al., _Critical Race Theory: The Key Writings that Formed the Movement_ (New York: New Press, 1995).

[23] The overlap between racism and anti-immigrant sentiment is also evident for racialized immigrant groups in other countries. Racialized immigrant groups are those that have been ascribed a new, stigmatized racial category upon immigration to a new country. In the United States, for example, public discourse about Mexican immigrants and Mexican Americans includes alarmist language about threat, population size, fertility patterns, and "reconquest" of the US Southwest. But Mexican immigrants and Mexican Americans also endure racial slurs and insults. Mexican immigrants without valid documentation have been unjustly referred to as dangerous criminals and gang members, even though there is no relationship between legal status and crime rates.

CHAPTER 6

Racism, Resistance, and Reframing Illegality

Here in the Dominican Republic, in my opinion, there is racism. Mainly against morenos [brown-skinned people]. Or los negros [the blacks]. Here there is racismo callado [quiet racism]. Racismo callado means that they're racist, but they don't want to admit it. I can be racist, and I hate you, but I don't let you know what's in my heart. But I do things to take you out, you understand? I don't want to do anything for you. I reject you. I do everything possible so that you have absolutely nothing all the time. So that you're always under me—like they say, pidiéndome cacao [begging from me]. That's racismo callado. That's why Haiti and the Dominican Republic will always have problems, because here in the Dominican Republic, there is a lot of racism.

—Antonio, resident of La Tierra

Quiet Racism

The case of people of Haitian descent in the Dominican Republic complicates the relationship between race, blackness, and nation by providing evidence of how state-level policy constructs differences and dictates sociopolitical belonging. When I inevitably get lost in the weeds of policies, programs, and procedures, the words of the people pull me back to the purpose of this work. Antonio, a Dominican of Haitian descent, poignantly explains the intersectional politics of belonging.[1] "Quiet racism," as he calls it, works behind the scenes at a structural level to ensure that people of Haitian descent *have absolutely nothing all the time.* Although the public-facing narrative is that the laws apply to all immigrant families, racial profiling ensures that people of Haitian descent are *always under* those the constitution deems Dominican. The subclass created by increasing conditionality on birthright citizenship is specifically for Dominicans of Haitian descent.

In the Dominican Republic, people of Haitian descent are a racialized labor source that is included in the economy and yet excluded from society. By creating a documentation program for Haitian immigrants that confers documents but no path to a naturalized legal status, the Dominican Republic gains exploitable labor without paying the costs of social integration. By establishing a Book of Foreigners for *Dominicans* of Haitian descent, the country can eliminate full social and political participation for generations, based solely on the circumstances of a child's birth.

It cannot be overstated that Dominicans of Haitian descent are not, in fact, foreigners—as the Book of Foreigners implies. But the naming and the labeling does the semantic work of moving Dominicans of Haitian descent from a position of inclusion to one of exclusion, strategically and politically grouping them with people who are immigrants. Of course, the legislation that increases conditionality on birthright citizenship applies only to those whose parents are unable to prove their legal residence. Still, the social implication is clear: Dominicans of Haitian descent—broadly speaking—do not belong in the Dominican Republic.

The politics of belonging incorporates intersectional social hierarchies based on race, skin color, gender, and socioeconomic status. Public discourse and interpersonal practices construct social boundaries, and intermediaries police them. In documentation offices, at military checkpoints, or on buses and sidewalks, people continually draw lines that push people of Haitian descent outside of the Dominican national imaginary. People with dark brown skin encounter harassment and have racial epithets thrown at them, as their skin color—associated with Haitians—represents foreignness. In a context where skin color and blackness have a complicated association with nationality, nonphenotypical characteristics, including last name and speech, also support discriminatory efforts to identify people of Haitian descent. In documentation offices, for example, people with Haitian last names derived from French rather than Spanish are racially profiled. Their documents are suspended because of their last name, impeding their chances for employment or education opportunities. As discrimination falls along gendered lines, women of Haitian descent have children deemed stateless by hospitals that ignore the rights of Dominican fathers. Although Dominican fathers can legally pass citizenship to their children, mothers without legal residence leave hospitals with babies cheated out of citizenship, as they have few options to document their Dominican-born children. Anti-Haitian policies operate as designed, keeping people of Haitian descent in their intended places—subjugated, subordinated, and living in second-class citizenship.

Irrespective of individuals, a system built on racism will reproduce itself. In this way, such systems perpetuate the racial inequalities they were designed to create. Racism justifies and rationalizes inequalities, even as human-rights violations abuses abound. All people have the right to nationality, the right to work and education, the right to vote, and the right to social protection and liberty.[2] In the Dominican Republic, Dominicans of Haitian descent affected by increased conditionality on birthright citizenship are denied these rights, as laws built on institutionalized racism serve to keep people of Haitian descent in their marginalized place. A racialized labor source, their presence in the country is only meant to be functional. As they venture into more visible social places outside the *batey*, the government responds with discriminatory and restrictive policies that create statelessness for generations.

Reframing Illegality

Before beginning this project, I did not understand legal status in all of its nuance. At a basic level, I understood that some immigrants have documents that protect them from deportation while others do not. After years of drawing time lines that outline policy changes, listening to stories that detail complicated lives, and cataloging the array of exceptions to supposed rules, I can no longer view illegality as binary. Watching people try to navigate a complex bureaucratic system meant to marginalize them was heart-wrenching. Haitian immigrants with barely enough money to buy food scraped together funds to try and enroll in the National Regularization Plan so that their children could enroll in the Book of Foreigners. Liminal legality describes the experiences of people whose legal status hangs in the balance between "documented" and "undocumented." Illegality is not a fundamental state of being. People move in and out of legal statuses as policies change around them, highlighting the importance of theoretical approaches that view legal status as a socially constructed category that varies based on local contextual factors.[3]

One contextual factor that contributes to the social construction of legal status is the local racial hierarchy. In a given country, or even in geographic regions within countries, the racial context dictates which groups are perceived as illegal—or as outsiders. In some geographic areas of the United States, for example, people who "look Mexican" encounter discrimination and harassment as illegality is regionally framed as Mexican.[4] In other regions, people who "look Middle Eastern" encounter discrimination as they interact with social institutions. Illegality is created and enforced along racial lines, and these examples illustrate the importance of examining local racial hierarchies to understand how immigrant families are carved outside of the national imaginary in different countries.

In addition to shifting my view of legality toward incorporating context and nuance, after this project I can no longer discuss illegality absent a critical eye toward labor systems. The human-rights violations and labor abuses are so pervasive that the need to create solutions centered on human dignity seem obvious. Yet abuses persist with little consequence. And so we must ask: Who benefits from illegality? As governments and businesses negotiate terms that prioritize profit, they create legal statuses that offer temporary reprieve from deportation or expulsion without fully incorporating that labor source into society. You can work, but your children cannot vote.

To understand illegality, we must understand race and labor.[5] Societies have incorporated racialized labor for centuries. To maintain race-based labor arrangements, racism must remain at the center of policies and practices. Otherwise workers might seem too much like people. The ideological work necessary to maintain racialized labor systems justifies exploitation. The race-labor logic model says, *That work is inferior, Haitian work. Since Haitians are inferior, they should be excluded from Dominican society.* This logic, though simplified, represents the ideological work that racism performs to support sociopolitical suppression and exploitation. Accordingly, any discussion of illegality must make visible the roles of racial hierarchies and labor systems.

Resistance . . . and More Resistance

To present this research comprehensively, I must also include a discussion of on-the-ground resistance. Strategic litigation has been a key form of resistance among domestic and international organizations advocating the protection of human rights for people of Haitian descent in the Dominican Republic. But in response to international sanctions resulting from the discriminatory denial of the right to nationality, Dominican policies regarding citizenship have become increasingly restrictive. For example, one year after the General Law of Migration (Ley General de Migración, No. 285-04) increased conditionality on birthright citizenship, the Inter-American Court of Human Rights[6] heard the case of two Dominican girls who had been denied birth certificates because they were of Haitian descent. In *Case of the Girls Yean and Bosico v. Dominican Republic*, the court ruled that the girls had been arbitrarily denied birth certificates because of their race and that the "in transit" exception to should not apply to the immigration status of individuals living in the country for an extended period. A critical legal win, the case of Yean and Bosico clarified that children could not be denied nationality by inheriting their parents' migration status.[7]

Following this critical win on the international stage, backlash against the Inter-American Court's ruling was swift as nationalist voices in the Dominican Republic further demarcated the line in the sand.[8] Dominican government officials criticized the ruling, saying it was part of an international conspiracy to undermine Dominican sovereignty, which in turn fueled nationalist anti-Haitian rhetoric. In the end, the Dominican government largely ignored the Inter-American Court's ruling and moved forward with a series of restrictive anti-Haitian policies that would culminate in present-day racialized statelessness.

Still, an emergent wave of activism among migrant-rights organizations has publicized unjust documentation policies and the inherent racism that they perpetuate. Civil-society organizations have denounced discriminatory practices, presenting reports to the Committee on the Elimination of Racial Discrimination.[9] The Movement of Dominican-Haitian Women (MUDHA) and the Caribbean Migrants Observatory (OBMICA) have actively engaged in domestic and international efforts to resist anti-Haitian policies and defend the rights of people of Haitian descent in the Dominican Republic. Further, cultural endeavors that highlight the presence and visibility of African ancestry among Dominicans push back against narratives that separate Dominicans and Haitians based on perceptions of divergent heritage. The women-led group Acción Afro-Dominicana works to uncover all forms of racism in the Dominican Republic while creating a community of consciousness with other women in the African diaspora.[10] The work of these organizations underscores the importance and effectiveness of collective resistance to structural discrimination.[11]

Many in the United States have a connection to the Dominican Republic in one form or another. Often, when I discuss this research, people tell me about a church mission trip or a vacation they took to the Dominican Republic. Or perhaps they know Dominicans in the United States and tell me about that relationship. Their stories typically include warm and joyful memories. But occasionally, they share a story that adds anecdotal evidence substantiating the existence of anti-Haitian racism. For example, after describing this book at a professional networking event, one woman said to me, "You know, I was on a service trip in the Dominican Republic, and we were riding a public bus. Then, out of nowhere, our guide starts pointing out people, saying, 'He's Haitian . . . she's Haitian . . . him . . . and him too. You can tell by the shape of their heads.' I was appalled!"

This is, in fact, appalling. But in moments like these, I question the moral authority with which people recount to me their "Dominican-racism stories." In the United States, we must reckon with our own forms of quiet racism against immigrants. Under our current government, nonwhite immigrants are under attack as US Immigration and Customs Enforcement (ICE) agents scan motel guest registries for "Latino-sounding" names.[12] This is the same kind of racial discrimination evident when documentation officials in the Dominican Republic deny birth certificates to people with Haitian last names. The case of people of Haitian descent in the Dominican Republic is not meant to make us feel better about our own brand of anti-immigrant racism. Rather, this case should provide countries across the globe with a mirror that reflects the injustices we have committed against racialized labor sources in our own countries.[13] Border regions across the world represent rich relationships and painful divisions. But they also provide an opportunity for nations to prioritize rules of engagement that center dignity and shared humanity. We must see our own reflections in the Dominican case and move toward greater inclusion and justice for immigrants marginalized by racism. Only then can we achieve human rights for all.

Notes

1 Evelyn Nakano Glenn, *Unequal Freedom: How Race and Gender Shaped American Citizenship and Labor* (Cambridge, MA: Harvard University Press, 2009), and Nira Yuval-Davis, *The Politics of Belonging: Intersectional Contestations* (London: SAGE Publications, 2011).

2 United Nations, "Human Rights," accessed November 30, 2019, https://www.un.org/en/sections/issues-depth/human-rights/.

3 Joanna Dreby, *Everyday Illegal*.

4 See, for example, García, "Racializing 'Illegality,'" and René D. Flores and Ariela Schachter, "Examining Americans' Stereotypes about Immigrant Illegality," *Contexts* 18, no. 2 (2019): 36–41.

5 For scholarship examining racialized labor, see, for example, Iyko Day, *Alien Capital: Asian Racialization and the Logic of Settler Colonial Capitalism* (Durham, NC: Duke University Press, 2016); Golash-Boza, *Deported*; Jung, *Coolies and Cane*; Laura López-Sanders, "Trapped at the Bottom: Racialized and Gendered Labor Queues in New Immigrant Destinations," UC San Diego Working Paper 176, March 2009 (text available online at https://escholarship.org/content/qt1r39d099/qt1r39d099.pdf); and SaunJuhi Verma, "Seasoning Labor: Contemporary

South Asian Migrations and the Racialization of Immigrant Workers," *Journal of Asian American Studies* 22, no. 1 (2019): 31–52.

[6] The Inter-American Court of Human Rights operates in conjunction with the Inter-American Commission on Human Rights. Together they comprise the human-rights-protection system of the Organization of American States, which serves to uphold and promote basic rights and freedoms in the Americas. The court rules on whether a country has violated an individual's human rights.

[7] Francisco Quintana, "Inter-American Court Condemns Unprecedented Situation of Statelessness in the Dominican Republic," European Network on Statelessness (website), October 27, 2014, https://www.statelessness.eu/blog/inter-american-court-condemns-unprecedented-situation-statelessness-dominican-republic.

[8] Samuel Martínez, "The Price of Confrontation: International Retributive Justice and the Struggle for Haitian-Dominican Rights," in *The Uses and Misuses of Human Rights: A Critical Approach to Advocacy*, ed. George J. Andreopoulos and Zehra F. Kabasakal Arat (New York: Palgrave Macmillan, 2014), 89–115.

[9] The Committee on the Elimination of Racial Discrimination (CERD) is a body of independent experts that monitors the implementation of rights related to racial discrimination under the Office of the UN High Commissioner for Human Rights (OHCHR). For specific recommendations to address anti-Haitian discrimination and documentation, see Open Society Justice Initiative and the Center for Justice and International Law, "Submission to the Committee."

[10] "República Dominicana: Mujeres afrodescendientes reclaman respeto a su identidad," September 8, 2016, Comunicaciones Aliadas, https://www.comunicacionesaliadas.com/republica-dominicana-mujeres-afrodescendientes-reclaman-respeto-a-su-identidad/.

[11] Centro Bono and Reconoci.do are also key organizations at the forefront of advocacy for documentation and citizenship rights among people of Haitian descent in the Dominican Republic.

[12] Flores and Schachter, "Examining Americans' Stereotypes."

[13] For a critical discussion of global race and racism, see Michelle Christian, "A Global Critical Race and Racism Framework: Racial Entanglements and Deep and Malleable Whiteness," *Sociology of Race and Ethnicity* 5, no. 2 (2019): 169–85. For a discussion of the global vestiges of slavery and how power produces historical memory, see works by Haitian anthropologist Michel-Rolph Trouillot, including *Silencing the Past: Power and the Production of History* (Boston: Beacon Press, 1995).

Discussion Questions

In Someone Else's Country

- Haitian immigrants and Dominicans of Haitian descent are systematically excluded from full participation in Dominican society.

  - What are examples of the systematic nature of their exclusion?
  - Who are the key stakeholders in this issue? What are their competing interests?

- Find another example from a different country that shows how race/ethnicity and legality intersect. What are similarities between your example and the Dominican Republic example? What are differences? Does the issue of citizenship emerge? Are there similar stakeholders?
- What are the connections between social exclusion along racial/ethnic lines and voting rights? Why are these connections important for political participation?

Racism

- If people created racism, what would it take for people to dismantle racism?

  - What would make dismantling racism challenging? What would make it more possible?

- How can individuals work together to share power and create a more equitable society? Organizations? Governments?
- What is your role in maintaining or dismantling systems built on racism— as an individual? A community member? A person who is part of an organization? A voter?

Legality

- "Legality is socially constructed." What does this mean?
- How can universal laws perpetuate inequality?
- How does "liminal legality" help us understand people's experiences with documentation more deeply than "documented" and "undocumented"?
- What is statelessness? Why is statelessness a human-rights violation?

Policy

- Haitian immigrants were recruited to the Dominican Republic for labor and then socially excluded. Many have lived and worked in the country for decades. What policy solutions could address their needs?

  ○ What are the necessary considerations for implementing these solutions?

- Dominicans of Haitian descent born to parents without valid documentation are denied full citizenship. What policy solutions could address their needs?

  ○ What are the necessary considerations for implementing these solutions?

- Besides the Dominican government, how do other institutions perpetuate inequality? Hospitals? Schools? Employers?

  ○ What policy solutions could address these inequities?

Research and the Researcher (Methodology)

The Insider-Outsider Perspective

When I began this work, I was very aware of my outsider status. Two specific examples remain with me. The first stems from a conversation between one of my dissertation advisors and her colleague. This colleague warned my advisor that I was putting myself in danger if I did my research in a Dominican *batey*. She told my advisor, "Outsiders do not go into *bateyes* without armed guards. Will your student have an armed guard when she goes?" Narratives like these perpetuate the idea that Haitian communities are violent. I took safety precautions, such as choosing not to stay in La Tierra past dark so that I could avoid taking public transportation alone at night. But I never felt unsafe in La Tierra. Being an outsider in some ways was balanced by my being an insider in other ways. Perhaps as a Black American I attracted less unwanted attention than a white foreigner might have. My status as a wife and mother also opened avenues of connection between myself and community members, and having previously lived in the Dominican Republic for an extended period afforded me a firm starting point when learning more about the country and culture.

The second example of my outsider status is the broad understanding that I was one of many foreigners who have come and gone in this space. People come to the Dominican Republic from all over the world to "help"—Canadian nuns, Mormon missionaries, Peace Corps volunteers, US church-mission trips, foundations that want to bolster education or provide school supplies, doctors who do surgeries on children with tonsillitis, photographers who want to document poor living conditions in *bateyes*. Some speak Spanish; others do not. Some stay for two weeks; others stay for two years. Somehow, I thought my presence was different. But I found myself placed squarely among the "foreigners who come and go," and it was uncomfortable. One of the families in La Tierra would tell me stories about Sarah, a *gringa*[1] from the United States who lived in the Dominican Republic for years and visited La Tierra often during her time in the country. At first, I felt irritated when they told me stories about her, primarily because I liked to think of myself as a unique and autonomous foreigner. But after some time, I became more aware of the similarities between myself and the collection of rotating foreigners.

> I have chosen to stop being annoyed whenever they bring up Sarah. I think I'm annoyed because foreigners are often lumped together, and I doubt that our purposes were the same. I also feel annoyed because I like to separate myself from the other foreigners who rotate in and out of these places in two weeks. But in so many ways, I'm the same.
>
> —Field notes, March 27, 2015

I stayed in the country longer than many foreigners do. I learned Spanish and Haitian Creole. I established working relationships with local organizations and drew on their expertise for my research. Still, my stay was temporary, and my observations are those of a well-intentioned outsider.

Research Questions, Data Collection, and Analysis

When I started this research, my primary research question was: What is the mental-health impact of changes to birthright citizenship? But over the course of my analyses, this book became less about mental health and more about the structural production of precarious legal status. People living in La Tierra wanted to understand how the country could benefit from their presence while also publicly shaming them for being there. Following the priorities of community members, the primary research questions for this book have changed. Now the book engages with the following questions: (1) How do policies produce liminal legality? (2) How do universal laws perpetuate racial inequality? (3) How do people experience the policies that affect them?

These questions provide a foundation for the data analysis and discussion in this book. Because of the undeniable impact of discriminatory legal changes on mental health, some of the narratives throughout the book reveal the depression and anxiety that people in the community experience as they make sense of their position in a country where they are needed and yet unwanted. But sometimes the worry and sadness they feel is about basic survival as people struggle to provide basic needs for themselves and their families. As I try to authentically tell the stories of people living in La Tierra, mental health is present, but the structural production of liminal legality is the primary focus of analyses.

Data Collection

This research was conducted in the classic tradition of participant observation, which allows ethnographers to understand the context and social forces shaping the experiences and interpretations of individuals. In addition to supporting community integration, participant observation provided an important and necessary check against self-reports derived from in-depth interviews. Further, since documentation may be a particularly sensitive subject, this method allowed me to build relationships and establish rapport over time. To get to know people, and to allow them to get to know me, I attended community functions, religious services, and group meetings in addition to spending time with individuals and families in their homes. Since family is an important way that people socially "place" others, my husband and children visited the community with me on occasion to provide a fuller picture of who I was. Community members were especially delighted to meet my father when he came to visit me in the country.

I completed fieldwork over ten consecutive months, between August 2014 and May 2015. My interpretations were also influenced by the time I had spent in the Dominican Republic as a Peace Corps volunteer from August 2008 until January 2010. Data-collection methods during my fieldwork included participant observation, in-depth interviews with local key informants and *batey* residents, a focus-group discussion, a depression-and-anxiety scale, and a community census. I am a fluent nonnative Spanish speaker, and I also completed a year-long Haitian Creole immersion course to familiarize myself with the language and culture before entering the field.

Before completing interviews with people in La Tierra, I completed semistructured key-informant interviews with fifteen people who'd had experience serving *batey* populations. Key-informant interviews are qualitative, in-depth interviews with people who are familiar with the population of interest. Interviews with key informants helped identify common concerns in *batey* communities. I also used key-informant interviews to shape language and word choice for subsequent interviews with *batey* residents. Key informants for this study included four academic researchers at Dominican universities, four representatives of nongovernmental organizations that work with Haitian immigrants in the Dominican Republic, six health-service providers who work in a clinic that serves *bateyes* in the region, and the principal of the public elementary school in the *batey*. Key informants were recruited using referrals from the US embassy, a local health clinic, and other qualified experts. Each interview lasted between thirty and sixty minutes and was conducted in the language preferred by the participant (Spanish or English).

In addition to key-informant interviews, I led a focus-group discussion in La Tierra. One month after I began visiting the field site, a pastor in La Tierra recruited twelve people to meet with me and to answer any questions I had. She introduced me to everyone and then said, "What do you want to talk about?" The meeting evolved into an impromptu focus group about documentation policy and racism. Attendees included six Haitian immigrants, five Dominicans of Haitian descent, and one Dominican. The conversation took place primarily in Spanish, with some comments in Haitian Creole. A participant sitting next to me translated Creole comments to Spanish to ensure that I understood.

Recruitment Process

For in-depth interviews with *batey* residents, I recruited participants using a snowball-sampling method, with particular attention to maximum variation in perspectives. With this variation in mind, I tried to balance the number of Haitian immigrants, Dominicans of Haitian descent, and men and women who completed interviews. Although this sampling strategy does not enable generalizability of findings to the broader *batey* population in the Dominican Republic, it does allow generalization to the theoretical processes that connect racism, documentation policy, and legal status.

I chose respondents using two strategies: an a priori, theory-driven framework and an emergent, or data-driven, framework. For example, a priori, I wanted to ensure that I balanced the sample on immigrant status based on existing literature theorizing differences between foreign-born and native-born populations. When I started data collection, however, I learned that the community was also divided based on religious affiliation. So, using a data-driven framework, I ensured that the sample included church members as well as those who were not church members. This approach produced a sample that included a range of community members' voices. Interviewees were paid 300 pesos (about US$7.00) at the end of my time in the country as a thank-you for their participation.

I conducted most of the interviews personally. However, since I am a nonnative Spanish speaker, I took extra steps to safeguard against the possibility that language bias obscured critical aspects of people's experiences. I also wanted to ensure variation in the language of interviewees. For this purpose, Malena Jean Lamas, a trained research assistant, conducted twenty of the interviews. Malena, a bilingual Dominican woman of Haitian descent, conducted all interviews completed in Haitian Creole. Having Malena conduct a set of

Photo B.1. The author with Malena Jean Lamas, the research assistant who supported data collection for this book

Source: Trenita Childers

interviews also helped to provide a reference point for addressing how my own positioning as an American might have affected the interview process. Malena also shared her insights with me and gave me a tour of her own community as a point of comparison for other *bateyes* I had visited.

Appendix C includes English and Spanish versions of the interview guide for this research. It is important to note that aspects of data collection incorporated three languages: Spanish, Haitian Creole, and English. I prioritized eliciting responses from people in their preferred language, but it is possible that subtleties got lost in translation. To mitigate this possibility, I discussed my interpretations with a local organization and also with participants in La Tierra. This approach triangulated findings and validated interpretations among community members.

Fifty-five people engaged in in-depth conversations about life in the *batey* and in the Dominican Republic. In-depth interviews lasted one hour on average and were completed in the language preferred by the participant (Spanish or Haitian Creole).

During each in-depth interview, I recorded depression and anxiety symptoms using items from three sources: culturally adapted Haitian Creole and Spanish versions of both the Beck Depression Inventory (BDI) and the Beck Anxiety Inventory (BAI), as well as the Zanmi Lasante Depression Symptom Inventory (ZLDSI), which was locally developed and validated in Haiti.[2] Questions about mental health symptoms provided additional information about how people experience policies that affect their day-to-day lives.

In addition to in-depth interviews and participant observation, I completed a community census during which I counted all households in the *batey* and collected basic demographic information. In March, after being in the field for seven months, I walked around the *batey* with youth in the community counting and spatially locating houses to produce a map of the *batey*.[3] During the door-to-door census-data collection, we asked how many individuals lived in the house; how many men, women, and children; and how many were born in Haiti versus the Dominican Republic. Since some houses were divided to include multiple families, we also asked whether housing was shared. Producing the map revealed the connections between housing and Haitian ethnicity. For example, Dominicans in the community lived mostly near one another toward the entrance of the *batey*. As you walk toward the back of the *batey*, closer to the sugarcane fields, families are primarily Haitian.

All forms of data collection—participant observation, in-depth interviews with local key informants and *batey* residents, the depression-and-anxiety scale, and the community census—inform the conclusions drawn in this book. The richness of the data gathered for this project creates a comprehensive picture of the lived experiences of people of Haitian descent in a Dominican *batey*.

Data Analysis

All interviews were audio recorded and transcribed. Interviews conducted in Spanish were transcribed in Spanish. Interviews conducted in Haitian Creole were translated from Haitian Creole to Spanish with the assistance of the bilingual research assistant who helped conduct interviews. For analyses, I used an inductive, grounded-theory approach, which is a systematic methodology that allows key themes to emerge from respondents. I entered ethnographic field notes and interview transcripts into NVivo 10 software to facilitate analysis.

Data analysis proceeded along several stages.[4] Analysis began with transcripts at the within-case level. Beginning intracase allows the analyst to develop a comprehensive understanding of the individuals' experiences. Once the within-case analysis was complete, analysis proceeded to a between-case examination comparing different experiences. Similarities between the within-case analysis and the between-case analysis provide greater evidence for the findings from the within-case examination. The final phase of analysis involved cross-group comparisons examining similarities and differences between Dominicans, Haitian immigrants, and Dominicans of Haitian descent.

To categorize data, I developed an "open-coding" schema focusing on structural racism and immigration policy to incorporate themes that respondents indicate are important but cannot be derived from extant research. The second coding phase involved "axial coding," which is the process of relating categories and concepts to one another. This phase allows the researcher to discern key relationships between variables. The final phase involves "selective coding," during which the researcher decides on a main "storyline" of the analysis.

The reliability and validity of the data collected for this study were based on best-practice criteria established as appropriate for ethnographic data. Recorded interviews were checked against interview protocols to ensure continuity between subjects and interview techniques. The use of multiple data-collection methods and my long-term engagement at the research site also strengthen validity, and member checking (or the process of testing interpretations and conclusions with participants) likewise contributes to validity. To ensure that accounts are rich, robust, and comprehensive, I triangulated findings with other data sources, including existing survey data and other research on the population under study. The long-term engagement of ethnographic researchers allows for a continual reflexive process during which theories are tested against emergent data and revised. Further, this engagement allowed me to check my assumptions against those of respondents to ensure a comprehensive and shared understanding of the social world under study.

Community-engaged research must do more than collect data to advance science. Researchers must also offer something back to the communities from which they learn. Before leaving the Dominican Republic, I shared preliminary findings from this research with three different audiences: a health clinic, an international-development agency, and La Tierra—the *batey* community where I collected data for this book. Each of these presentations provided the opportunity to solicit feedback from research participants and organizations that serve *batey* communities.

Notes

[1] *"Gringa"* is a term used primarily for white Americans.

[2] I vetted items measuring depression and anxiety with local mental-health professionals, a partner health-research organization, and *batey* residents prior to conducting interviews.

[3] To protect the field site's anonymity, the community map is not included in this book.

[4] Following Burton's process of "structured discovery" (Burton et al., "Critical Race Theories," and Burton et al., "The Role of Trust in Low-Income Mothers' Intimate Unions," *Journal of Marriage and Family* 71, no. 5 [2009]: 1107–24).

Interview Guide

English

Name: _____ Date: _____

Age: _____

Sex: M / F

Nationality: Dominican / Haitian / Dominican of Haitian descent

Years in Dominican Republic: _____

Religion: Catholic / Christian / Evangelical / none

Language: Spanish / Haitian Creole / other _____

Highest education level: _____

Color: white / *indio* / *moreno* / Black / other _____

Documentation: *cédula* / passport / *ficha* / birth certificate / none

Number of children: _____

Ages: _____

Do they live with you? yes / no

Housing type: house / barracks / shared house / room in a house

Bathroom: toilet / latrine (Shared? yes / no) / no bathroom

Number of people in your home: _____

Time living in your home: _____

General Questions

Could you describe a typical day for you?

Tell me about the last time you had a really good day. What happened?

Tell me about the last time you had a really bad day. What happened?

Family

Tell me about your family.

Probe: Who are your parents? Where do they live? Do you have children?

Where were your parents born? (If born in Haiti) When did they move to the Dominican Republic? Why did they move?

Where were you born? (If born in Haiti) When did you move to the Dominican Republic? Why did you move?

How would you compare your life here to your life in Haiti?

Do you have family in Haiti? Do you still communicate with them? If so, how?

Have you always lived in La Tierra?

Labor Market

What do you do to earn money for yourself or your household?

What are your job duties? If you have a small business, what do you make or sell?

Probe: (If employed) How did you find your job? (If a student) What would you like to do after you graduate?

What is your work schedule?

Probe: (If unemployed) What kind of employment have you had in the past?

Documentation

Recently there has been a lot in the news about documentation. What do you think about it?

Have you had problems with documentation?

Probe: What kinds of problems? What have you tried to do to resolve the problems?

How does the situation with documentation make you feel?

How does it make you feel to have/not have a *cédula*?

Do you know people who have had problems with documentation? What kinds of problems have they had? What do they do to resolve their problems?

Do you know anyone, an organization or person, who is helping people with documentation problems?

Identity, Color, Racism

Do you believe that life is different for white and Black people? Can you describe an example?

Probe: Is it different for you? For others?

Probe: Is it different at work? In school? Within families?

Do you believe that being Dominican/Haitian is an important part of how you see yourself?

Probe: Why or why not?

Do you feel connected to Haiti? Do you feel connected to other people of Haitian descent?

Probe: What makes you feel connected/disconnected?

Some people say that the Dominican Republic is a racist country. What do you think?

Discrimination[1]

I have a list of experiences that some people have. Tell me if you have ever had these experiences as I read each one.

1. Sometimes people treat you with less courtesy or respect than others.

   What do you think was the main reason for that experience?

2. People act like they think you are not intelligent.

   What do you think was the main reason for that experience?

3. Have you ever been unfairly fired from a job?

   What do you think was the main reason for that experience?

4. Have you ever been humiliated in front of others? At work? At school? Can you describe an example?

   What do you think was the main reason for that experience?

5. Have you ever heard an offensive joke or insult? Can you describe an example?

Mental Health and Coping[2]

I have a list of problems that people might have. After I read each one, please tell me how much the problem has bothered you in the past seven days, including today.

0 = never, 1 = a little, 2 = sometimes, 3 = often, 4 = very frequently

faintness or dizziness	0 1 2 3 4
chest pains	0 1 2 3 4
nausea or upset stomach	0 1 2 3 4
trouble breathing because of nerves	0 1 2 3 4
loss of feeling in parts of your body	0 1 2 3 4
loss of appetite	0 1 2 3 4
feeling lonely	0 1 2 3 4
feeling sad	0 1 2 3 4
feeling hopeless about the future	0 1 2 3 4
feeling like nothing matters	0 1 2 3 4
feeling restless or worried	0 1 2 3 4
trouble sleeping	0 1 2 3 4
feeling tense or weighed down	0 1 2 3 4
feeling nervous when left alone	0 1 2 3 4
feeling like you are under pressure	0 1 2 3 4

What do you do when you feel sad or worried?

Can you share an example of when that helped you?

Closing

We have discussed several topics. Is there anything else you would like to share? Is there anything I didn't ask that you would like to discuss?

Español

Nombre: _____   Fecha: _____

Edad: _____

Sexo: M / F

Nacionalidad: dominicana(o) / haitiana(o) / dominicana(o) de ascendencia haitiana

Años en RD: _____

Religión: católico / cristiano / evangélico

Idiomas: español / kreyòl / otro

Curso más alto de escuela: _____

Color: blanca(o) / india(o) / morena(o) / negra(o) / otra _____

Documentación: cédula/ pasaporte / ficha / carnet / acta de nacimiento / ninguna

Número de hijos: _____

Edades: _____

¿Viven con Ud.? sí / no

Tipo de casa: casa / apartamento / pieza un cuarto / habitación

Baño: inodoro / letrina (¿Compartido? sí / no) / no tiene

Número de personas en su hogar: _____

Tiempo viviendo en este hogar: _____

Preguntas Generales

¿Me puedes describir un día típico o normal para ti?

¿La última vez que tuviste un día muy bueno, qué pasó?

¿La última vez que tuviste un día muy mal, qué pasó?

La Familia

Háblame de tu familia.

Sonda: ¿Quiénes son tus padres? ¿Dónde viven? ¿Tienes hijos?

¿Dónde nacieron tus padres?

(Si nacieron en Haití) ¿Cuándo se mudaron a la República Dominicana? ¿Por qué se mudaron?

¿Nació usted aquí?

(Si nació en Haití) ¿Cuándo te mudaste a la República Dominicana? ¿Por qué te mudaste? ¿Cómo compararía su vida aquí a su vida en Haití?

¿Tiene familia en Haití? ¿Todavía se comunica con ellos? ¿Cómo?

¿Siempre ha vivido en La Tierra?

Mercado Laboral

¿Qué haces para ganar fondos para ti mismo o para tu hogar?

¿Cuáles son sus deberes en este trabajo? (Si es comerciante) ¿Qué haces?

Sonda: (Si trabaja) ¿Cómo te enteraste de este trabajo? (Si es estudiante) ¿Qué quieres hacer después de graduarse?

¿Qué es tu horario de trabajar?

(Si está desempleado) ¿Qué tipo de trabajo has tenido en el pasado?

Documentación

Hoy en día, hay muchas noticias de documentación. ¿Qué es tu opinión de lo que está pasando?

¿Has tenido problemas con la documentación?

Sonda: ¿Qué tipo de problemas? ¿Qué has tratado de hacer para resolver el problema?

¿Qué tipo de sentimientos le provoca su situación de documentación?

¿Como te sientes a tener/no tener su cédula cédula/documentos?

¿Usted conoce a otros que han tenido problemas con la documentación?

Sonda: ¿Qué tipo de problemas? ¿Qué hizo para resolver el problema?

¿Conoce a alguien, institución o promotor, que está ayudando a las personas que tienen problemas?

Identidad/Color/Racismo

¿Crees que la vida es diferente para los negros y los blancos? ¿Me puedes describir un ejemplo?

Sonda: ¿Para ti? ¿Para otras personas?

Sonda: ¿En el trabajo? ¿En la escuela? ¿En la familia?

¿Crees que ser dominicano/haitiano es una parte importante de cómo te ves a ti mismo? ¿Por qué/por qué no?

¿Te sientes conectado/a a Haití? ¿Te sientes conectado/a a otras personas de ascendencia haitiana?

¿Te sientes conectado/a a la RD?

Sonda: ¿Qué te hace sentir conectado/a?

Hay algunos que dicen que el estado dominicano es racista. ¿Qué es tu opinión?

Discriminación

Tengo una lista de algunas experiencias que algunas personas tienen. Dime si alguna vez has tenido la experiencia al leer cada uno.

1. A veces la gente te trata con menos cortesía o respeto que los demás.

   ¿Cuál crees que fue la razón principal de esta experiencia?
   Sonda: Su linaje u origen nacional, su género, su raza, su edad, su religión, su altura, su peso, algún otro aspecto de su apariencia física; su orientación sexual, su educación o el dinero/cuarto que tienes

2. Las personas actúan como si ellos piensan que no soy inteligente.

   ¿Cuál crees que fue la razón principal de esta experiencia?
   Sonda: Su linaje u origen nacional, su género, su raza, su edad, su religión, su altura, su peso, algún otro aspecto de su apariencia física; su orientación sexual, su educación o el dinero/cuarto que tienes

3. ¿En cualquier momento en tu vida, has sido despedido de empleo injustamente?

   ¿Cuál crees que fue la razón principal de esta experiencia?
   Sonda: Su linaje u origen nacional, su género, su raza, su edad, su religión, su altura, su peso, algún otro aspecto de su apariencia física; su orientación sexual, su educación o el dinero/cuarto que tienes

4. ¿Alguna vez has sido humillada/o delante de los demás en el trabajo/ escuela? ¿Me puedes describir un ejemplo?

   ¿Cuál crees que fue la razón principal de esta experiencia?
   Sonda: Su linaje u origen nacional, su género, su raza, su edad, su religión, su altura, su peso, algún otro aspecto de su apariencia física; su orientación sexual, su educación o el dinero/cuarto que tienes

5. ¿Alguna vez has oído insultos o bromas que te ofenda? ¿Me puedes describir un ejemplo?

   ¿Cuál crees que fue la razón principal de esta experiencia?
   Sonda: Su linaje u origen nacional, su género, su raza, su edad, su religión, su altura, su peso, algún otro aspecto de su apariencia física; su orientación sexual, su educación o el dinero/cuarto que tienes

Salud Mental y Afrontamiento

Aquí tengo una lista de los problemas que la gente podría tener. Al leer cada uno a usted, dime cuánto te ha molestado el problema en los últimos siete días, incluyendo hoy.

0 = no, ni un poco, 1 = un poco, 2 = de vez en cuando, 3 = mucho 4, = muchísimo

¿Durante los últimos siete días, cuánto has molestado:

el desmayo o el mareo	0 1 2 3 4
el dolor en el corazón o en el pecho	0 1 2 3 4
la náusea o el malestar de estómago	0 1 2 3 4
problemas para respirar debido a los nervios	0 1 2 3 4
pérdida de sensibilidad en partes de su cuerpo	0 1 2 3 4
pérdida de apetito	0 1 2 3 4
sentirse sola/o	0 1 2 3 4
sentirse triste	0 1 2 3 4
sintiéndose desesperado por el futuro	0 1 2 3 4
sentirse como nada importa	0 1 2 3 4
sentirse inquieta/o preocupada/o	0 1 2 3 4
problemas para dormir	0 1 2 3 4
sentirse tensa/o o sobrecargada/o	0 1 2 3 4
sentirse nerviosa/o cuando se deja sola/o	0 1 2 3 4
sentir que estás bajo presión	0 1 2 3 4

¿Qué haces cuando te sientes triste/pensativo/inquieto?

¿Puede compartir un ejemplo de cuándo eso le ayudó?

Terminando/Finalizando

Hemos hablado de muchos temas. ¿Hay algo más que te gustaría compartir? ¿Hay algo que no te haya pedido que quieras discutir?

Notes

1 Discrimination questions adapted from the Everyday Discrimination Scale (EDS). See Nancy Krieger et al., "Experiences of Discrimination: Validity and Reliability of a Self-Report Measure for Population Health Research on Racism and Health," *Social Science & Medicine* 61, no. 7 (2005): 1576–96; David R. Williams, Hector M. González, Stacey Williams, Selina A. Mohammed, Hashim Moomal, and Dan J. Stein, "Perceived Discrimination, Race and Health in South Africa: Findings from the South Africa Stress and Health Study," *Social Science and Medicine* 67, no. 3 (2008): 441–52 (text available online at https://scholar.harvard.edu/files/davidrwilliams/files/2008-perceived_discrimination_race-williams.pdf); and Michelle J. Sternthal, Natalie Slopen, and David R. Williams, "Racial Disparities in Health," *Du Bois Review: Social Science Research on Race* 8, no. 1 (2011): 95–113 (text available online at https://www.ncbi.nlm.nih.gov/pmc/articles/PMC5993442/).

2 Mental-health questions adapted from the Beck Depression Inventory (BDI), the Beck Anxiety Inventory (BAI), and the Zanmi Lasante Depression Symptom Inventory (ZLDSI).

Key Terms

acta de nacimiento: birth certificate

alcalde: mayor, community leader

anba fil: under the wire; refers to the process of entering the Dominican Republic without valid documentation

anti-Haitian racism: systemic discrimination against people of Haitian descent, designed to maintain hierarchical systems that impede people of Haitian descent from political, economic, and social participation in the Dominican Republic

batey (s), *bateyes* (pl): a company town or sugar mill plantation

bilateral agreement: an agreement between two countries

birthright citizenship: the status of becoming a citizen by virtue of being born in a given territory, as opposed to the acquisition of citizenship via other means, such as a naturalization processes for immigrants

blanqueamiento: whitening

Book of Foreigners: a registry created in 2007 by the Dominican Republic's Central Electoral Board for people born in the Dominican Republic who cannot document their parents' legality; registration restricts access to sociopolitical participation for native-born persons

capataz de corte: supervisor of cane cutting

cédula, cédula de identidad: Dominican identification card

Central Electoral Board (CEB): the Dominican civil-registry office that provides documentation services

certificado de nacido vivo: certificate of live birth

chiripero: a person who performs odd jobs to earn income

citizenship: the status of a person who is legally recognized as belonging to a nation; confers social, political, and civil rights, including the right to vote and access to social services

colmado: a convenience store; *colmados* are found across the Dominican Republic

colorism: a form of discrimination in which people are treated differently based on skin color (for example, people within the same racial group include people who are treated better or worse based on how light or dark their skin is); this can happen within or across racial groups (for example, people of Asian descent may privilege lighter skin, and whites may prefer to hire people of Asian descent with lighter skin)

Comisión Nacional de los Derechos Humanos: the National Human Rights Commission

critical race theory: an approach to studying race and racism that views race as a socially constructed concept; it emphasizes the intersections between race, law, and power

Dominican Constitutional Court: a judicial body established by the 2010 Dominican constitution that includes thirteen judges tasked with enforcing the Dominican constitution; their landmark decision in 2013 set legal precedent for denying Dominicans of Haitian descent their citizenship

ethnicity: shared culture, including language, ancestry, practices, and beliefs; for example, although they are both racially categorized as Black in the United States, Nigerian Americans and African Americans have different ethnicities

ficha: work identification card provided to Haitian agricultural laborers by Dominican sugar mills

General Law on Migration: a Dominican law established in 2004 classifying people without valid documentation as "in transit," thereby excluding their Dominican-born children from being eligible for birthright citizenship

guest-worker program: a bilateral migrant-labor program that supplies low-wage workers from sending countries to receiving countries

guagua: a public transportation bus

güira: a metallic Dominican percussion instrument played rhythmically with a stiff brush

La Tierra: the pseudonym for the *batey* where this research was completed

liminal legality: a theoretical framework that emphasizes the processes and systems by which government institutions create the gray areas of legality between what we call "documented" and "undocumented"; key facts of liminal legality include financial barriers, heightened monitoring, and vulnerability to private and public actors

luz: electricity

mayordomo: *batey* superintendent

morena/o: brown-skinned person; skin-color classification

nationality: the status of belonging to a particular nation, whether by birth or naturalization

National Regularization Plan for Foreigners with Irregular Migration Status (PNRE): a new framework created in the Dominican Republic in 2013 to regularize the status of migrants with unauthorized legal status residing in the Dominican Republic; the PNRE did not specify exactly how people would access this path to regularization, leaving them with a temporary and unstable legal status

Naturalization Law 169-14: a naturalization process created in 2014 for two groups born in the Dominican Republic; Group A, Dominican-born people whose citizenship was stripped, would have their Dominican citizenship restored, while Group B, Dominican-born people whose births were never registered, would be naturalized through a procedure requiring them to declare themselves Haitian nationals and register in the Book of Foreigners

picadores: cane cutters

race: physical differences that groups and cultures consider socially significant; for example, although they have different cultures, Nigerian Americans and African Americans would both be racially categorized as Black in the United States based on their physical appearance

racialized social system: a social hierarchy that perpetuates differential access to social and material resources based on race

racialization: a social process that confers racial identities and associated social and material resources based on the existing racial hierarchy in a given context; emphasizes the social construction of race and racism

racial profiling: targeting people as objects of suspicion and heightened scrutiny based on their race or ethnicity

Resolution 12: guidance issued in 2007 that instructed civil-registry officers to stop conferring Dominican identity documents to "children of foreign parents who had received birth certificates under irregular circumstances"; initiated the retroactive stripping of citizenship from Dominicans of Haitian descent

sans: small microlending business among women in Dominican communities

social construction: a sociological theory that people create the social realities we experience; this concept is evidenced by the ways that sociopolitical phenomena vary over time and across geographic contexts

stateless: a person who is not recognized by any nation as a citizen; they are denied social, political, and civil rights, including the right to vote and access to social services

structural racism: the complex systems that develop and maintain race-based hierarchies and inequality, resulting in differential access to opportunities and resources in government, education, and workplaces

yola: a small boat that transports passengers from the Dominican Republic to Puerto Rico

Bibliography

Agadjanian, Victor, Cecilia Menjívar, and Natalya Zotova. "Legality, Racialization, and Immigrants' Experience of Ethnoracial Harassment in Russia." *Social problems* 64, no. 4 (2017): 558–76.

AlMomento.net. "Una organización denuncia hay 'ataques racistas' contra haitianos en la RD." June 18, 2019. https://almomento.net/una-organizacion-denuncia-hay-ataques-racistas-contra-haitianos-en-la-rd/.

Alrabe, Khaled, Jamie Armstrong, B. Shaw Drake, Kimberly Fetsick, Elizabeth Gibson, Tabitha King, Young-Min Kwon, and Franziska Veh. "Left Behind: How Statelessness in the Dominican Republic Limits Children's Access to Education." Georgetown Law Human Rights Institute. March 2014. https://www.law.georgetown.edu/human-rights-institute/wp-content/uploads/sites/7/2018/03/left-behind.pdf.

Amnesty International. "Dominican Republic: Withdrawal from Top Regional Human Rights Court Would Put Rights at Risk." November 6, 2014. https://www.amnesty.org/en/latest/news/2014/11/dominican-republic-withdrawal-top-regional-human-rights-court-would-put-rights-risk/.

———. "No Nationality, No Rights: Stateless People in the Dominican Republic." May 9, 2016. https://www.amnesty.org/en/latest/campaigns/2016/05/stateless-people-in-the-dominican-republic/.

———. "'Without Papers, I Am No One': Stateless People in the Dominican Republic." 2015. https://www.amnestyusa.org/files/without-papers_stateless-people-dominican-republic.pdf.

Andreopoulos, George J., and Zehra F. Kabasakal Arat. *The Uses and Misuses of Human Rights: A Critical Approach to Advocacy.* New York: Palgrave Macmillan, 2014.

André, Richard. "The Dominican Republic and Haiti: A Shared View from the Diaspora." A conversation with Edwidge Danticat and Junot Díaz. In "Higher Education and Competitiveness." *Americas Quarterly* 8, no. 3 (2014): 28–35. https://www.americasquarterly.org/content/dominican-republic-and-haiti-shared-view-diaspora.

Andrews, George Reid. *Blackness in the White Nation: A History of Afro-Uruguay.* Chapel Hill: University of North Carolina Press, 2010.

Aranda, Elizabeth, and Elizabeth Vaquera. "Racism, the Immigration Enforcement Regime, and the Implications for Racial Inequality in the Lives of Undocumented Young Adults." *Sociology of Race and Ethnicity* 1, no. 1 (2015): 88–104. Available online at https://www.academia.edu/11015509/Racism_the_Immigration_Enforcement_Regime_and_the_Implications_for_Racial_Inequality_in_the_Lives_of_Undocumented_Young_Adults.

Armenta, Amada. "Racializing Crimmigration: Structural Racism, Colorblindness, and the Institutional Production of Immigrant Criminality." *Sociology of Race and Ethnicity* 3, no. 1 (2017): 82–95.

Asad, Asad L., and Matthew Clair. "Racialized Legal Status as a Social Determinant of Health." *Social Science and Medicine* 199 (2018): 19–28.

Asociación Scalabriniana al Servicio de la Movilidad Humana (ASCALA). "Living Conditions in the Dominican Bateyes." August 17, 2015. https://ascala2.wordpress.com/2015/08/17/living-conditions-in-the-dominican-bateyes/.

Associated Press. "Dominican Migrant: We Ate Flesh to Survive; A Small Group Turned to Cannibalism after Being Stranded in Mid-ocean." NBC News, November 4,

2008. http://www.nbcnews.com/id/27531105/ns/world_news-americas/t/dominican
-migrant-we-ate-flesh-survive/#.XeKOApNKipo.

———. "Dominicans Saved from Sea Tell of Attacks and Deaths of Thirst." *New York Times*, August 12, 2004. https://www.nytimes.com/2004/08/12/world/dominicans -saved-from-sea-tell-of-attacks-and-deaths-of-thirst.html.

Baluarte, David. "The Perpetuation of Childhood Statelessness in the Dominican Republic." *World's Stateless Children.* Institute on Statelessness and Inclusion. 2017. http:// children.worldsstateless.org/3/litigating-against-childhood-statelessness/the-perpet uation-of-childhood-statelessness-in-the-dominican-republic.html.

Baptiste, Nathalie, and Foreign Policy in Focus. "Terror, Repression and Diaspora: The Baby Doc Legacy in Haiti." *The Nation*, October 23, 2014. https://www.thenation .com/article/terror-repression-and-diaspora-baby-doc-legacy-haiti/.

Bashi, Vilna. "Globalized Anti-blackness: Transnationalizing Western Immigration Law, Policy, and Practice." *Ethnic and Racial Studies* 27, no. 4 (2004): 584–606.

———. *Survival of the Knitted: Immigrant Social Networks in a Stratified World.* Stanford, CA: Stanford University Press, 2007.

Bashi, Vilna, and Antonio McDaniel. "A Theory of Immigration and Racial Stratification." *Journal of Black Studies* 27, no. 5 (1997): 668–82.

Basok, Tanya, and Martha L. Rojas Wiesner. "Precarious Legality: Regularizing Central American Migrants in Mexico." *Ethnic and Racial Studies* 41, no. 7 (2018): 1274–93.

Beaman, Jean. *Citizen Outsider: Children of North African Immigrants in France.* Oakland: University of California Press, 2017.

Belton, Kristy A. "Rooted Displacement: The Paradox of Belonging among Stateless People." *Citizenship Studies* 19, no. 8 (2015): 907–21.

———. *Statelessness in the Caribbean: The Paradox of Belonging in a Postnational World.* Philadelphia: University of Pennsylvania Press, 2017.

Bernier, Barbara L. "Sugar Cane Slavery: Bateyes in the Dominican Republic." *New England Journal of International and Comparative Law* 9 (2003): 17.

Blake, Jillian. "Haiti, the Dominican Republic, and Race-Based Statelessness in the Americas." *Georgetown Journal of Law and Modern Critical Race Perspectives* 6 (2014): 139.

Bloemraad, Irene. "Being American/Becoming American: Birthright Citizenship and Immigrants' Membership in the United States." Special issue, *Who Belongs? Immigration, Citizenship, and the Constitution of Legality* 60 (2013): 55–84. Text available online at https://sociology.berkeley.edu/sites/default/files/faculty/bloemraad/ Bloemraad_Being_Becoming_American_2013.pdf.

Bloemraad, Irene, Anna Korteweg, and Gökçe Yurdakul. "Citizenship and Immigration: Multiculturalism, Assimilation, and Challenges to the Nation-State." *Annual Review of Sociology* 34 (2008): 153–79.

Bonacich, Edna, Sabrina Alimahomed, and Jake B. Wilson. "The Racialization of Global Labor." *American Behavioral Scientist* 52, no. 3 (2008): 342–55.

Bonilla-Silva, Eduardo. *Racism without Racists: Color-Blind Racism and the Persistence of Racial Inequality in the United States.* Lanham, MD: Rowman & Littlefield, 2006.

———. "Rethinking Racism: Toward a Structural Interpretation." *American Sociological Review* 62, no. 3 (1997): 465–80. Text available online at https://sph.umd .edu/sites/default/files/files/Bonilla-Silva%201996%20Rethinking%20Racism%20 Toward%20Structural%20Interpretation.pdf.

Boon-Kuo, Louise. "Visible Policing Subjects and Low Visibility Policing in Australia: Migration and Race in Australia." In *Race, Criminal Justice, and Migration Control:*

Enforcing the Boundaries of Belonging, edited by Mary Bosworth, Alpa Parmar, and Yolanda Vázquez, 93–107. Oxford: Oxford University Press, 2018.

Bosworth, Mary, Alpa Parmar, and Yolanda Vázquez, eds. *Race, Criminal Justice, and Migration Control: Enforcing the Boundaries of Belonging.* Oxford: Oxford University Press, 2018.

Bou, Irene Rial. *Di Perejil* [Say parsley]. Producciones Oya. Lanham, MD: National Film Network, 2006. DVD.

Bowling, Ben, and Sophie Westenra. "Racism, Immigration, and Policing." In *Race, Criminal Justice, and Migration Control: Enforcing the Boundaries of Belonging*, edited by Mary Bosworth, Alpa Parmar, and Yolanda Vázquez, 61–77. Oxford: Oxford University Press, 2018.

Brown, Hana E. "Race, Legality, and the Social Policy Consequences of Anti-immigration Mobilization." *American Sociological Review* 78, no. 2 (2013): 290–314. https://journals.sagepub.com/doi/10.1177/0003122413476712.

Burton, Linda M., Andrew Cherlin, Donna-Marie Winn, Angela Estacion, and Clara Holder-Taylor. "The Role of Trust in Low-Income Mothers' Intimate Unions." *Journal of Marriage and Family* 71, no. 5 (2009): 1107–24.

Burton, Linda M., Eduardo Bonilla-Silva, Victor Ray, Rose Buckelew, and Elizabeth Hordge Freeman. "Critical Race Theories, Colorism, and the Decade's Research on Families of Color." *Journal of Marriage and Family* 72, no. 3 (2010): 440–59. Text available online at http://cds.web.unc.edu/files/2013/01/Burton-Bonilla-Silva-Ray-Buckelew-Hordge-Freeman-Decade-Review1.pdf.

Caldwell, Kia Lilly. *Negras in Brazil: Re-envisioning Black Women, Citizenship, and the Politics of Identity.* New Brunswick, NJ: Rutgers University Press, 2007.

Camejo, Mary Jane, Amy Wilentz, National Coalition for Haitian Refugees, Americas Watch Committee, and Caribbean Rights, and Human Rights Watch. *Harvesting Oppression: Forced Haitian Labor in the Dominican Sugar Industry.* Edited by Kenneth Roth and Anne Fuller. New York: Americas Watch, The National Coalition for Haitian Refugees, Caribbean Rights, 1990. https://www.hrw.org/reports//pdfs/d/domnrep/domrep.906/domrep906full.pdf.

Candelario, Ginetta E. B. *Black Behind the Ears: Dominican Racial Identity from Museums to Beauty Shops.* Durham, NC: Duke University Press, 2007.

Caribbean Community (CARICOM). "Crisis Related to Dominicans of Haitian Descent and Haitian Migrants in the Dominican Republic." October 13, 2015. https://caricom.org/dominicans-of-haitian-descent-and-haitian-migrants-in-the-dominican-republi.

Cebulko, Kara. "Documented, Undocumented, and Liminally Legal: Legal Status during the Transition to Adulthood for 1.5–Generation Brazilian Immigrants." *The Sociological Quarterly* 55, no. 1 (2014): 143–67.

Celucien, L. Joseph, Jean Eddy Saint Paul, and Glodel Mezilas, eds. *Between Two Worlds: Jean Price-Mars, Haiti, and Africa.* Lanham, MD: Rowman & Littlefield, 2018.

Central Romana Corporation, Consorcio Azucarero Central, and Consorcio Azucararo de Empresas Industriales. "Labor Conditions in the Dominican Sugar Industry: Moving Progress Forward." April 2016. https://static1.squarespace.com/static/57f5349f03596e786d9ae6f4/t/58a037263e00be6bfe5e5458/1486894889614/DSI+Update+2+04+16.pdf.

Chacón, Jennifer M. "Producing Liminal Legality." *Denver University Law Review* 92, no. 4 (2014): 709–67. Text available online at https://poseidon01.ssrn.com/delivery.php?ID=541021002118115123084101087022092089109025032011016032119084097076096096025066083106001060102005041111018116099067085083127112042034007076000096064094084115004027030084017057103116

15101099120000608406408208911502500301609507202609601002 50 72003083116094&EXT=pdf.

Charles, Jacqueline. "U.S. Expresses 'Deep Concern' over Dominican Court Citizenship Ruling." *Miami Herald*, December 18, 2013. https://www.miamiherald.com/news/ nation-world/world/americas/haiti/article1958632.html.

———. "Thousands March in Haiti over Dominican Racism." *Miami Herald*, February 25, 2015. https://www.miamiherald.com/news/nation-world/world/americas/haiti/ article11180039.html.

Chavez, Leo Ralph. *The Latino Threat: Constructing Immigrants, Citizens, and the Nation*. 2nd ed. Stanford, CA: Stanford University Press, 2013.

Chen, Edith Wen-Chu. "'You Are Like Us, You Eat Plátanos': Chinese Dominicans, Race, Ethnicity, and Identity." *Afro-Hispanic Review* 27, no. 1 (2008): 23–40.

Chetty, Raj G. "The Tragicomedy of Anticolonial Overcoming: Toussaint Louverture and the Black Jacobins on Stage." *Callaloo* 37, no. 1 (2014): 69–88.

Christian, Michelle. "A Global Critical Race and Racism Framework: Racial Entanglements and Deep and Malleable Whiteness." *Sociology of Race and Ethnicity* 5, no. 2 (2019): 169–85.

Cobas, José A., Jorge Duany, and Joe R. Feagin. *How the United States Racializes Latinos: White Hegemony and Its Consequences*. New York: Routledge, 2009.

Comunicaciones Aliadas. "República Dominicana: Mujeres afrodescendientes reclaman respeto a su identidad." September 8, 2016. https://www.comunicacionesaliadas.com/ republica-dominicana-mujeres-afrodescendientes-reclaman-respeto-a-su-identidad/.

Consejo Estatal del Azúcar de la República Dominicana. "Historia del Consejo Estatal del Azúcar (CEA)." Accessed February 3, 2020. http://www.cea.gob.do/index.php/ sobre-nosotros/historia.

Crenshaw, Kimberlé, Neil Gotanda, Gary Peller, and Kendall Thomas. *Critical Race Theory: The Key Writings that Formed the Movement*. New York: New Press, 1995.

Curnutte, Mark. "Labor Dept. Finds Bitterness in Sugar Workers' Lives." *Cincinnati Enquirer*, published at *USA Today*, October 3, 2013. https://www.usatoday.com/ story/news/nation/2013/10/03/sugar-workers-human-labor-rights/2919687/.

Day, Iyko. *Alien Capital: Asian Racialization and the Logic of Settler Colonial Capitalism*. Durham, NC: Duke University Press, 2016.

Davidson, Christina Cecelia. "Disruptive Silences: The AME Church and Dominican-Haitian Relations." *Journal of Africana Religions* 5, no. 1 (2017): 1–25.

DeChalus, Camila. "PhD Student Faces Deportation to Liberia, Where She Has Never Lived." *Roll Call*. March 18, 2019. https://www.rollcall.com/news/facing-depor tation-to-liberia-where-she-has-never-lived?fbclid=IwAR1OZjrjVCJP2I2W8RP 582gThvvoAM2hfT0wUVvILICXNWkOD9hO1VSFCXk.

De Genova, Nicholas. *Working the Boundaries: Race, Space, and "Illegality" in Mexican Chicago*. Durham, NC: Duke University Press, 2005.

de la Fuente, Alejandro, and George Reid Andrews. *Afro-Latin American Studies: An Introduction*. Cambridge: Cambridge University Press, 2018.

Derby, Lauren Hutchinson. *The Dictator's Seduction: Politics and the Popular Imagination in the Era of Trujillo*. Durham, NC: Duke University Press, 2009.

Derby, Robin L. H., and Richard Lee Turits. "Historias de Terror y los Terrores de la Historia: La Masacre Haitiana de 1937 en la República Dominicana." *Estudios Sociales* 26, no. 92 (1993): 65–76. Text available online at http://www.sscnet.ucla .edu/history/derby/derby_historiads_terror.pdf.

Dev, Atul. "India Is Testing the Bounds of Citizenship." *The Atlantic*, August 31, 2019. https://www.theatlantic.com/international/archive/2019/08/india-citizenship -assam-nrc/597208/.

Diario Libre. "Queman barrio haitiano." October 30, 2008. https://www.diariolibre .com/actualidad/queman-barrio-haitiano-CODL175412.

Dominican Today. "Dominican Republic Police Say Compatriots Lynched Haitian." February 12, 2015. https://dominicantoday.com/dr/local/2015/2/12/Dominican-Repub lic-police-say-compatriots-lynched-Haitian/.

Dominican Today. "Deadline for Foreigners to Seek Regularization Expired Sun." August 27, 2018. https://dominicantoday.com/dr/local/2018/08/27/deadline-for-foreigners -to-seek-regularization-expired-sun/.

Donnella, Leah. "Brexit: What's Race Got to Do with It?" NPR, *Code Switch*, June 25, 2016. https://www.npr.org/sections/codeswitch/2016/06/25/483362200/brexit -whats-race-got-to-do-with-it.

Downs, Kenya. "Haitian's Lynching Renews Protests against Dominican Citizenship Law." NPR, *Code Switch*. February 14, 2015. https://www.npr.org/sections/ codeswitch/2015/02/14/384344141/haitians-lynching-renews-protests-against-do minican-citizenship-law.

Dreby, Joanna. *Everyday Illegal: When Policies Undermine Immigrant Families.* Oakland: University of California Press, 2015.

Duany, Jorge. "Racializing Ethnicity in the Spanish-Speaking Caribbean: A Comparison of Haitians in the Dominican Republic and Dominicans in Puerto Rico." *Latin American Caribbean Ethnic Studies* 1, no. 2 (2006): 231–48.

Dulitzky, Ariel E. "A Region in Denial: Racial Discrimination and Racism in Latin America." In *Neither Enemies nor Friends: Latinos, Blacks, Afro-Latinos*, edited by Suzanne Oboler and Anani Dzidzienyo, 39–59. New York: Springer, 2005.

El Nacional. "Apresan jóvenes por quemar bandera haitiana." February 13, 2015. https://elnacional.com.do/apresan-jovenes-por/.

Espiritu, Yến Lê. *Asian American Women and Men: Labor, Laws, and Love.* 2nd ed. Lanham, MD: Rowman & Littlefield, 2008.

Evertsz, Franc Báez. *Braceros haitianos en la República Dominicana.* 2nd ed. Santo Domingo, DR: Instituto Dominicano de Investigaciones Sociales, 1986.

Farmer, Paul. "On Suffering and Structural Violence: A View from Below." *Daedalus* 125, no. 1 (1996): 251–83. Text available online at http://www2.kobe-u.ac.jp/ ~alexroni/IPDreadings%202017/IPD%202017_10/On%20suffering%20and%20 structural%20violence.pdf.

FitzGerald, David Scott, and David Cook-Martín. *Culling the Masses: The Democratic Origins of Racist Immigration Policy in the Americas.* Cambridge, MA: Harvard University Press, 2014.

Fletcher, Laurel, and Timothy Miller. "New Perspectives on Old Patterns: Forced Migration of Haitians in the Dominican Republic." *Journal of Ethnic and Migration Studies* 30, no. 4 (2004): 659–79. Text available online at https://www.academia.edu/2632059/ New_Perspectives_on_Old_Patterns_Forced_Migration_of_Haitians_in_the.

Flores, René D., and Ariela Schachter. "Examining Americans' Stereotypes about Immigrant Illegality." *Contexts* 18, no. 2 (2019): 36–41.

Food and Nutrition Security Platform. "Progressing with Solidarity." Accessed February 3, 2020. https://plataformacelac.org/en/programa/243.

Fondo de Población de las Naciones Unidas (UNFPA). "El acceso de inmigrantes y descendientes a la salud y la protección social en la República Dominicana:

Segunda Encuesta Nacional de Inmigrantes, ENI-2017." September 2018. https://dominicanrepublic.unfpa.org/sites/default/files/pub-pdf/El%20acceso%20de%20inmigrantes%20y%20descendientes%20a%20la%20salud%20y%20la%20proteccón%20social%20en%20la%20República%20Dominicana.pdf.

Fumagalli, Maria Cristina. *On the Edge: Writing the Border between Haiti and the Dominican Republic.* Liverpool: Liverpool University Press, 2015.

García, San Juanita. "Racializing 'Illegality': An Intersectional Approach to Understanding How Mexican-Origin Women Navigate an Anti-immigrant Climate." *Sociology of Race and Ethnicity* 3, no. 4 (2017): 474–90.

García-Peña, Lorgia. *The Borders of Dominicanidad: Race, Nation, and Archives of Contradiction.* Durham, NC: Duke University Press, 2016.

Gleeson, Shannon, and Roberto G. Gonzales. "When Do Papers Matter? An Institutional Analysis of Undocumented Life in the United States." *International Migration* 50, no. 4 (2012): 1–19. Text available online at https://digitalcommons.ilr.cornell.edu/cgi/viewcontent.cgi?article=2247&context=articles.

Glenn, Evelyn Nakano. *Unequal Freedom: How Race and Gender Shaped American Citizenship and Labor.* Cambridge, MA: Harvard University Press, 2009.

Global Health Data Exchange. "Dominican Republic Demographic and Health Survey 2013." Institute for Health Metrics and Evaluation. Last modified January 29, 2020. http://ghdx.healthdata.org/record/dominican-republic-demographic-and-health-survey-2013.

Golash-Boza, Tanya Maria. *Deported: Immigrant Policing, Disposable Labor, and Global Capitalism.* New York: New York University Press, 2015.

———. *Yo Soy Negro: Blackness in Peru.* Gainesville: University Press of Florida, 2012.

Golash-Boza, Tanya, and Pierrette Hondagneu-Sotelo. "Latino Immigrant Men and the Deportation Crisis: A Gendered Racial Removal Program." *Latino Studies* 11, no. 3 (2013): 271–92. Text available online at https://www.researchgate.net/publication/263325706_Latino_Immigrant_Men_and_the_Deportation_Crisis_A_Gendered_Racial_Removal_Program.

Goldberg, David Theo. *The Racial State.* Malden, MA: Blackwell Publishing, 2002.

González, Ivet. "Women of Haitian Descent Bear the Brunt of Dominican Migration Policy." Inter Press Service, February 5, 2016. http://www.ipsnews.net/2016/02/women-of-haitian-descent-bear-the-brunt-of-dominican-migration-policy/.

Gonzales, Roberto G. *Lives in Limbo: Undocumented and Coming of Age in America.* Oakland: University of California Press, 2016.

Grasmuck, Sherri, and Rosario Espinal. "Market Success or Female Autonomy? Income, Ideology, and Empowerment among Microentrepreneurs in the Dominican Republic." *Gender and Society* 14, no. 2 (2000): 231–55.

Guardian. "Dominican Republic Extends Residency Deadline ahead of Mass Deportation." June 17, 2015. https://www.theguardian.com/world/2015/jun/17/dominican-republic-deadline-residency-haiti.

Guzmán, Elena. "Checkpoint Nation: In the Dominican Republic, Haitian Descendants Face Profiling and Scrutiny Deep within the Country's Borders." North American Congress on Latin America (NACLA). March 22, 2019. https://nacla.org/news/2019/03/22/checkpoint-nation.

Haney-López, Ian F. *White by Law: The Legal Construction of Race.* New York: New York University Press, 1997.

Haney, William M., Peter Rhodes, Eric Grunebaum, Christopher Hartley, and Paul Newman. *The Price of Sugar.* Waltham, MA: Uncommon Productions, 2007. DVD.

Hernández, Tanya Katerí. *Racial Subordination in Latin America: The Role of the State, Customary Law, and the New Civil Rights Response.* Cambridge: Cambridge University Press, 2013.

Herrera, Juan. "Racialized Illegality: The Regulation of Informal Labor and Space." *Latino Studies* 14, no. 3 (2016): 320–43.

Hintzen, Amelia. "'A Veil of Legality': The Contested History of Anti-Haitian Ideology under the Trujillo Dictatorship." *New West Indian Guide/Nieuwe West-Indische Gids* 90, nos. 1–2 (2016): 28–54. Text available online at https://brill.com/view/journals/nwig/90/1-2/article-p28_2.xml?language=en.

Hordge-Freeman, Elizabeth. "'Bringing Your Whole Self to Research': The Power of the Researcher's Body, Emotions, and Identities in Ethnography." *International Journal of Qualitative Methods* 17, no. 1 (2018): 1609406918808862.

———. *The Color of Love: Racial Features, Stigma, and Socialization in Black Brazilian Families.* Austin: University of Texas Press, 2015.

Howard, David. *Coloring the Nation: Race and Ethnicity in the Dominican Republic.* Oxford: Signal Books, 2001.

Human Rights Watch. "'Illegal People': Haitians and Dominico-Haitians in the Dominican Republic." April 2002, 14, no. 1 (b). https://www.hrw.org/reports/pdfs/d/domnrep/domrep0402.pdf.

Hunter, Margaret. "The Persistent Problem of Colorism: Skin Tone, Status, and Inequality." *Sociology Compass* 1, no. 1 (2007): 237–54.

Institute on Statelessness and Inclusion. "The World's Stateless Children." January 2017. https://files.institutesi.org/worldsstateless17.pdf.

Instituto Azucarero Dominicano (Inazucar). "Central Romana Corporation." 2017. https://www.inazucar.gov.do/index.php/ingenios/central-romana.

———. *Informe Zafra Azucarera, 2017/2018.* Santo Domingo, DR: Inazucar, 2018. http://www.inazucar.gov.do/files/informes-zafra/2017-2018/INFORME_FINAL_DE_ZAFRA_2017-2018_-.pdf.

Inter-American Commission on Human Rights (IACHR). "IACHR Welcomes Willingness of Dominican Republic to Comply with Recommendations." Press release. Organization of American States (website). June 29, 2017. https://www.oas.org/en/iachr/media_center/PReleases/2017/087.asp.

———. Report No. 68/05. October 13, 2005. Organization of American States (website). http://cidh.org/annualrep/2005eng/DominicanRep.12271eng.htm.

International Justice Resource Center. "In the Case of Dominican and Haitian People Expelled v. the Dominican Republic, IACTHR Finds Multitude of Human Rights Violations." October 28, 2014. https://ijrcenter.org/2014/10/28/in-the-case-of-dominican-and-haitian-people-expelled-v-the-dominican-republic-iacthr-finds-multitude-of-human-rights-violations/.

Jimenez, Manuel. "Dominican Government Gives Details of Naturalization Plan for 'Foreigners.'" Reuters, November 30, 2013. http://www.reuters.com/article/2013/12/01/us-dominicanrepublic-citizenship-idUSBRE9B000O20131201.

Joseph, Celucien L., Jean Eddy Saint Paul, and Glodel Mézilas, eds. *Between Two Worlds: Jean Price-Mars, Haiti, and Africa.* Lanham, MD: Lexington Books, 2018.

Jung, Moon-Ho. *Coolies and Cane: Race, Labor, and Sugar in the Age of Emancipation.* Baltimore, MD: Johns Hopkins University Press, 2009.

Kaiser, Bonnie N., Hunter M. Keys, Jennifer Foster, and Brandon A. Kohrt. "Social Stressors, Social Support, and Mental Health among Haitian Migrants in the Dominican Republic." *Revista Panamericana de Salud Pública* 38, no. 2 (2015): 157–62. Text available online at https://www.scielosp.org/article/rpsp/2015.v38n2/157-162/.

Kanaar, Michelle. "Dominican Republic: The Haitian Sugar Workers Denied Their Pensions." *Equal Times*, December 16, 2015. https://www.equaltimes.org/dominican -republic-the-haitian?lang=en#.XXeyKy5Kipo.

———. "Dominican System Snarls Pensions for Haitian Workers." *Miami Herald*, October 21, 2015. https://www.miamiherald.com/news/nation-world/world/americas/haiti/article40778388.html.

Kaplan, Marion A. *Dominican Haven: The Jewish Refugee Settlement in Sosúa, 1940– 1945*. New York: Museum of Jewish Heritage, 2008.

Kasinitz, Philip, John H. Mollenkopf, Mary C. Waters, and Jennifer Holdaway. *Inheriting the City: The Children of Immigrants Come of Age*. New York: Russell Sage Foundation, 2009.

Katz, Jonathan M. "The Dominican Time Bomb." *New York Times*, July 2, 2015. https://www.nytimes.com/2015/07/02/magazine/the-dominican-time-bomb.html.

Keys, Hunter M., Bonnie N. Kaiser, Jennifer W. Foster, Rosa Y. Burgos Minaya, and Brandon A. Kohrt. "Perceived Discrimination, Humiliation, and Mental Health: A Mixed-Methods Study among Haitian Migrants in the Dominican Republic." *Ethnicity and Health* 20, no. 3 (2015): 219–40.

Keys, Hunter M., Gregory S. Noland, Madsen Beau De Rochars, Thomas H. Taylor, Stephen Blount, and Manuel Gonzales. "Perceived Discrimination in *Bateyes* of the Dominican Republic: Results from the Everyday Discrimination Scale and Implications for Public Health Programs." *BMC Public Health* 19 (2019): 1513. https://bmcpublichealth.biomedcentral.com/articles/10.1186/s12889-019-7773-2.

Krieger, Nancy, Kevin Smith, Deepa Naishadham, Cathy Nelson Hartman, and Elizabeth M. Barbeau. "Experiences of Discrimination: Validity and Reliability of a Self-Report Measure for Population Health Research on Racism and Health." *Social Science & Medicine* 61, no. 7 (2005): 1576–96.

Lanham, David, and Amy Liu. "Not Just a Typographical Change: Why Brookings Is Capitalizing Black." Brookings Institution. September 23, 2019. https://www.brookings.edu/research/brookingscapitalizesblack/.

Lindskoog, Carl. *Detain and Punish: Haitian Refugees and the Rise of the World's Largest Immigration Detention System*. Gainesville: University Press of Florida, 2018.

López-Sanders, Laura. "Trapped at the Bottom: Racialized and Gendered Labor Queues in New Immigrant Destinations." UC San Diego Working Paper 176. March 2009. Text available online at https://escholarship.org/content/qt1r39d099/qt1r39d099.pdf.

Lozano, Wilfredo. "República Dominicana en la mira: Inmigración, exclusión social y despojo ciudadano." *Nueva Sociedad*, no. 251 (2014): 7–16. https://nuso.org/media/articles/downloads/4024_1.pdf.

Lozano, Wilfredo, and Bridget Wooding, eds. *Los retos del desarrollo insular: Desarrollo sostenible, migraciones y derechos humanos en las relaciones domínico-haitianas en el siglo XXI*. Santo Domingo, DR: FLACSO and CIES, 2008.

Lustig, Nora, Judith Morrison, and Adam Ratzlaff. "Splitting the Bill: Taxing and Spending to Close Ethnic and Racial Gaps in Latin America." Inter-American Development Bank. 2019. https://publications.iadb.org/publications/english/document/Splitting_the_Bill_Taxing_and_Spending_to_Close_Ethnic_and_Racial_Gaps_in_Latin_America.pdf.

Maldonado, Marta Maria. "'It Is Their Nature to Do Menial Labour': The Racialization of 'Latino/a Workers' by Agricultural Employers." In *Latino Identity in Contemporary America*, edited by Martin Bulmer and John Solomos, 101–20. New York: Routledge, 2014.

Mariner, Joanne. *Dominican Republic: "Illegal People"; Haitians and Dominico-Haitians in Dominican Republic.* New York: Human Rights Watch, 2002.

Marosi, Richard. "Hardship on Mexico's Farms, a Bounty for U.S. Tables." Photography and video by Don Bartletti. *Los Angeles Times*, December 7, 2014. https://graphics .latimes.com/product-of-mexico-camps/.

Martínez, Samuel. "From Commoditizing to Commodifying Human Rights: Research on Forced Labor in Dominican Sugar Production." *Humanity: An International Journal of Human Rights, Humanitarianism, and Development* 6, no. 3 (2015): 387–409.

———. "From Hidden Hand to Heavy Hand: Sugar, the State, and Migrant Labor in Haiti and the Dominican Republic." *Latin American Research Review* 34, no. 1 (1999): 57–84.

———. *Peripheral Migrants: Haitians and Dominican Republic Sugar Plantations.* Knoxville: University of Tennessee Press, 1995.

———. "The Price of Confrontation: International Retributive Justice and the Struggle for Haitian-Dominican Rights." In *The Uses and Misuses of Human Rights: A Critical Approach to Advocacy*, edited by George J. Andreopoulos and Zehra F. Kabasakal Arat, 89–115. New York: Palgrave Macmillan, 2014.

Martínez, Samuel, and Bridget Wooding. "El antihaitianismo en la República Dominicana: ¿Un giro biopolítico?" *Migración y Desarrollo* 15, no. 28 (2017): 95–123. Text available online at https://www.redalyc.org/pdf/660/66053147004.pdf.

Matibag, Eugenio D., and Teresa Downing-Matibag. "Sovereignty and Social Justice: The 'Haitian Problem' in the Dominican Republic." *Caribbean Quarterly* 57, no. 2 (2011): 92–117. Text available online at https://lib.dr.iastate.edu/cgi/view content.cgi?referer=https://www.google.com/&httpsredir=1&article=1089&con text=language_pubs.

Mayorga-Gallo, Sarah. *Behind the White Picket Fence: Power and Privilege in a Multiethnic Neighborhood.* Chapel Hill: University of North Carolina Press, 2014.

McIlwaine, Cathy. "Legal Latins: Creating Webs and Practices of Immigration Status among Latin American Migrants in London." *Journal of Ethnic and Migration Studies* 41, no. 3 (2015): 493–511.

McPherson, Alan. *The Invaded: How Latin Americans and Their Allies Fought and Ended U.S. Occupations.* New York: Oxford University Press, 2014.

Menjívar, Cecilia. "Liminal Legality: Salvadoran and Guatemalan Immigrants' Lives in the United States." *American Journal of Sociology* 111, no. 4 (2006): 999–1037. Text available online at https://www.researchgate.net/publication/249177038_Liminal_ Legality_Salvadoran_and_Guatemalan_Immigrants'_Lives_in_the_United_States.

Menjívar, Cecilia, and Leisy J. Abrego. "Legal Violence: Immigration Law and the Lives of Central American Immigrants." *American Journal of Sociology* 117, no. 5 (2012): 1380–1421. Text available online at https://kuscholarworks.ku.edu/bitstream/ handle/1808/21439/Menjivar_2012.pdf?sequence=1&isAllowed=y.

Mills, Charles W. *The Racial Contract.* Ithaca, NY: Cornell University Press, 2014.

Mintz, Sidney Wilfred. *Sweetness and Power: The Place of Sugar in Modern History.* New York: Penguin, 1986.

Mitchell-Walthour, Gladys L., and Elizabeth Hordge-Freeman. *Race and the Politics of Knowledge Production: Diaspora and Black Transnational Scholarship in the United States and Brazil.* New York: Palgrave Macmillan US, 2016.

Michener, Jamila. *Fragmented Democracy: Medicaid, Federalism, and Unequal Politics.* Cambridge: Cambridge University Press, 2018.

Morales, Maria Cristina. "The Ethnic Niche as an Economic Pathway for the Dark Skinned: Labor Market Incorporation of Latina/o Workers." *Hispanic Journal of Behavioral Sciences* 30, no. 3 (2008): 280–98.

Movimiento de Mujeres Domenico-Haitianas, Inc. (MUDHA). "La líder: Sonia Pierre." MUDHA (website). Accessed March 3, 2018. http://mudhaong.org/quienes-somos/la-lider-sonia-pierre/.

Moya Pons, Frank. *The Dominican Republic: A National History*. Princeton, NJ: Markus Wiener Publishers, 2010.

Ngai, Mae M. *Impossible Subjects: Illegal Aliens and the Making of Modern America*. Updated edition. Princeton, NJ: Princeton University Press, 2014.

Oficina Nacional de Estadísticas (ONE). *Segunda encuesta nacional de inmigrantes [ENI-2017]: Versión resumida del informe general*. Santo Domingo, DR: ONE, 2018. Text available online at https://www.refworld.org.es/pdfid/5b1ef7a54.pdf.

Olmos, Daniel. "Racialized Im/Migration and Autonomy of Migration Perspectives: New Directions and Opportunities." *Sociology Compass* 13, no. 9 (2019): e12729.

Omi, Michael, and Howard Winant. *Racial Formation in the United States*. London: Routledge, 2014.

Open Society Justice Initiative and the Center for Justice and International Law. "Submission to the Committee on the Elimination of Racial Discrimination: Review of the Dominican Republic." January 2013. https://tbinternet.ohchr.org/Treaties/CERD/Shared%20Documents/DOM/INT_CERD_NGO_DOM_13708_E.pdf.

Organisation for Economic Co-operation and Development (OECD). "The Dominican Republic's Migration Landscape." In *Interrelations between Public Policies, Migration and Development in the Dominican Republic*, 37–55. Paris: OECD Publishing, 2017. https://read.oecd-ilibrary.org/development/interrelations-between-public-policies-migration-and-development-in-the-dominican-republic/the-domini can-republic-s-migration-landscape_9789264276826-6-en#page1.

Ortega, Eddy Olivares. "La cédula y su caducidad." *Acento*, January 17, 2015. https://acento.com.do/2015/opinion/8213611-la-cedula-y-su-caducidad/.

Parmar, Alpa. "Policing Belonging: Race and Nation in the UK." In *Race, Criminal Justice, and Migration Control: Enforcing the Boundaries of Belonging*, edited by Mary Bosworth, Alpa Parmar, and Yolanda Vázquez, 108–24. Oxford: Oxford University Press, 2018.

Paschel, Tianna S. *Becoming Black Political Subjects: Movements and Ethno-racial Rights in Colombia and Brazil*. Princeton, NJ: Princeton University Press, 2016.

Peguero, Valentina. *Immigration and Politics in the Caribbean: Japanese and Other Immigrants in the Dominican Republic*. Translated by Linda Crawford. Coconut Creek, FL: Caribbean Studies Press, 2008.

Pesqueira, Diego, "Acusan 3 en caso mueren 24 haitianos perdieron la vida en tráfico ilegal." *Hoy*, January 12, 2006. https://hoy.com.do/acusan-3-en-caso-mueren -24-haitianos-perdieron-la-vida-en-trafico-ilegal-2/.

Petrozziello, Allison J. *Haitian Construction Workers in the Dominican Republic: An Exploratory Study on Indicators of Forced Labor*. Washington, DC: US Department of Labor, Bureau of International Labor Affairs, 2012. Text available online at https://digitalcommons.ilr.cornell.edu/cgi/viewcontent.cgi?article=2813&context =key_workplace.

Petrozziello, Allison J., Amelia Hintzen, and Juan Carlos González Díaz. *Género y el riesgo de apatridia para la población de ascendencia haitiana en los bateyes de la República Dominicana*. Santo Domingo, DR: OBMICA, 2014.

——. "(Re) Producing Statelessness Via Indirect Gender Discrimination: Descendants of Haitian Migrants in the Dominican Republic." *International Migration* 57, no. 1 (2019): 213–28.

Pierre, Jacques. *Omega*. Preface by Josaphat-Robert Large. Gainesville, FL: Classic Editions, 2012.

Quintana, Francisco. "Inter-American Court Condemns Unprecedented Situation of Statelessness in the Dominican Republic." European Network on Statelessness (website). October 27, 2014. https://www.statelessness.eu/blog/inter-american-court-condemns-unprecedented-situation-statelessness-dominican-republic.

Ray, Victor. "A Theory of Racialized Organizations." *American Sociological Review* 84, no. 1 (2019): 26–53.

República Dominicana. Decreto No. 327-13 de 2013, Plan nacional de regularización de extranjeros en situación migratoria irregular en la República Dominicana (National Regularization Plan for Foreigners with Irregular Migration Status). Presidential decree 327-13 of November 29, 2013. Dominican Republic. Text available online at http://www.scribd.com/doc/188044925/Decreto-327-13.

——. Ley No. 285 de 2004 sobre migración [Dominican Republic]. August 15, 2004. Text available online at https://www.refworld.org/docid/46d6e07c2.html.

Reyes, Maxwell. "Queman bandera haitiana en Santiago." *El Sol de Santiago*, February 11, 2015. https://elsoldesantiago.com/queman-bandera-haitiana-en-santiago/.

Rincón, Domingo, and Natalia Riveros. *Facilitando el acceso al registro civil dominicano a descendientes de parejas mixtas: Protocolo para su acompañamiento legal*. Santo Domingo, DR: Centro para la Observación Migratoria y el Desarrollo Social en el Caribe (OBMICA), 2018. http://obmica.org/images/Publicaciones/Libros/Protocolo-2018-FINAL.pdf.

Riveros, Natalia. *Estado de la cuestión de la población de los bateyes dominicanos en relación a la documentación*. Santo Domingo, DR: Observatorio Migrantes del Caribe, 2014.

Rohter, Larry. "Jose Pena Gomez, 61, Rare Black Dominican Figure, Dies." *New York Times*, May 12, 1998. https://www.nytimes.com/1998/05/12/world/jose-pena-gomez-61-rare-black-dominican-figure-dies.html and https://nacla.org/article/dominican-elections-loser-take-all.

Roediger, David R., and Elizabeth D. Esch. *The Production of Difference: Race and the Management of Labor in U.S. History*. New York: Oxford University Press, 2014.

Romero, Mary. "The Inclusion of Citizenship Status in Intersectionality: What Immigration Raids Tells Us about Mixed-Status Families, the State and Assimilation." *International Journal of Sociology of the Family* 34, no. 2 (2008): 131–52. Text available online at https://www.researchgate.net/publication/254147161_The_Inclusion_of_Citizenship_Status_in_Intersectionality_What_Immigration_Raids_Tells_Us_About_Mixed-Status_Families_the_State_and_Assimilation.

Rosario, Mariela. "Lynching of Haitian Man Highlights Tension in Dominican Republic." *Latina*, May 11, 2009. http://www.latina.com/lifestyle/news-politics/lynching-haitian-man-highlights-tension-dominican-republic.

Sáenz, Rogelio, and Karen Manges Douglas. "A Call for the Racialization of Immigration Studies: On the Transition of Ethnic Immigrants to Racialized Immigrants." *Sociology of Race and Ethnicity* 1, no. 1 (2015): 166–80.

Sagás, Ernesto. *Race and Politics in the Dominican Republic*. Gainesville: University Press of Florida, 2000.

Sagás, Ernesto, and Orlando Inoa. *The Dominican People: A Documentary History*. Princeton, NJ: Markus Wiener Publishers, 2003.

Scheiber, Noam. "Why Wendy's Is Facing Campus Protests (It's about the Tomatoes)." *New York Times*, March 7, 2019. https://www.nytimes.com/2019/03/07/business/economy/wendys-farm-workers-tomatoes.html.

Seamster, Louise, and Jessica Welburn. "How a Racist System Has Poisoned the Water in Flint, Mich." *The Root*, January 9, 2016. https://www.theroot.com/how-a-racist-system-has-poisoned-the-water-in-flint-mi-1790853824.

Simmons, David. "Structural Violence as Social Practice: Haitian Agricultural Workers, Anti-Haitianism, and Health in the Dominican Republic." *Human Organization* 69, no. 1 (2010): 10–18.

Simmons, Kimberly Eison. *Reconstructing Racial Identity and the African Past in the Dominican Republic*. Gainesville: University Press of Florida, 2009.

Soley, Ximena, and Silvia Steininger. "Parting Ways or Lashing Back? Withdrawals, Backlash and the Inter-American Court of Human Rights." Special issue 2, "Resistance to International Courts." *Journal of International Journal of Law in Context* 14 (2018): 237–57.

Sternthal, Michelle J., Natalie Slopen, and David R. Williams. "Racial Disparities in Health." *Du Bois Review: Social Science Research on Race* 8, no. 1 (2011): 95–113. Text available online at https://www.ncbi.nlm.nih.gov/pmc/articles/PMC5993442/.

Stinchcomb, Dawn F. *The Development of Literary Blackness in the Dominican Republic*. Gainesville: University Press of Florida, 2004.

Tavernier, LaToya A. "The Stigma of Blackness: Anti-Haitianism in the Dominican Republic." *Socialism and Democracy* 22, no. 3 (2008): 96–104.

Thornton, Brendan Jamal, and Diego I. Ubiera. "Caribbean Exceptions: The Problem of Race and Nation in Dominican Studies." *Latin American Research Review* 54, no. 2 (2019): 413–28. https://larrlasa.org/articles/10.25222/larr.346/.

Torres-Saillant, Silvio. "The Tribulations of Blackness: Stages in Dominican Racial Identity." *Latin American Perspectives* 25, no. 3 (1998): 126–46.

Trouillot, Michel-Rolph. *Silencing the Past: Power and the Production of History*. Boston: Beacon Press, 1995.

Turits, Richard Lee. "A World Destroyed, a Nation Imposed: The 1937 Haitian Massacre in the Dominican Republic." *Hispanic American Historical Review* 82, no. 3 (2002): 589–635.

Twine, France Winddance. *Racism in a Racial Democracy: The Maintenance of White Supremacy in Brazil*. New Brunswick, NJ: Rutgers University Press, 1998.

United Nations. "Human Rights." Accessed November 30, 2019. https://www.un.org/en/sections/issues-depth/human-rights/.

United Nations Committee on the Elimination of Racial Discrimination. "Consideration of Reports Submitted by States Parties Under Article 9 of the Convention: Concluding Observations of the Committee on the Elimination of Racial Discrimination: Dominican Republic." United Nations. May 16, 2008. Text available online at https://www.refworld.org/publisher,CERD,,DOM,4885cf9dd,0.html.

United Nations Department of Economic and Social Affairs (UNDESA). "International Migration Stock 2015." Database. United Nations. 2015. http://www.un.org/en/development/desa/population/migration/data/estimates2/estimates15.shtml.

[United Nations High Commissioner for Refugees (UNHCR)] Agencia de la ONU para los Refugiados (ACNUR). "Tendencias globales: Desplazamiento forzado en 2015; Forzados a huir" [Global trends: Forced displacement in 2015; Forced to flee]. United Nations High Comissioner for Refugees (UNHCR/ACNUR). http://www.acnur.org/fileadmin/scripts/doc.php?file=fileadmin/Documentos/Publicaciones/2016/10627.

United Nations High Commissioner for Refugees (UNHCR). "Dominican Republic Urged Not to Deport Stateless Dominicans." June 19, 2015. https://www.unhcr .org/en-us/news/latest/2015/6/5584221a6/dominican-republic-urged-deport-state less-dominicans.html.

Valenzuela, Miguelina, Cristina Rodríguez, and Carlos Despradel. *Un siglo de historia: Central Romana Corporation*. La Romana: Central Romana Corporation, Ltd., 2012. http://centralromana.com.do/Central_Romana_Un_Siglo_De_Historia/mobile/.

Verité. "Research on Indicators of Forced Labor in the Supply Chain of Sugar in the Dominican Republic." 2012. https://www.verite.org/wp-content/uploads/2016/11/ Research-on-Indicators-of-Forced-Labor-in-the-Dominican-Republic-Sugar-Sec tor_9.18.pdf.

Verma, SaunJuhi. "Seasoning Labor: Contemporary South Asian Migrations and the Racialization of Immigrant Workers." *Journal of Asian American Studies* 22, no. 1 (2019): 31–52.

Viruell-Fuentes, Edna A. "'It's a Lot of Work': Racialization Processes, Ethnic Identity Formations, and Their Health Implications." *Du Bois Review: Social Science Research on Race* 8, no. 1 (2011): 37–52.

Wade, Peter. *Race and Ethnicity in Latin America*. 2nd ed. London and New York: Pluto Press, 2010.

Waters, Mary C. *Black Identities: West Indian Immigrant Dreams and American Realities*. Cambridge, MA: Harvard University Press, 2009.

Weiss, Adam. "Strategic Litigation to Address Childhood Statelessness." World's Stateless Children (website). Institute on Statelessness and Inclusion. 2017. http://children .worldsstateless.org/3/litigating-against-childhood-statelessness/strategic-litigation -to-address-childhood-statelessness.html.

Wigginton, Sheridan. "Character or Caricature: Representations of Blackness in Dominican Social Science Textbooks." *Race Ethnicity and Education* 8, no. 2 (2005): 191–211.

Williams, David R., Hector M. González, Stacey Williams, Selina A. Mohammed, Hashim Moomal, and Dan J. Stein. "Perceived Discrimination, Race and Health in South Africa: Findings from the South Africa Stress and Health Study." *Social Science and Medicine* 67, no. 3 (2008): 441–52. Text available online at https:// scholar.harvard.edu/files/davidrwilliams/files/2008-perceived_discrimination_ race-williams.pdf.

Wooding, Bridget. "Contesting Dominican Discrimination and Statelessness." *Peace Review* 20, no. 3 (2008): 366–75. Text available online at https://www.researchgate.net/ publication/233461016_Contesting_Dominican_Discrimination_and_Statelessness.

———. "Haitian Immigrants and Their Descendants Born in the Dominican Republic." *Oxford Research Encyclopedia of Latin American History*. Oxford University Press. Online publication January 2018. https://oxfordre.com/latinamerican history/view/10.1093/acrefore/9780199366439.001.0001/acrefore-97801993 66439-e-474?rskey=PWgo27&result=188.

Wooding, Bridget, and Richard David Moseley-Williams. *Needed but Unwanted: Haitian Immigrants and Their Descendants in the Dominican Republic*. London: Catholic Institute for International Relations, 2004.

World Bank. "The World Bank in Dominican Republic: Overview." Last updated September 25, 2019. https://www.worldbank.org/en/country/dominicanrepublic/overview.

Wright, Micah. "An Epidemic of Negrophobia: Blackness and the Legacy of the US Occupation of the Dominican Republic." Special issue, "Dominican Black Studies." *The Black Scholar* 45, no. 2 (2015): 21–33.

Wucker, Michele. "The Dominican Republic's Shameful Deportation Legacy." *Foreign Policy*, October 8, 2015. https://foreignpolicy.com/2015/10/08/dominican -republic-haiti-trujillo-immigration-deportation/.

Yeoh, Brenda S. A., and Heng Leng Chee. "Migrant Wives, Migrant Workers, and the Negotiation of (Il)Legality in Singapore." In *Migrant Encounters: Intimate Labor, the State, and Mobility across Asia*, edited by Sara L. Friedman and Pardis Mahdavi, 184–205. Philadelphia: University of Pennsylvania Press, 2015.

Yuval-Davis, Nira. *The Politics of Belonging: Intersectional Contestations*. London: SAGE Publications, 2011.

———. "Women, Citizenship and Difference." *Feminist Review* 57, no. 1 (1997): 4–27.

Index

Acción Afro-Dominicana, 130

acta de nacimiento, 79

activism: for *cédulas*, 103–4; counterprotests, 109–10; for human rights, 73; by MUDHA, 77, 97–98; in politics, 105; religion and, 135; resistance as, 127–31

Africa, 9

alcalde, 57, 115

anba fil, 62–63

ancestry, 23n8, 40

anti-Haitian racism: in birthright citizenship, 99; *cédulas* and, 98–99; colorism for, 115–18; in culture, 109; in documentation, 71; in Dominican Republic, 1–7, 10–14, 16–19, *18*; financial barriers from, 83–87; by government, 14, 52, 111–12; ideology of, 10–14; illegality and, 127–31; in immigration, 92–93; last names in, 118–19; in La Tierra, 51, 127; liminal legality as, 78; lynching and, 109–11; for *morenos*, 22; policy for, 134; politics of, 99–104; racialization for, 112–15; racial profiling, 122–23; social exclusion and, 4–5; speech for, 119–22; in sugar mills, 37–38

ASCALA. *See* Scalabrinianic Association for the Service of Human Mobility

authority: for employment, 78–79; of *fichas*, 63; in politics, 70; in sugarcane labor, 61–62; of sugar mills, 57, 63, 69

axial coding, 140

BAI. *See* Beck Anxiety Inventory

Balaguer, Joaquín, 19, 64, 76n31, 90

barracks, *33–34*

bateyes, 8, 48n2; communities in, 55–56, 139; crime in, 135; culture of, 112, 137, 139; exploitation of, 53–54; for government, 63–64; history of, 30–31; labor in, 31, 36–38; *motochonchistas* in, 120; race in, 113–14; racialization in, 128; snowball-sampling method in, 137–38; variations in, 38. *See also* La Tierra

BDI. *See* Beck Depression Inventory

Beck Anxiety Inventory (BAI), 139

Beck Depression Inventory (BDI), 139

bilateral agreements, 4, 53–54, 69, 72, 73

birthright citizenship: anti-Haitian racism in, 99; birth certificates, 1, 19–20, 79–80, 86; in courts, 16–17; employment and, 16; *fichas* and, 114; immigration and, 103; policy for, 2, 4–5, 82–83; for *prietos*, 116; racial profiling in, 119; second-class citizenship and, 128; social exclusion from, 89–90

blanqueamiento, 12

Book of Foreigners: bureaucracy of, 20; citizenship in, 99; civil-registry audits with, 80, 81; employment and, 84–85; history of, 4–5, 15, *15*, 17, 18; for liminal legality, 104–5; politics of, 21, 78; structural racism in, 99, 100

botellóns, 39

braceros, 7–8, 74n12

Brexit, 9

bribery, 120–21

bureaucracy: of Book of Foreigners, 20; of *cédulas*, 94–96, 118; of documentation, 57, 90–91; of *fichas*, 70; psychology of, 83–85

buscones, 62

CAC. *See* Consorcio Azucarero Central

CAEI. *See* Consorcio Azucarero de Empresas Industriales

calmados, 35

capataz de corte, 31, 61

capitalism, 5

Caribbean Community (CARICOM), 104

Caribbean Migrants Observatory (OBMICA), 130

CARICOM. *See* Caribbean Community

cartulinas, 46

Case of the Girls Yean and Bosico v. Dominican Republic, 130

CEA. *See* Consejo Estatal del Azúcar

CEB. *See* Central Electoral Board

cédulas: activism for, 103–4; anti-Haitian racism and, 98–99; birth certificates and, 79–80; bureaucracy of, 94–96, 118; CEB and, 16–17, 113; *cédula de cartóns*, 63; changes to, 62–63; for citizenship, 49n16; decision-making and, 105; deportation and, 65–66; for documentation, 88–89; for education, 37, 110; *fichas* and, 93; for government, 19–20, 73; for labor, 67–68; for marriage, 44; politics of, 78; for voting, 101–2; for work, 2

Center for Justice and International Law (CEJIL), 98

Central Electoral Board (CEB), 15–17, 77, 79–80, 88, 113

Central Romana Corporation, Ltd., 30

CERD. *See* Committee on the Elimination of Racial Discrimination

certificado de nacido vivo, 79

children: education for, 40; *fichas* for, 80, 87. *See also* families

China, immigrants from, 12

chiriperos, 37, *43*, 58, 90

Circular 17. *See* Resolution 12

Trenita Brookshire Childers is a health-services researcher at the American Institutes for Research. Dr. Childers's primary research interests include health equity, plain-language writing, and community-engaged methods. Previously, Dr. Childers was a Peace Corps volunteer in the Dominican Republic. She holds a PhD from the Department of Sociology at Duke University and a BA in sociology from Davidson College. She lives in Raleigh, North Carolina, with her loving husband and three adorable sons.